Misremembering *the* Holocaust

THE LIBERATION OF BUCHENWALD AND THE LIMITS OF MEMORY

GEORGE R. MASTROIANNI

Revised edition © 2023 George Mastroianni.

The right of George Mastroianni to be identified as the author of this work has been asserted. All rights reserved.

No part of this book may be reproduced, stored in a retrieval system, or transmitted in any form, or by any means (electronic, mechanical, photocopying, recording or otherwise) without the prior written permission of the author, except in cases of brief quotations embodied in review articles. It may not be edited, amended, lent, resold, hired out, distributed or otherwise circulated, without the publisher's written permission.

Permission may be sought directly from the author.

ISBN: 978-0-5786-2575-1

Cover design and interior formatting by Andy Meaden / meadencreative.com

ACKNOWLEDGEMENTS

I am deeply indebted to Herr Bernd Schmidt of Weimar, Germany for his invaluable assistance in writing this book. Herr Schmidt has worked for many years to help bring to public awareness the role played by the Allies in creating the conditions that made the liberation of Thuringia, and Buchenwald, possible. Bernd was instrumental in creating the memorial to 6th Armored Division soldiers that presently stands in Hottelstedt, a few kilometers northwest of Buchenwald. Herr Schmidt was also the moving force in memorializing the work of the 120th Evacuation Hospital, the unit that provided definitive care to Buchenwald survivors in the weeks after liberation. Bernd helped place the plaque honoring the 120th at the Ettersberg Castle, where the 120th was quartered while at Buchenwald. Bernd played a key role in recognizing the part played by the 80th Infantry Division in accepting the surrender of the city of Weimar and managing the occupation. Herr Schmidt and Helen Patton, granddaughter of General George S. Patton, together memorialized the contributions of American soldiers to the liberation of Thuringia at Ottmanshausen, Hottelstedt, and Weimar. Bernd was awarded the United States Army Outstanding Civilian Service Award on March 2, 2001, by Major General Charles C. Campbell, US Army. The citation reads:

"In recognition of special service from April 1998 to October 2000, Mr. Schmidt devoted countless hours to researching, planning, and executing the inauguration of the first memorials to U.S. soldiers in the former East Germany. As a result of his tireless efforts, these memorials will stand now as a reminder of the sacrifices made for freedom. At his urging, the city of Weimar hosted 80th Infantry Division veterans and their families in 1999 for celebrations commemorating the peaceful surrender of their town. This invitation provided the veterans and the citizens of Weimar with an unprecedented opportunity to revisit those historical events. His commitment to honor the U.S. Army's role in securing freedom in this part of Germany has indeed brought – as Mr. Schmidt himself has said, "A light on the darkest part of history".

The award was signed by Larry R. Jordan, Lieutenant General, Deputy Commanding General of United States Army Europe and Seventh Army.

I was privileged to spend some time with Herr Bernd Schmidt in Weimar and at Buchenwald in 2019 while researching this book. He has been unfailingly gracious and generous in our correspondence, and was an incomparable guide to Weimar and Buchenwald.

My friend and colleague Max Cameron helped me research the activities of the 97th Infantry Division and the 303rd Infantry Regiment, and was especially helpful in doggedly pursuing information about James V. DeMarco; it was Max who put me in touch with PFC DeMarco's relative. I am also grateful to Thierry Arsicaud, who created and maintains the "Echo Delta" mapping website that I used to convert WWII US military grid references to modern latitude and longitude coordinates.

Archival research was conducted by Geoff Lentini of Golden Arrow Research, LLC, and Dieter Stenger of Stenger Historica.

Dagmar Herzog, Connor Sebestyen, Adam Seipp, and Flint Whitlock provided extremely helpful comments on an earlier draft of this manuscript which improved this one immensely. Their generosity and courtesy are much appreciated.

David Frey and Jennifer Ciardelli provided invaluable assistance: David discussed the issues central to this book with me before I began, and helped me refine the concept; Jen's assistance at the United States Holocaust Memorial Museum has been extremely helpful.

Other books by George R. Mastroianni:

A Warrior's Guide to Psychology and Performance

Of Mind and Murder: Toward a More Comprehensive Psychology of the Holocaust

Contents

Introduction	xi
1 What was Buchenwald?	**1**
The Camp System – A "Lager Archipelago"	4
The Role of the SS	5
Prisoner Organization	6
Buchenwald at the End of WWII and Beyond	9
2 The Liberation	**11**
The Prisoner's View	12
Liberation Day – The American View	12
Liberation Day – The German View	16
Liberation Day Timeline – What Happened?	30
Liberation Day Timeline – What Did Not Happen?	31
After Liberation	31
How False Memories Are Made	33
3 Buchenwald in East Germany: The Role of Collective Memory	**38**
A Soviet Version	52
4 Buchenwald in America: Social Memory	**55**
Survivor's Memories of Black Liberators	69
Rabbi Lau	69
Benjamin Bender	71
Alex Gross	72
Henry Oster	75
The Trouble with Testimony	78

5 Buchenwald in America: Individual Memory and Public Outreach   81

   Harry Herder, Jr.   82
   Leo D. Hymas   88
   Rick Carrier   96
   J. Ray Clark   105
   Others   107
   Survivor Memoirs   107
   Jack Werber   107
   Other Discrepancies   110
      How many ovens?   110
      Arbeit macht frei or Jedem das seine?   111
      Eisenhower at Buchenwald   113
      Radio calls?   114
   EPILOGUE   116

6 Memory and History   122

   Finding the Truth   125
   Memory   126
   Encoding and the Camps   127
   Storage   130
   Retrieval   132
   Retrieval and Reconstruction   133
   False Memories May Have Both Individual and Social Origins   135
   Involuntary Impostor Syndrome   139
   The Public Fate of False Memories of the Holocaust   141
   The Record Corrected: Selbstbefreiung and Liberators: Fighting on Two Fronts in WWII   142
   Under the Radar, Into the Crosshairs   143
      No Gun Ri   144

Appendix 153

- Leon Adler 153
- Andy Anderson 153
- Kenneth Berthold 153
- Don Cote 154
- Martin Damgaard 154
- Leslie Leonard Fleisher 154
- Arthur Goldberg 155
- Sol Goldstein 155
- Herbert Gorfinkle 156
- Barry Lewis 156
- John Macinko 156
- George "Butch" Newsom 157
- Lucien Rego 157
- Tony Rossetti 157
- Don Schoo 158
- Milton Silva 158
- Works Cited 159

Index 163

INTRODUCTION

I have a relative who is several years younger than her two older sisters, who are quite close in age. One day the older girls were involved in a minor fender-bender on a visit to the local mall in their father's car. On returning home, they concocted a story to conceal the truth from their father: a man in a white car had pulled in to their driveway to turn around, striking their Dad's car in the process, then sped away. The older girls then coached the youngest daughter, who had been home all along, to support them and repeat the story, complete with convincing details, to the father. The plan was carried out, and the collective filial deceit was successful: the older girls escaped detection and potential punishment.

Fast-forward several decades. At a family gathering, the youngest daughter, now forty-something, recalls the time that Dad's car was struck in the driveway by the guy in the white car. The older sisters come clean and somewhat sheepishly remind her that in fact, that did not happen: the story was fabricated by them to evade their responsibility for the accident. But the youngest sister is adamant: she *remembers* the squealing tires, the white car speeding down the street. Her memory of the incident is false, because the car was damaged at the mall, not in the driveway. But it is still, as far as she knows and believes, her memory of what happened to her. In relating the story, she is not lying: she has simply mistakenly integrated the tall tale created by her sisters into her own experience. The drilling and repetition and elaborate detail to achieve the illusion of veracity has deposited vivid visual memories in her brain that linger yet.

This example of one of the ways our memories can fail to represent the past accurately is harmless, even amusing. Human memory does not provide us with a perfect record of our experiences, and most of us probably carry with us a few memory failures like the one above: we may not even be aware of them. In general, the minor discrepancies and inconsistencies in our memories cause no great mischief, as the important events in our lives can be readily cross-checked, documented and corroborated. There are circumstances, though, in which these minor failings can become quite important. Eyewitness testimony in crimes is a good example: psychologist Elizabeth Loftus[1] has shown that eyewitnesses to events frequently get even important details wrong.

Oral histories documenting the experiences of individuals who have participated in or witnessed historically significant events can help us appreciate the human dimension of those events. More than a dry recitation of dates and facts, such testimony can transport us to another time and place through the experiences of one who was there, and we can better imagine what it must have been like to have been there. But eyewitnesses to history can also sometimes get things wrong. Because history by definition happened in the past, it can often be quite difficult to find other eyewitnesses or other methods of corroboration to sort out contradictions or discrepancies in individual testimonies.

In most areas of study this state of affairs may be annoying, insofar as it is frustrating that we may not know what "really" happened at a given time and place. In Holocaust studies, though, there is a potentially more serious consequence when contradictions and uncertainty find their way into discussions of Holocaust history. Holocaust doubters and deniers seize on any example of inaccuracy or confusion in the historical record to justify invalidating the entire record. If Holocaust researchers or historians can be wrong about Fact A, the argument goes, then might they be wrong about Facts B and C, also? And if they might be wrong about Facts A, B, and C, perhaps they are wrong about the whole thing.

This is not a book about Holocaust denial. It is a book about the ways one day in one place in WWII has been remembered and misremembered: the day American troops first entered a Nazi concentration camp with a large remaining population of prisoners. The camp was Buchenwald. The day was April 11, 1945. General Dwight D. Eisenhower visited a sub-camp of Buchenwald, Ohrdruf, on April 12, 1945: the horrific scenes he encountered there affected him deeply. He soon became aware of Buchenwald and, though he never visited the camp, determined to publicize Buchenwald and the atrocities the Nazis had committed there to make clear to the ordinary soldier and citizen that even if it was not always clear what they had been and were fighting for, there need be no doubt as to what they had been and were fighting against[2]. Liberation of the camps helped validate the moral imperative justifying the monumental effort and sacrifice that had been demanded of so many for so long, and Buchenwald soon became the best-known of the American-liberated camps.

Buchenwald was occupied by Americans for more than two months, from

---

[1] Gerry, Maryanne, and Hayne, Harlene. *Do Justice and Let the Sky Fall: Elizabeth F. Loftus and Her Contributions to Science, Law, and Academic Freedom (Psychology Press Festschrift Series)*, (London, Psychology Press, 2006).

[2] Flint Whitlock. *Buchenwald: Hell on a Hilltop*, (Brule, WI, Cable Publishing, 2014), p. 267.

mid-April 1945 until early July of the same year. Especially during the early weeks of occupation, Allied authorities encouraged and facilitated visits to Buchenwald by officials and dignitaries from Allied countries, by reporters and photographers, and by thousands of Allied troops. Eisenhower's purpose in publicizing Buchenwald so widely seems to have been to encourage Allied soldiers and citizens to personally associate themselves and their efforts with the ending of the horrific ordeal suffered by so many in the Nazi camp system. At the time, little special significance was attached to the identities of the particular American soldiers who had first reached the camps as they were "liberated"[3]. There was very little fighting associated with the arrival of American troops at the camps, and chance and proximity were the main determinants of which soldiers were the first into the camps.

Journalists waiting at the main gate to the Buchenwald prisoner area for a tour, April 18, 1945. Photo used with permission of the United States Holocaust Memorial Museum. (Note that the time on the clock is NOT 3:15 – this will be important later)

"Liberation" was thus seen as a collective achievement that helped to provide some moral and psychological closure to years of sacrifice and suffering. At war's end, Allied authorities encouraged the broadest possible participation in adopting a sense of responsibility for the moral good that had been achieved. After all, the particular soldiers who entered the camps were often only in them for a very short time, as Allied forces were moving rapidly to exploit the German collapse. These soldiers were often not the ones who spent weeks working in the horrific conditions of the camps, trying their best to save as many of the victims of Nazi barbarity as might be saved. As well, they were supported by hundreds of thousands of other soldiers who made their advance across Europe possible; by American workers and citizens who toiled and sacrificed to produce the necessities of war; by sailors who transported those necessities across the Atlantic at their peril; by aviators who provided strategic and tactical air support. And it should be said, by the Russians who had sacrificed millions in their grinding war against the Nazis in the east, destroying staggering amounts of Nazi combat power in the years since Hitler invaded the Soviet Union on June 22, 1941.

When the war ended, the soldiers returned home, and the business of picking up where they had left off began. The liberation of the camps, and the Holocaust more broadly, were not topics of intense public interest in the United States. Interest in exactly how and by whom Buchenwald (or Flossenburg, or Dachau, or Mauthausen) had been liberated only began to grow in the United States decades later. The aging of the generation that fought World War II, the appearance of the ABC miniseries *Holocaust* in 1978, and other factors contributed to an explosion of interest in the 1980's and 1990's in events that had been largely forgotten. As public interest in the details of liberation increased, more and more veterans and survivors began to contribute their own stories and claims about their experiences with the camps. Many of these stories conflicted with "official" versions of the events, and with one other. In some cases, individual veterans and survivors seem to have constructed more or less elaborate memories of the liberation of Buchenwald that appear to be largely or completely false. In other cases, individual memories have become enmeshed in social and political dynamics resulting in false narratives, such as the Oscar-nominated PBS film *Liberators: Fighting on Two Fronts in WWII*, which was withdrawn from public viewing because it was determined that the central claim of the film, that it was African-American soldiers who liberated Buchenwald, could not be proven. In East Germany, soon after the end of the war, the *Selbstbefreiung* – "self-liberation"

---

[3] Though the fact was noted in the 6th AD newspaper – United States Holocaust Memorial Museum, https://collections.ushmm.org/search/catalog/irn503807, retrieved 29 December 2018.

– myth had been cultivated and was actively promulgated for decades. This view of the liberation revised Americans out of the picture entirely, falsely giving credit for the liberation to German Communists who dominated the prisoner hierarchy at Buchenwald.

Books such as Jan Gross' *Golden Harvest* and Dan Porat's *The Boy*[4] begin with singular, but striking images and use these as a point of departure from which to explore larger issues. Gross' book focuses on a photograph of Polish people scavenging for gold on the site of the Treblinka killing center after WWII. Porat's book begins with an iconic photograph of a little boy with his hands upraised, an invitation to a broader story. My hope for the present volume is that it will draw attention to one event, the liberation of Buchenwald, but that it will also invite attention to larger issues about memory and history[5].

We will never know what happened in every corner of the camp at every moment on that day: at best we can hope to forge a provisional consensus as to the sequence and timing of the events that we now see as historically significant. Once we agree on the general outlines of the events of April 11, 1945 at Buchenwald, we can begin to explore the manifold ways in which these events have been remembered, and misremembered. Chapter One provides a brief description of Buchenwald: why and when it was built, how it functioned and changed over the course of its existence. Chapter Two offers a detailed look at the day of liberation: I will propose a kind of least-common-denominator timeline of the events that occurred on liberation day of which we can be relatively certain. Chapter Three examines the *Selbstbefreiung*, or self-liberation myth and the role it played in East Germany as an example of social memory. Chapter Four considers the case of the film *Liberators: Fighting on two Fronts in WWII* as an instance of social and collective memory processes in the US. Chapter Five focuses on individual memory as a way of understanding how and why individuals sometimes misremember important events and will provide numerous examples of individuals whose memories of Buchenwald are flawed in various ways, from people who were definitely at Buchenwald but have gotten some details wrong, to people who were not present at the liberation but have constructed what appear to be elaborate false narratives of the liberation. Chapter Six addresses the intersection of psychology and history in this important area of memory.

---

[4] Jan Gross with Irena Grudzinska Gross, *Golden Harvest*, (Oxford and New York, Oxford University Press, 2012).

[5] David Frey of the *Center for Holocaust and Genocide Studies* at West Point suggested this connection to me.

I wrote earlier that this is not a book about Holocaust denial. It is a book about memory, individual testimony and oral history, and the liberation of Buchenwald. The book will recite a long list of mistakes people have made in their memories of Buchenwald, and also mistakes made by Holocaust institutions and museums in presenting the story of the liberation. Survivors, liberators, observers, and scholars have all made mistakes in talking about the liberation of Buchenwald. Some of these mistakes are minor and inconsequential, while others completely contradict what we know about the events of April 11, 1945. Some of these mistakes are mainly individual phenomena, while others appear to represent the operation of larger-scale social and political factors. Insofar as I also wrote earlier that Holocaust deniers may seize on discrepancies of this sort to justify their abhorrent views, I should explain why I have chosen to expose these failures of memory in this way. Would it not be better to simply not mention the many inconsistencies that exist in Holocaust scholarship and literature? If a respected institution doing good works has made minor mistakes in presenting the story of the liberation, would it not be best to quietly correct the mistakes and move on without mention?

Others have wrestled with this question before me. Later we will encounter the story of Deli Strummer, a Holocaust survivor, whose public outreach efforts for the Baltimore Jewish Council were ended in 2000 after an investigation by Lawrence Langer and Raul Hilberg led to the conclusion that significant aspects of her testimony were mistaken. I have concluded that the best course of action is not merely to mention the many ways that the liberation of Buchenwald has been misremembered, but to embrace and try to explain them: to contextualize these instances as the same sort of errors, distortions, omissions, and embellishments that riddle our own recollections of our own lives. Human memory is not structured and does not function in a way that could possibly be expected, under most circumstances, to produce anything like a clean and consistent record of recollections of the liberation of Buchenwald. If there is any lesson to be drawn from the material brought together in this book, I hope that it will be this: the existence of inconsistencies, errors, and discrepancies in human memories about an event tells us little or nothing about the likelihood that the event really happened, or happened in a particular way. Instead, these errors, mistakes and distortions tell us something about the circumstances under which these memories were formed, stored, and recalled, and perhaps a bit about the people to whom these memories belong.

1 WHAT WAS BUCHENWALD?

Buchenwald[6] was a Nazi concentration camp that operated from late 1937 until April 11, 1945. The camp was located on the Ettersberg, a mountain a few miles northwest of Weimar, a symbolic seat of German culture: the official name of the camp was *Konzentrationslager Buchenwald, Post Weimar*"[7]. Buchenwald was a camp initially intended to house prisoners subject to *Schutzhaft*, or protective custody. Protective custody came to Germany with the Reichstag Fire Decree in February, 1933, permitting the arrest and detention of persons who were not necessarily accused of any crime, but who were considered a potential threat to state security[8]. Criminals, political prisoners, homosexuals, Roma and Sinti, Jehovah's witnesses, and the so-called "work-shy" were among the groups targeted by the Nazis for protective custody. Many Jews were sent to Buchenwald after the November 9, 1938 pogrom in Germany known as *Kristallnacht*. The population of the camp expanded and diversified after the invasion of Poland on September 1, 1939, as people from the newly conquered territories were sent there, and began to increase dramatically and diversify still further after the German invasion of the Soviet Union on June 22, 1941.

The growing need for slave laborers to support the Nazi war effort led to an influx of prisoners into the Nazi camp system as the demands of the war became greater and greater. Many of the camps provided slave laborers to support war-related industrial production. As the war in the east turned decisively against Germany after the fall of Stalingrad in early 1943, and Russian troops continued

---

[6] "Buchenwald" is German for "beech forest". The camp was also operated as "Soviet Special Camp No. 2" from 1945 until 1950.

[7] Gedenkstätte Buchenwald (Eds). *Buchenwald Concentration Camp 1937-1945: A Guide to the Permanent Historical Exhibition*. (Gottingen: Wallstein Verlag, 2004).

[8] United States Holocaust Memorial Museum, https://www.ushmm.org/learn/timeline-of-events/1933-1938/reichstag-fire-decree, retrieved 30 December 2018. It was the state and the German people who were ostensibly being "protected", not the individual detained under the decree.

to push west, many prisoners confined in camps threatened by the Russians were eventually evacuated from those camps and marched or transported westward and southward. These movements accelerated in late 1944 and early 1945, and are often referred to as "death marches", as prisoners were transported in horrific conditions in open trains or unheated railcars, or simply marched on foot and shot or beaten when they failed to keep up. Mortality rates were very high, as many of these prisoners had already endured forced labor and starvation at the camps from which they were evacuated. Many such prisoners arrived at Buchenwald in the fall of 1944 and the chaotic spring of 1945.

The main gate to the prisoner area at Buchenwald as it looks today. Note that the clock is now permanently set to 3:15. (Author's photograph, used with permission).

When Allied troops began to encounter Nazi concentration camps in the spring of 1945, many of the camp populations had increased dramatically because of these movements, and conditions in camps such as Buchenwald, Bergen-Belsen (liberated by the British) and others were unspeakably bad. This led to some confusion among the soldiers that liberated or visited the camps, as they were largely unaware of the complicated history of the camps and the ways the camps had changed over time. Many naturally assumed that the camps had always existed in the state in which they were liberated. Moreover, many of them learned later about the extermination camps, such as Auschwitz, and may have misinterpreted the presence of features such as the crematoria at Buchenwald and Dachau as suggesting that all the Nazi camps served the same purposes.

Buchenwald was a sprawling facility that contained barracks and other facilities for prisoners, barracks and other facilities for the SS guards and camp administration. The Little Camp, which was constructed in 1943, was originally intended as a transit camp for short-term housing of inmates who were to be transferred to other labor camps. It later became a kind of camp-within-a-camp, where living conditions were most horrific.

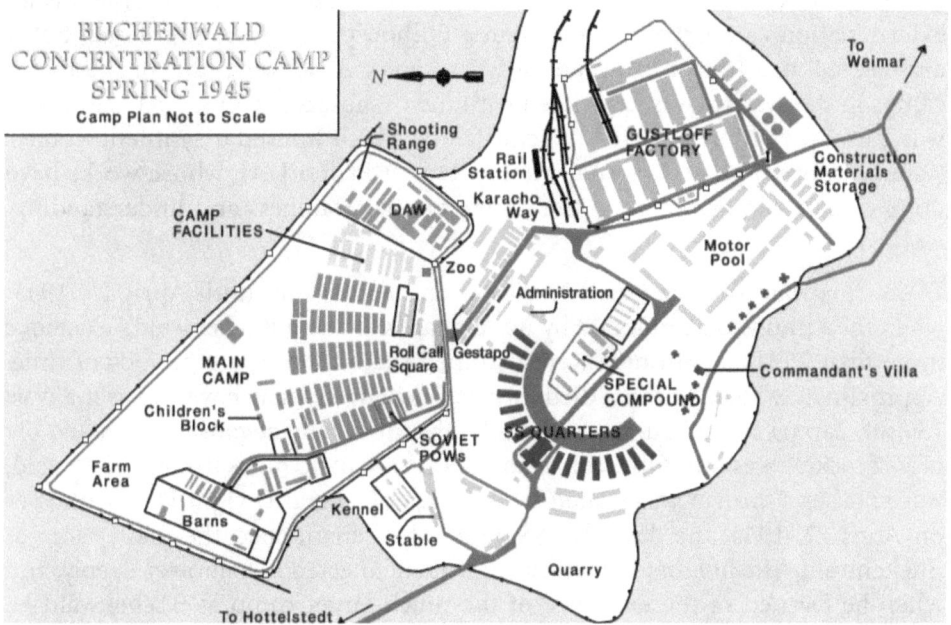

A plan of Buchenwald. The prisoner area lies on the north side of the camp (to the left in this plan), while the Gustloff Werke, an armaments manufacturer that hired slave labor from the SS, occupied the large complex on the east side of the camp, toward the top of this plan. The main gate to the prisoner area, which contains the "JEDEM DAS SEINE" gate and camp clock, is just above the words "Roll Call Square". The SS administrative and military facilities were located on the southern and western portions of the camp; the quarry was on the southwest corner of Buchenwald. (Plan used with permission from the United States Holocaust Memorial Museum).

The Camp System – A "Lager Archipelago"[9]

There were thousands of camps in the Nazi system. Some camps were labor camps, where people were forced to work for the Nazi regime. Other camps were transit camps, places where people were held for short periods of time before being sent on to further destinations. Still others were extermination camps, or killing centers. Some camps, such as Buchenwald, were established and existed until the end of the Third Reich; others, such as Sobibor and Treblinka, were established for limited purposes, such as the killing of specific populations of Jews and were closed when that purpose had been fulfilled. Auschwitz, probably the best-known camp in the Nazi system, served multiple purposes: it was an extermination camp, where more than a million people were murdered, but it also served as a transit camp and a work camp. Auschwitz, like all the major camps in the system, was associated with many sub-camps. One such sub-camp was Auschwitz-Monowitz, or Auschwitz III, which housed a synthetic-rubber ("Buna" rubber) plant. It was at Monowitz that Primo Levi, whose works have done so much to bring life in the camps to our awareness and understanding, worked.

Buchenwald operated as a Nazi concentration camp until April 11, 1945, when the camp was abandoned by its SS guards. During Buchenwald's existence more than 250,000 prisoners were confined there for varying periods of time. Approximately 56,000 people died there[10]. Buchenwald may have had as many as 139 sub-camps. Mittelbau-Dora, an underground facility devoted to the assembly of V-2 rockets was one; Ohrdruf, a small camp about 40 miles from Buchenwald, was another. Ohrdruf was visited by American General Dwight D. Eisenhower on April 12, 1945, the day after SS guards had abandoned the main camp at Buchenwald. The horrors witnessed at Ohrdruf affected Eisenhower deeply, and when he learned of the existence of the much larger camp at Buchenwald he decided to publicize the camp and the atrocities committed there as widely as he could, though he himself never visited the main camp. Buchenwald is the source of some of the most-widely-known images from the Holocaust: lampshades said to be made from human skin and shrunken heads were displayed on a table at the camp, for example, and photographs of the display were widely distributed.

---

[9] Alexander Solzhenitsyn used the term "Gulag Archipelago" to refer to the complex of Soviet camps and prisons. This variation of Solzhenitsyn's term helps capture the large number and variety of Nazi-run camps through which many prisoners passed.

[10] Hackett, David A. The Buchenwald Report. (Boulder: Westview Press, 1995) p. 65.

The Role of the SS

Nazi concentration camps were administered by the SS (*Schutzstaffel*), which had originated as Hitler's elite personal guard. The SS was and is notorious as the organization most directly responsible for implementing Hitler's Final Solution. The SS was also a business: the labor of inmates was exploited in many of the camps to enrich the SS and the Nazi state. At Buchenwald, inmates worked in a quarry and other facilities for the *Deutsche Erd- und Steinwerke GmbH* (German Earth and Stone Works, or DEST) and the *Deutsche Ausrüstungs Werke* (German Equipment Company, or DAW), which were SS organizations. Inmates were also hired from the SS by the *Gustloff Werke*, a small-arms manufacturer and producer of parts for the V-2 rocket, and the Zeiss optics company in nearby Jena, which assembled binoculars using slave labor from the camps.

Inmates were exploited as an expendable and replaceable resource by the SS to maximize revenue. Camp administrators minimized costs by providing horrendous living conditions, inadequate food, clothing, medical care, and sanitation to prisoners, while extracting as much labor as possible from them, often under extremely dangerous conditions. High disease, injury, and mortality rates among inmates were not seen as reasons to question or punish SS camp administrators, but corruption sometimes was. There were many opportunities for personal enrichment in the environment of the camps, and SS soldiers and officers who were too open or profligate about their corruption, diverting to personal use resources that should have gone to the SS or the state, risked severe punishment. The first SS Commandant of Buchenwald, Karl Koch, was relieved of his duties as Commandant in 1941 for corruption and was eventually executed by the SS in 1945, shortly before the German surrender. He was succeeded as Commandant by Hermann Pister, who remained in command until the camp was abandoned by the Nazis in April, 1945.

Inmates at Buchenwald were also subjected to horrific medical experimentation by SS doctors. Typhus was endemic throughout the Nazi camp system, largely because the SS failed to provide adequate sanitary facilities in the camps, and so there was interest in finding ways to prevent and treat the disease. Prisoners were infected with typhus in order to test various treatments: survivors of the research were often murdered[11]. Research was also conducted on homosexuality at Buchenwald. A Danish physician, Carl Vaernet, believed

---

[11] For more information on the program of human experimentation on inmates at Buchenwald (and elsewhere), see Baumslag, Naomi. *Murderous Medicine: Nazi Doctors, Human Experimentation, and Typhus.* (Washington DC, Baumslag, 2005), and Weindling, Paul. *Victims and Survivors of Nazi Human Experiments: Science and Suffering in the Holocaust.* (London, Bloomsbury, 2015).

homosexuality to be an organic disorder resulting from testosterone deficiency, and experimented with implants and injections to "cure" the condition[12].

Prisoner Organization

Internal organization and conditions varied in Nazi camps, depending on many factors. Generally speaking, though, the SS relied heavily on inmates to occupy positions of responsibility and authority in the day-to-day running of the camps. Many of the tasks performed by inmates were dirty, dangerous, or unpleasant jobs, but prisoners also served as managers and administrators: at Buchenwald inmates could influence or determine important decisions, such as which work assignments other inmates received, or which prisoners would be assigned to which transports out of the camp. Assignment to some of these transports meant near-certain death. Transportation to Auschwitz was often tantamount to a death sentence: many prisoners from Buchenwald were also sent to Dora-Mittelbau, a sub-camp of Buchenwald where V-2 rockets were assembled. Conditions were very bad at Dora, an underground complex, and prospects for survival were worse there than at many other camps.

Social relations in Nazi concentration camps shared many of the same features found in other societies. There were social hierarchies, formal and informal rules, and there was social change as time passed. The development of a social hierarchy within the ranks of the prisoners was facilitated by the Nazi obsession with categorizing and classifying people. Prisoner uniforms were marked with an elaborate system of color-coded identifying badges. These badges identified the category to which the inmate belonged, as well as the prisoner's national origin. At Buchenwald, two especially important categories of prisoners were the "greens" and the "reds". Prisoners who wore an inverted green triangle on their uniforms were criminals; those identified by an inverted red triangle were political prisoners, mainly Communists, Socialists, and other political opponents of the Nazi regime. Jews, identified by two overlapping yellow triangles resembling a star of David, "Gypsies" (Roma and Sinti) and homosexuals (identified with a pink triangle) were at the bottom of the prisoner hierarchy.

---

[12] United States Holocaust Memorial Museum, Holocaust Encyclopedia Buchenwald, https://encyclopedia.ushmm.org/content/en/article/buchenwald, retrieved 30 December 2018.

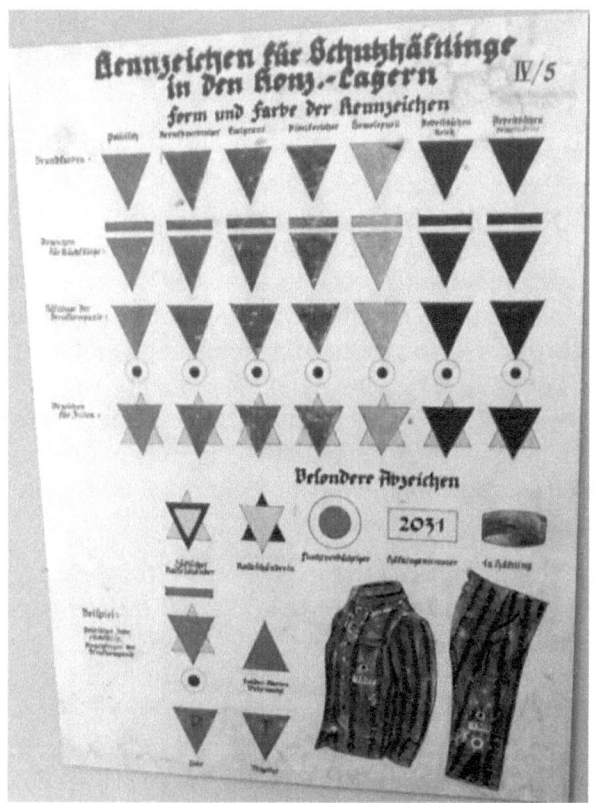

Poster of identifying insignia for prisoners.
(Author's photo used with permission from the *Buchenwald Gedenkstätte*.)

In addition to these visible markings, prejudices and stereotypes continued to operate in camp society just as they did outside:

"While geographical origins could form the basis of relationships built around a shared culture, language, and customs, they could also do the opposite and signal seemingly insurmountable discrepancies. For example, Alexander Kuliesiewicz recounts the story of a dying Goral who, even in the moment of his death, felt compelled to express his disdain for his fellow Polish prisoners from the cities, whom he dismissed as "damned spoiled brats" with their "fancy talk". In another account, Jewish Greek women recall that they were referred to as "Grecko klepsi klepsi" in Auschwitz and Ravensbrück because of their skillful thefts in the camp – which entailed not only taking useful things from the property room but also supposedly robbing their fellow prisoners. Other stereotypes held that Polish women were vulgar and dirty,

French women were vain, Greek women were clever thieves but also clean, orderly, and disciplined, Belgian women were naïve, non-Jewish Ukrainian women were cruel, Czech women were energetic, and so on.

National and geographic classifications went hand in hand with a socially evaluated status that worked like a positive or negative sign in mathematics. This evaluation factor, in turn, was overlaid with the significance of a prisoner's triangle color, which represented an additional intensifying or weakening sign. In the case of Jews and "Gypsies", however, their classification was so dominant that it completely outweighed any national or cultural aspects in how they were perceived – for example, a Jewish Pole would be viewed as a Polish Jew, or a prisoner's nationality would be so negligible that he or she would be viewed and identified solely as a Jew. The same applies to "Gypsies", whose geographic origins seem to have been entirely of secondary importance, probably not least because they were suspected of being permanently rootless wanderers."[13]

In the early years of Buchenwald's existence, the prisoner hierarchy was dominated by the greens. Criminal inmates occupied the most powerful positions and exercised control over important aspects of camp life. At some point, perhaps in 1942, reds took over, and so-called "politicals" remained in control of the prisoner-led component of camp functioning until the liberation in 1945. The reds were dominated by German Communists: this is relevant to the question of what exactly happened at the time of liberation because Buchenwald was located in what would become the German Democratic Republic (the now-former East Germany). The role played by inmates, led by German Communists, in the liberation of the camp would become, as we shall see, an important and controverted issue in later years. Maja Suderland puts it this way:

"In the wake of the "third Reich", this strongly polarized (and polarizing) debate about the role of the prisoner functionary painted a black-and-white image of "red" prisoner functionaries as "good" and others - particularly greens – as "evil". This notion also found its way into the divergent discourse of the German Democratic Republic and the Federal Republic of Germany, in which the role of communists was judged in accordance with the ideological underpinnings of each state (cf. Detlef Garbe in Abgeleitete Macht 1998:13)[14]

---

[13] Suderland, Maja. *Inside Concentration Camps: Social Life at the Extremes* (Cambridge: Polity Press, 2013) p. 191.

[14] Ibid., p. 200..

Buchenwald at the End of WWII and Beyond

As the tide of war shifted increasingly against the Third Reich, large numbers of prisoners evacuated from other camps were sent to Buchenwald. Prisoners who arrived at Buchenwald were housed first in an area of Buchenwald known as the Little Camp, fenced off from the main camp. Typhus and dysentery were endemic among the prisoners being shuttled about by the Nazis, as sanitary conditions at the camps were horrific. Most of the tens of thousands of prisoners who arrived at Buchenwald later in the war arrived sick and starving, and conditions in the Little Camp were much, much worse than conditions in the main camp. Some Americans who visited Buchenwald soon after its liberation remarked on the dramatic differences between prisoners and conditions in the main camp as compared to those in the Little Camp. Those in the main camp appeared comparatively healthy and well-fed, while those in the Little Camp were often little more than living skeletons. Movement between the Little Camp and the main camp was largely controlled by the prisoner functionaries at Buchenwald.

Buchenwald was bombed by American forces on August 24, 1944. This raid was intended to cripple the industrial facilities at Buchenwald and spare the prisoner areas, a goal which was largely met. There were, however, many inmate casualties in addition to the SS and other Germans who were killed or wounded in the raid. The nearby town of Weimar was also bombed on February 9, 1945, and sustained considerable damage.

Buchenwald was occupied by Americans until July 3, 1945, whereupon it was turned over to the Soviet Union. Within a short time the Soviets began to use Buchenwald for their own detainees. Detention of Nazi sympathizers after the war was anticipated by the Allies for security reasons, and many of the prisoners held at Buchenwald fell into this category. Others were political prisoners, who were seen as a threat to Communist rule. Buchenwald became known as Soviet Special Camp No. 2, administered by the NKVD, the Soviet internal security agency. Between 1945 and 1950 approximately 25,000 people were interned there, and approximately 8,000 died. During this period the Little Camp was closed, and the prisoners were housed in the main camp. As during the Nazi era, day-to-day life in the camp was largely prisoner-run. Soviet Special Camp No. 2 was closed in early 1950, a few months after the German Democratic Republic was founded on October 7, 1949.

This brief sketch is intended merely to acquaint the reader with the basic history of Buchenwald. My purpose in this book is to focus on the day of liberation and the way that day has been remembered by various parties. If this book should stimulate interest in learning more about the camp's history over the twelve years, more or less, that it existed as a place where people were imprisoned, there are fortunately many excellent sources. For a general overview of the Nazi camp system, written by a Buchenwald survivor, Eugen Kogon's T*he Theory and Practice of Hell*[15] is a good start. Maja Suderland's excellent *Inside Concentration Camps*[16] provides a sophisticated analysis of the social structure and function in Nazi camps. Primo Levi's many works offer an invaluable look at life in the Nazi camps through the eyes of a sensitive and articulate observer: *The Drowned and the Saved*[17], and *If This is a Man*[18] are among his best-known works. *The Society of Terror: Inside the Dachau and Buchenwald Concentration Camps*[19] by Paul Martin Neurath also provides an intimate and informative portrait of daily life in the camps. *The Buchenwald Report*[20], which was originally prepared by a group of inmates led by Kogon in the weeks after liberation, was lost to history for many years but surfaced and was published in English in 1995 by David Hackett. *Buchenwald Concentration Camp 1937-1945: A Guide to the Permanent Historical Exhibition*[21], compiled by Harry Stein and edited by the Gedenkstätte Buchenwald, contains a detailed history of the camp's development. A trilogy by Flint Whitlock, which includes: *Buchenwald: Hell on a Hilltop*[22], T*he Beasts of Buchenwald, and Survivor of Buchenwald* is extremely informative and helpful. There are also a number of survivor memoirs and testimonies, many of which will be discussed in later Chapters.

---

[15] Kogon, Eugen. *The Theory and Practice of Hell: The German Concentration Camps and the System Behind Them*. (New York: Farrar, Staruss and Giroux, 1950).

[16] Suderland, Maja. *Inside Concentration Camps: Social Life at the Extremes* (Cambridge: Polity Press, 2013).

[17] Levi, Primo. *The Drowned and the Saved*. (New York, Simon and Schuster, 1988).

[18] Levi, Primo. *If This is a Man*. (London, Abacus, 2013).

[19] Neurath, Paul Martin. (Christian Fleck and Nico Stehr, Eds.) *The Society of Terror: Inside the Dachau and Buchenwald Concentration Camps*. (Boulder: Paradigm Publishers, 2005).

[20] Hackett, David A. *The Buchenwald Report*. (Boulder: Westview Press, 1995).

[21] Gedenkstaette Buchenwald (Eds.) *Buchenwald Concentration Camp 1937-1945: A Guide to the Permanent Historical Exhibition*. (Gottingen: Wallstein Verlag, 2004).

[22] Whitlock, Flint. Buchenwald: *Hell on a Hilltop*. (Brule, Wisconsin, Cable Publishing, 2014).

2 THE LIBERATION

Buchenwald was first visited by American troops on April 11, 1945. At this late stage of the war in Europe, German forces were collapsing rapidly. German Army Group B, commanded by Field Marshal Walter Model, had successfully prevented Allied troops from crossing the Rhine and penetrating into the industrial heartland of Germany until late March, 1945. By April 1, Model's forces were encircled by the American Ninth Army (part of 21st Army Group, commanded by Field Marshal Bernard Montgomery) in the north, and the American First Army (part of the 12th Army Group, commanded by General Omar Bradley) in the center, in what was known as the Ruhr Pocket. General George Patton's Third Army, assigned to 12th Army Group, positioned further south, was able to race across Germany from west to east south of the collapsing Ruhr Pocket, and 21st Army Group moved across Germany from west to east north of the Ruhr pocket. Allied forces continued to eliminate German resistance within the Ruhr Pocket, and eventually, more than 300,000 German soldiers surrendered there. Field Marshal Model took his own life on April 21, 1945, rather than surrender himself.

The first American soldiers to visit Buchenwald were part of Patton's Third Army, which was racing eastward to meet Soviet forces pushing westward. While German resistance to the Allied advance continued, the armored divisions leading the American advance across central and southern Germany made rapid progress, covering many miles each day and capturing large numbers of prisoners. It was during this period that elements of the 4th and 6th Armored Divisions, part of Patton's Third Army, happened upon Buchenwald. Before delving too deeply into the many accounts of the liberation of Buchenwald that appear to deviate from what the historical record shows happened on April 11, 1945, it is necessary to grasp the nettle and attempt to construct a timeline that represents the best guess we can make about what exactly did happen.

The Prisoner's View

The account of the day of liberation from *The Buchenwald Report*, which was written by prisoners in the weeks immediately after the liberation of the camp in April, 1945, lays out the timeline of events on April 11, 1945. The key events began at around 10:30 AM, when the camp Commander, SS Colonel Hermann Pister, summoned the senior prisoner functionary, Camp Elder Hans Eiden, and informed him that the SS would abandon Buchenwald and leave it in his hands. At approximately noon, an announcement was made over the Buchenwald public-address system to the effect that all SS-men should evacuate the camp immediately. During the afternoon of the 11th, inmates reported hearing small-arms fire and the sounds of tanks engaged in combat and moving around the camp. The prisoners consolidated control of the camp after the SS had fled, raising a white flag over the main gate to the prisoner area of the camp. The clock over the main gate today memorializes this event as having occurred at 3:15 PM, the time to which it is now permanently set. Shortly after the flag was raised, American troops entered the camp from the northwest, the direction of the village of Hottelstedt. The exact time of their arrival is unknown, but estimates place it variously at around 4:00 PM or 5:00 PM[23].

Liberation Day – The American View

At the United States Holocaust Memorial Museum (USHMM) in Washington D.C, there is an exhibit memorializing the American liberators of Nazi concentration camps. The US Army Center for Military History has established certain criteria to be used in identifying Army units as "liberators" of Nazi camps. These criteria are that the units must have arrived at the camp within 48 hours of the first entry of American troops, and that the units be Army Divisions[24]. The Divisions recognized on the USHMM website[25] as having liberated Buchenwald are the 6th Armored Division and the 80th Infantry Division, assigned to George S. Patton's Third Army. As we will see below, the Fourth Armored Division should also be included. The account of the liberation by the 6th Armored Division soldiers is relatively straightforward.

---

[23] Hackett, David A. *The Buchenwald Report*. (Boulder: Westview Press, 1995) pp. 103-104; 332-334

[24] Divisions during World War II varied in strength depending on their function (Armor, Infantry) but generally would have contained 10,000-20,000 troops.

[25] United States Holocaust Memorial Museum, Liberating Unit Histories and Insignia, https://www.ushmm.org/information/exhibitions/online-exhibitions/special-focus/liberation/liberating-unit-histories-and-insignia, retrieved October 6 2019.

Flags of some of the Army Divisions recognized as concentration camp liberators at the United States Holocaust Memorial Museum. This photograph is from the annual Days of Remembrance ceremony at the United States Capitol Rotunda. (Photograph used with permission from the US Holocaust Memorial Museum).

Captains Robert Bennett and Frederic Keffer, both soldiers in the 9th Armored Infantry Battalion, 6th Armored Division, 3rd Army, were interviewed at Mittweida, Germany on April 21, 1945 (ten days after the liberation of Buchenwald) by Lieutenant Colonel Hollis C. Alpert. In a section of the interview transcript entitled "THE DISCOVERY OF BUCHENWALD" Keffer and Bennett provided this account of the liberation:

"CT 9[26] unknowingly provided the liberation of the camp that later became famous, or rather infamous, as a symbol of the chill-blooded cruelty of the German Nazi state, along with other such camps in which deliberate starvation of thousands of political prisoners was accomplished, in which many thousands of others were burned, beaten, hung and shot to death. BUCHENWALD (J4375[27]) contained 21,000 prisoners at the time of its

---

[26] Combat Team 9, the organization to which the 9th Armored Infantry Battalion was assigned. CT 9 was assigned to Combat Command A, 6th Armored Division.

[27] WWII map references found in US operational records for Europe are to the "Nord du Guerre" grid, an element of the Modified British System. This system is explained here, (https://www.echodelta.net/mbs/eng-welcome.php) an immensely valuable website. Buchenwald was in the grid square labelled "wJ". Using the Coordinate Translator found on this site (https://www.echodelta.net/mbs/eng-translator.php) these WWII references can be converted to latitude and longitude and plotted using modern mapping utilities. This location is actually about three kilometers directly west of the camp.

capture; it had originally held 60,000. There is reason to believe that the prompt arrival of the 6th Armored Division (and specifically) CT 9 [sic] on the scene saved many hundreds and perhaps thousands of lives. The newspaper and magazines have given much space to the horrows [sic] of BUCHENWALD, but little was told about the manner in which it was liberated. Unfortunately, the detailing of that leberation [sic], will probably come as something of an anti-climax.

CT 9 was passing along a road near ETTERSBURG [sic] (J4876[28]) when several Allied PWs came running down the road toward the column. It was about 1600, the afternoon of April 11. Capt Frederic Keffer, the Battalion S-2[29], in speaking to some of these prisoners learned of a large camp in the woods slightly to the south, which held a number of prisoners of the Germans. He was told also that most of the SS troops who administered the camp had fled, but that some had been held in an uprising of the prisoners when rumors of the nearness of American armored units had filled the camp. Capt Keffer took his S-2 Sergeant and two of the prisoners and went in a peep [sic] to investigate. He drove through the entrance of the camp and literally thousands of the prisoners surrounded him in a cheering mob. He was lifted from the peep [sic] and carried about the camp on the shoulders of the crowd like a conquering hero. They'd toss him into the air, catch him, and toss him again. Capt Keffer finally got tired of that sort of thing and insisted that he be let down. He then assured some of the prisoners that others would be along shortly, asked them to stay where they were, and escaped in his jeep. He was told the name of the camp, which was BUCHENWALD, but it had little meaning for him at that time. While at the camp he was shown some of the SS guards, who were securely staked down alive to the ground. These guards were later kept in custody by the prisoners, and some of the Russians and Poles organized expeditions into the surrounding villages to track down some of the SS who had escaped. Some were found and brought back to the camp, but no harm to them was actually witnessed by any of the Americans who visited the camp. Probably the prisoners who had been kept in a state of brutal enslavement did not wish to see them die too speedily. (This last information was given me by MG officers of XX Corps who paid many visits to BUCHENWALD)."[30]

---

[28] This location is approximately two kilometers northeast of Buchenwald, just south of the village of Ettersberg.

[29] The S-2 is the Intelligence officer; Bennett was the S-3, Operations Officer.

[30] National Archives and Records Administration, Record Group 407, Entry 284, Box 24096.

This story is repeated in George Hofmann's book *The Super Sixth*, though this version adds two more soldiers and has them entering through a hole in the fence rather than driving through the main gate:

"It was in the neighborhood of 1600 when Keffer, Gottschalk, Ward, and Hoyt, plus two of the escaped Russian prisoners, drove into the camp through a hole cut in the fence by the escaping Russians. Then they passed through a double, barbed-wire fence, 12 feet high and electrically charged."[31]

The prisoner account suggests that the Americans entered the camp from the northwest, along the road from the village of Hottelstedt that passes very close to the camp. The interview and summary presented by Hoffman both suggest that the encounter with the Russian prisoners took place near Ettersberg, which is east of Hottelstedt. There is no direct road from Ettersberg to Buchenwald, so it is quite possible that the soldiers drove back west to Hottelstedt, and then turned south to get to Buchenwald. Jürgen Möller reproduces a copy of a message from the 9th Armored Infantry Battalion (Keffer's unit) to 6th Armored Division G-2 logged at 6:10 PM on April 11 that states: "CONCENTRATION CAMP 463572 HAS SOME POLITICAL INCLUDING GERMAN HAVE BEEN INSTRUCTED TO STAY IN PLACE AWAITING MG[32]". The position noted is about 130 meters northwest of the *Effektenkammer*, the building in which prisoners' belongings were stored, which houses the present-day museum at Buchenwald.

The United States Holocaust Memorial Museum also reports that, "During its advance into central Germany, the 80th Infantry Division entered the Buchenwald concentration camp on April 12, 1945, to provide relief to the 6th Armored Division, which had arrived the day before.[33]" Evidence shows that the 4th Armored Division was also active in the discovery and occupation of Buchenwald: while the USHMM website does not credit the 4th Armored Division as a liberator of Buchenwald, it is so credited by the US Army Center for Military History[34], and as we shall see, was at Buchenwald on the 11th and requested help from the 80th Infantry Division to secure Buchenwald.

---

[31] George F. Hofmann. *The Super Sixth: History of the 6th Armored Division in World War II and its post-war Association*. (Louisville, Kentucky: Sixth Armored Division Association, 1975).

[32] Moeller, Juergen. *Konzentrationslager Buchenwald Weimar im April 1945: Die amerikanische Besetzung von Weimar Wer befreite Buchenwald?*, (Bad Langensalza, Verlag Rockstuhl, 2017), p. 38.

[33] The 80th Infantry Division, USHMM, https://encyclopedia.ushmm.org/content/en/article/the-80th-infantry-division, retrieved 9 January 2019.

[34] Letter from Terence J. Gough, Chief, Staff Support Branch, US Army Center for Military History to Mr. Bernd Schmidt, October 6, 1995. "Three divisions, the 4th and 6th Armored Divisions and the 80th Infantry Division, that were assigned to the Third U.S. Army are credited with the liberation of Buchenwald concentration camp on April 11 and 12, 1945."

Liberation Day– The German View

The *Buchenwald Gedenkstätte* is the memorial organization that administers the site of Buchenwald today. The version of events presented by the *Buchenwald Gedenkstätte* agrees with the USHMM version with respect to the late-afternoon arrival of the team from the 6th Armored Division. There are some differences between the way the story of the liberation is presented at the *Buchenwald Gedenkstätte* and in many American accounts, however. The *Buchenwald Gedenkstätte* appears to place the arrival of the 80th Infantry at Buchenwald on the 13th of April, for example:

"**12 April 1945**

The city of Weimar is occupied by units of the 80th Infantry Division. Initial contact is made with the camp now under the command of the International Camp Committee.

13 April 1945, 11:30 am

Lt. Colonel Edmund A. Ball of the 80th Infantry Division takes command of the camp; a company of the 317th Infantry Regiment is assigned to protect it. Ball meets with 21 representatives of the International Camp Committee, is briefed on the situation and decides what is to be done next. Following a memorial service in honour of Franklin D. Roosevelt, who had died the previous day, the inmates turn in their weapons."[35]

The *Buchenwald Gedenkstätte* also clearly identifies the 4th Armored Division as having been involved in combat with German forces in and around Buchenwald on April 11th *before* the arrival of the team from the 6th Armored Division. The timeline for April 11, 1945, as presented on the *Buchenwald Gedenkstätte* website is reproduced (with permission) below:

"**11 April 1945**

Morning

Units of the 4th and 6th Armored Divisions of the Third U.S. Army continue their advance from the area around Gotha towards the east via Erfurt.

around 10:00 a.m.

Camp senior Hans Eiden and Franz Eichhorn are ordered to report to the camp gate. Concentration camp commandant Pister announces the withdrawal of the SS to Eiden and instructs him to take control of the camp when this plan goes into effect.

---

[35] *Buchenwald Gedenkstätte*, https://www.buchenwald.de/en/469/, retrieved 31 December 2018.

10:00 a.m.

The "enemy alarm" siren sounds. The order "All members of the SS out of the camp immediately!" is given over the loudspeakers.

10:30 a.m.

The international camp committee mobilizes the resistance groups and distributes illegally obtained weapons.

11:00 a.m.

Infantry fire of American troops northwest of the camp.

around noon

The members of the SS command staff flee. The watchtower personnel abscond.

1:00 p.m.

The first two tanks of the 4th Armored Division of the Third U.S. Army approach from the direction of Hottelstedt.

2:00 p.m.

Heavy machine-gun fire at the north-western edge of the camp; twelve American tanks are sighted near the service courtyard. Four American tanks circuit the camp to the north of the grounds. Heavy fighting between American troops and the SS to the west of the camp.

2:30 pm

Tanks of the 37th Tank Battalion of the 4th Armored Division overrun the SS and command staff area without stopping. The SS has been militarily defeated.

2:45 p.m.

The armed resistance groups gather downhill from the roll call square.

3:00 p.m.

Otto Roth, the head of the military resistance groups, and two electricians enter the gate building by way of a ladder and occupy it without encountering resistance. The camp senior Hans Eiden follows them, hoists a white flag, and informs the camp of the situation in a short loudspeaker announcement.

4:00 p.m.

As planned, and without a struggle, the international resistance groups have taken control of the various areas of the camp and captured 76 prisoners in the process.

4:45 p.m.

Representatives of ten nations gather. They appoint a camp council and various commissions to ensure survival.

around 5:00 p.m.

Two scouts of the 4th Armored Division arrive at the camp gate in a jeep. Lieutenant Emmanuel Desard and Sergeant Paul Bodot - both Frenchman [sic] - learn of the combat operations from the liberated inmates. Lieutenant Desard appoints the camp senior head of the camp. He reports to the division staff what he has discovered: a liberated camp, armed and organized inmates.

around 5:10 p.m.

A reconnaissance troop of the 9th Infantry Battalion, part of Combat Team 9 of the 6th Armored Division, enters the camp at the northern end of the grounds. Captain Frederic Keffer, Sergeant Herbert Gottschalk, Sergeant Harry Ward and Private James Hoyt are greeted as liberators. Like Desard and Bodot, they remain for only a short time"[36].

Most contemporary reports mention sounds of gunfire and vehicles passing near the camp on the morning and afternoon of April 11th. The *Buchenwald Gedenkstätte*'s very specific claim that the 37th Tank Battalion (commanded at the time by Lieutenant Colonel Creighton Abrams, later Commander of US forces in Vietnam and namesake of the M-1 Abrams Main Battle Tank) fought the SS at Buchenwald and overran the camp itself is consistent with this entry in the After-Action Report of the 37th Tank Battalion, 4th Armored Division for April 11, 1945:

> "A/37[37] and C/10 continued on the main route of march and encountered direct AT fire in the vicinity of Daasdorf and Haberndorf.
>
> B/37 and A/10 took an alternate route Northeast from Ottstedt to 445758 and then East through the woods, coming out at 520765. They liberated a PW camp with 800-1000 Russian and French Prisoners; encountered bazooka fire on East edge of woods.

---

[36] *Buchenwald Gedenkstätte*, https://www.buchenwald.de/en/473/, retrieved 31 December 2018.

[37] These abbreviations identify the company-level units involved. "A/37" is A Company, 37th Tank Battalion; "C/10" is C Company, 10th Armored Infantry Battalion.

A/37 and C/10 were ordered to return to Ottstedt and continue along B/37's route of advance.

After breaking out of the woods B/37 and A/10 were momentarily stopped while D/37 and Assault Guns took the lead.

D/37 and Assault Guns ran into bazooka and small arms at Denstedt; they cleaned the town and then proceeded to Schwabsdorf which they outposted for the night.

A/37 and C/10 outposted Ulrichshaben; B/37 and A/10 outposted Sussenborn, and C/37 and B/10 cut roads leading into Grosskromsdorf from the West or rear."[38]

The two locations specified in the message (wJ445758 and wJ 520765) are located a few kilometers northwest and northeast of Buchenwald, respectively. Jürgen Möller's well-researched and informative book *Konzentrationslager Buchenwald Weimar: Wer Befreite Buchenwald?* (Who liberated Buchenwald?) provides a detailed look at the movements of the American units in the area of Buchenwald on the day of liberation. Drawing heavily on US military records, Möller makes the case that it was the actions of the 4th Armored Division units that set the stage for the arrival of the Keffer patrol later in the day. Möller suggests that it was the arrival of B/37 and A/10 that immediately precipitated the flight of the SS guards from Buchenwald and led to the release of the Russian prisoners who then encountered Keffer while pursuing the guards in the vicinity of Ettersberg. The 4th Armored Division units played a pivotal role in events that day, and apparently arrived before the 6th Armored Division personnel. The 37th Tank Battalion After-Action Report makes clear that they were at Buchenwald on April 11, 1945 without naming the camp; Möller notes that in the "much later-written Combat History of the 4th Armored Division" Buchenwald was mentioned by name. Möller concludes that the 4th and 6th Armored Divisions "gebührt die gleiche Ehre" (deserve the same honor) as liberators of Buchenwald[39].

There are other indications that the 4th Armored Division was present at Buchenwald on the 11th. A message in the 6th Armored Division G-1 Journal to XX Corps G-1 logged at 1110 on 11 April clearly places 4th Armored Division soldiers at the camp several hours before the reported arrival of the Keffer party from 6th Armored Division:

---

[38] 37th Tank Battalion After Action report, Ike Skelton Combined Arms Research Library, http://cgsc.cdmhost.com/cdm/ref/collection/p4013coll8/id/3721, retrieved 1 July 2019.

[39] Moeller, Juergen. *Konzentrationslager Buchenwald Weimar im April 1945: Die amerikanische Besetzung von Weimar Wer befreite Buchenwald?*, (Bad Langensalza, Verlag Rockstuhl, 2017), p. 38.

"...AT ETTERSBURG 21000, MAJORITY FRENCH ESTIMATED THREE HUNDRED ARMED THEMSELVES WITH DISCARDED GERMAN WEAPONS. ONE MARCEL PAUL (FR) PRESENT IN CAMP IS ACCUSED OF RESPONSIBILITY OF DEATHS OF 17,000 FRENCHMEN. INFO FROM AN ENGLISH OFFICER PRESENT IN CAMP. PWD TEAM OF 4 Δ ADMINISTERING THE CAMP 3 KM SW OF TOWN. FOOD AND MEDICAL SITUATION CRITICAL. URGENTLY NEED ASSISTANCE. REQUEST INF DIV TO TAKE OVER."[40]

This message says clearly that a "PWD team" of the 4th Armored Division (the triangle seen in the message represents the triangular shoulder patch associated with US armored divisions) was administering the camp as early as the morning of the 11th. "PWD" may refer to a Psychological Warfare Division or Department. It is not immediately clear exactly who the members of this "PWD team" were.

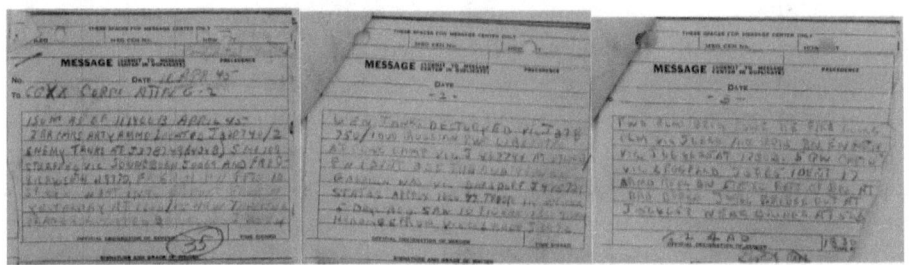

Another reference to Fourth Armored Division activity at Buchenwald appears in a message containing an intelligence summary sent from 4th Armored Division G-2 at 1830 on April 11 to CG XX Corps G-2 containing the following; "750/1000 Russian PWs liberated at conce camp vic J467744".[41] This may refer to the same incident noted in the 37th Tank Battalion after-action report, which also specifies "Russian and French prisoners" and gives a similar number (800-1000). There is also a message from CCB, 4th Armored Division, to the 4th AD G-2 dated 11 April and signed at 5:19 PM that states, "FWD ELMS LOC 5075 – 1700 HRS. APPROX 1000 RUSSIAN PWS LIBERATED AT LARGE CONC. CAMP (4 KM NW WEIMAR) VIC 467744." This message clearly places the 4th Armored Division at Buchenwald on April 11. The position wJ5075 is approximately 3.5 kilometers east of Buchenwald, south of the village of Kleinobringen and north of Weimar. That these elements of the 4th AD were only 3.5 kilometers (2 miles)

---

[40] National Archives and Records Administration, Records Group 407, Box 12529. The reference to Marcel Paul is curious. Paul was a French Communist who became a prominent politician after the war. He was accused of misusing his position as a camp functionary after the war, but was never charged or tried.

[41] National Archives and Records Administration, Records Group 407, Entry 427, Box 12365

east of Buchenwald at 5 PM may suggest that their visit to the camp had also occurred relatively late in the afternoon.

This display of US Army field equipment at the *Buchenwald Gedenkstätte* contains a uniform with the triangular shoulder patch of the 4th Armored Division. (Author's photograph. Used with permission).

LT Emmanuel Desard and Sergeant Paul Bodot were Free French interpreters assigned to the 4th Armored Division G-2 section. These soldiers reportedly arrived at Buchenwald in a jeep late on the afternoon of the 11th, made contact with Hans Eiden, the ranking prisoner functionary, placed him in charge of the camp, and issued him a pass to identify him to "Allied officers". The pass, a photograph of the jeep, and a description of the scene by Paul Bodot are in the collection of the *Buchenwald Gedenkstätte*. This visit is also mentioned on the website of the *Association Francaise Buchenwald Dora et Kommandos*, which discusses the role of the French Resistance at Buchenwald, but fixes their arrival at 5:30 PM:

> "5h30 – Une jeep américaine avec deux combattants français à bord, le lieutenant Desard et le sergent Bodot, arrive au camp, guidée par des détenus en armes"[42].

Jürgen Möller discusses the presence of these two soldiers at Buchenwald on April 11, 1945, and notes that while the timeline presented by the *Buchenwald Gedenkstätte* places Desard/Bodot and the Keffer party at Buchenwald at the same time, there was apparently no contact between them.

---

[42] Association Francaise Buchenwald Dora et Kommandos, https://asso-buchenwald-dora.com/le-camp-de-buchenwald/histoire-du-camp-de-buchenwald/, retrieved 31 December 2018.

Paul Bodot in the jeep in which he and Lt Emmanuel Desard visited Buchenwald. Copyright Paul Bodot – Association francaise Buchenwald Dora. Used with permission.

There is indeed a message in the 4th Armored Division files dated April 11 (but not time-stamped) signed by a Lt Desard that offers considerable detail about Buchenwald, correctly identifying the camp by name:

"CONCENTRATION CAMP BUCHENWALD (4775) OCCUPIED By 21,400 political prisoners: about 7000 FRENCH, others are GERMAN ANTI-NAZIS, RUSSIANS, POLES, SPANIARDS. ABOUT 20,000 have been evacuated during past 3 days. MEDICAL SIT: 3000 sick, many in critical state; 3000 invalids incl blind. Hospital and doctors present but no medicine or med materials or disinfectants on hand. Situation desperate. Help urgently required. FOOD SIT: Sufficient for 2 days but no bread at all on hand – Special Assault groups had been organized to overpower the guards. Before our arrival the guard posts were taken and 125 SS were captd and are still in custody of the camp. The leadership of the camp is in the hands of a well organized committee comprising all nationalities represented. DESARD Lt"[43]

---

[43] National Archives and Records Administration, Records Group 407, Entry 427, Box 12365.

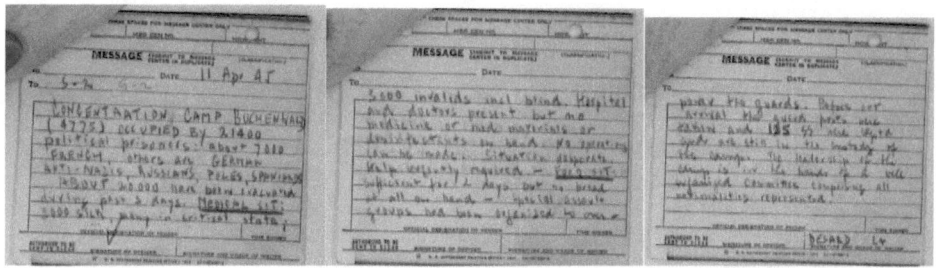

National Archives and Records Administration, Records Group 407, Entry 427, Box 12365.

The *Buchenwald Gedenkstätte* has a pass on display in the permanent exhibition at Buchenwald said to have been issued by Desard to Hans Eiden, the camp elder. Captain Davidson's report to XX Corps Headquarters (see below) about Buchenwald, sent the morning of the 12th, also refers to a pass: "Pass given to leader and two others to take groups out to obtain transportation and food and ordered to hold all people intact". The handwriting on the Desard pass in the collection of the *Buchenwald Gedenkstätte* and that on the Desard message in the 4th Division files do not, on causal inspection, appear to be the same (though I am no expert), and there is a clear and marked difference in the quality of the English in the two documents: the Desard message in the 4th Division files is composed in flawless English, while the pass at Buchenwald exhibits quite poor English:

"ALL ALLIED OFFICERS THE BEARER EIDEM IS LEADER OF ALL THE POLITIC PRISONNERS OF THE BUCHENWALD CONCENTRATION CAMP – PLEASE GIVE TO HIM PASS LT DESARD [ILLEGIBLE]".

> **MESSAGE** (SUBMIT TO MESSAGE CENTER IN DUPLICATE)
>
> ALL ALLIED OFFICERS
>
> THE BEARER EIDEM IS LEADER OF ALL POLITIC PRISONER OF THE BUCHENWALD CONCENTRATION CAMP PLEASE GIVE TO HIM PASS
>
> LT DESARD

Photo courtesy of the *Buchenwald Gedenkstätte*.

The pass is very difficult to read, and the above is what I see upon inspection of photographs of the pass and visual inspection of the pass (I believe a facsimile of the original is on display) as it sits in the display case at Buchenwald. The date "April 11" is much fainter than the other writing, and the identifying information below the name "Desard" is lower case and faint, while the rest of the pass is upper case. Perhaps these differences may be explained by haste when Desard wrote the pass, perhaps some of the writing was added later, or perhaps someone else wrote it out on his authority, or perhaps the pass was subjected to some kind of restoration at some point.

Soldiers from the 6th Armored Division were also at Buchenwald on the evening of the 11th. Captains Edmund Coates and Charles Davidson from the Sixth Armored Division General Staff appear to have arrived after Keffer and his party had left Buchenwald According to the 6th Armored Division G-1 Journal for 1900 (7 PM) on the 11th: "Asst G-1 departed for concentration camp containing 21000 political PW's. Checked on food and medical supplies and organized camp."[44] The 6th Armored Division G-2 log also summarizes a message received at 2345 (11:45 PM) on the 11th: "Res Comd: Coats informs me Comd SS garrison at Weimar. Telephone concentration camp at Ettersburg said unless talked to commander of camp personally he would send troopers. 21,000 people in camp with 1 day food supply a little medicine. Request you notify G-1.[45] It seems quite probable that Coates, the Asst G-1, was accompanied by Captain Davidson, 6th AD Assistant G-5. Early the following morning, Captain Davidson sent out three messages to XXth Corps in quick succession describing conditions at Buchenwald, Buttstadt, and Bad Sulza.

There is also further evidence of 4th Armored Division activity at and around Buchenwald on the 11th and 12th of April. At 0645 on the 12th of April, 4th AD G-2 transmitted the below message to XX Corps:

"MARKED MAP CAPTD TODAY VIC 466744 THOUGHT RELIABLE SHOWS SS WIKING MOVING S TOWARD RASTENBURG FR GENERAL DIR QUERFURT/REQ INFO ON THIS OUTFIT".[46]

At 0725 6th AD G-2 logged a summary:

"4th AD: Captured map shows SS Wiking moving S from F, QUERFURT D6916 to SASTENBURG J5893."[47]

The location of the map's reported capture is about 75 meters east of the road from Weimar to Buchenwald and about 150 meters south of the Buchenwald railyard; the timing of the messages suggests it may have been captured on the 11th. "Rastenberg" appears to be the correct spelling of the village referenced in the message, as the town of Rastenberg is about 30 km northeast of Weimar, which corresponds to the grid coordinates wJ5893. Querfurt is about 26 km northeast of Rastenberg.

Still another claim to priority in liberating Buchenwald is that of Egon W. Fleck and 1LT Edward A. Tenenbaum. Fleck and Tenenbaum were definitely at Buchenwald, as representatives of the Publicity and Psychological Warfare section at 12th Army Group Headquarters. Fleck and Tenenbaum submitted a report to their headquarters on April 24, 1945, entitled, "Buchenwald: A Preliminary Report". Curiously, the report itself does not specify the date on which the authors arrived at Buchenwald. David Hackett, in *The Buchenwald Report*, describes the

---

[44] National Archives and Records Administration, Records Group 407, Entry 427, Box 12529.
[45] National Archives and Records Administration, Records Group 407, Entry 427, Box 12529.
[46] National Archives and Records Administration, Records Group 407, Entry 427, Box 12365.
[47] National Archives and Records Administration, Records Group 407, Entry 427, Box 12529.

arrival of Fleck and Tenenbaum at Buchenwald on April 11 at approximately 5:30 PM. Hackett has Fleck and Tenenbaum remaining overnight at Buchenwald, and being awakened by a serenade from a brass band on the morning of the 12th, a detail mentioned in Fleck and Tenenbaum's report.[48]"

There is also a reference to Fleck and Tenenbaum as the first liberators of Buchenwald on the United States Holocaust Memorial Museum website documenting an artifact contributed by the Tenenbaum family:

"Pair of binoculars thrown at Lt. Edward Tenenbaum during the liberation of Buchenwald concentration camp in April 1945. Edward served in the OSS and the US Army during the Second World War (1939-1945). He was the first American officer to enter Buchenwald at liberation, a participant in the liberation of Ohrdruf, and author of the Buchenwald Report."[49]

Yet another claim for the priority of Fleck and Tenenbaum comes from Jorge Semprun, the well-known Spanish writer and Buchenwald survivor:

"He remembers how, alongside other Buchenwald inmates, he was a 22-year-old communist resistant taking up arms and fighting to at last bring down the gates of hell on 11 April 1945. 'The irony of the story,' begins Semprun, 'is that the American GIs had beaten and dispersed the Buchenwald garrison and charged victoriously onto Weimar. But it was only five days later, on 16 April, when two soldiers, Egon W. Fleck and Edward A. Tenenbaum, who had stayed behind entered the camp alone - so effectively, Buchenwald concentration camp was only really freed by American Jews of German origin!' Situated only a stone's throw from Weimar, the home of German poet Goethe, the Buchenwald camp chronicle did not stop with the nazi [sic] defeat"[50].

Semprun's version is not corroborated by any other reports of which I am aware. Semprun's account pushes the arrival of Americans at Buchenwald to the 16th, which is simply wrong, and invents a battle for Buchenwald and Weimar that did not take place. While Fleck and Tenenbaum do not specifically cite the date on which they arrived in Buchenwald, their report contains the following passage:

---

[48] Hackett, *Buchenwald Report*, p. 5.

[49] United States Holocaust Memorial Museum, Binoculars thrown at US soldier during concentration camp liberation, https://collections.ushmm.org/search/catalog/irn559440, retrieved 31 December, 2018. The caption of the photograph describing Tenenbaum as the first officer to arrive at Buchenwald may simply be the information that accompanied the donation of the artifact, not a determination by the USHMM.

[50] CafeBabel, Jorge Semprun, https://cafebabel.com/en/article/jorge-semprun-buchenwald-concentration-camp-survivor-65-years-on-5ae007aaf723b35a145e2402/, retrieved 31 December 2018.

"The writers first learned of the liberation of BUCHENWALD as they were riding down a forest road with an American column. They turned a corner onto a main highway, and saw thousands of ragged, hungry-looking men, marching in orderly formations, marching East. These men were armed, and had leaders at their sides. Some platoons carried German rifles. Some platoons had PANZERFAUSTS on their shoulders. Some carried "potato masher" hand grenades. They laughed and waved wildly as they walked. Or their captains saluted gravely for them. They were of many nationalities, a platoon of French, followed by a platoon of Spaniards, platoons of Russians, Poles, Jews, Dutch, mixed platoons. -Some wore striped convicts suits, some ragged uniforms of the United Nations, some shreds of civilian clothes. These were inmates of BUCHENWALD, walking out to war as tanks swept by at 25 miles per hour. 3. They were ordered to return to their camp by a tank officer. They did so, though many seemed disappointed. They wanted to know where the Germans were. They wanted to kill. The interrogators turned back towards BUCHENWALD, which lay close on the main road. At the gates of the camp were sentries. In the camp was a Camp Commandant, a German inmate. In the camp were 21,000 survivors who cheered at the sight of an American uniform, rushed out to shake hands, and threw valuable binoculars from their slave workshops at the passing troops. Yet in the camp there reigned order. Meals were served. Armed guards - inmates - patrolled the somber grounds, and wildly excited groups of men calmed at a word from those in authority. 4. That evening the interrogators attended a meeting of the Camp Directorate and of the Council. Then they were provided with beds in Block 50, the Typhus Experiment Laboratory, where victims of typhus injections were observed as they died. In the morning they were awakened by a brass band, which serenaded them until they appeared at the windows, to be cheered by several thousand inmates. Later they were present at a huge parade of part of the camp's inhabitants, and addressed them over a loudspeaker system. It was an incredible experience, as hard to forget as the sight of the camp's crematorium, the fresh corpses, and the living dead of the so-called "small camp." It was the rebirth of humanity in a bestial surrounding"[51].

---

[51] Egon Fleck and Edward Tenenbaum, *Buchenwald: A Preliminary Report*. https://archive.org/details/EdwardTenenbaumEgonFleckPreliminaryBuchenwaldReport/page/n8, retrieved 7 July 2019.

Pair of binoculars received by 1LT Edward Tenenbaum from prisoners at Buchenwald. Gift of Jeanette Tenenbaum. Photograph used with permission from the United States Holocaust Memorial Museum.

Fleck and Tenenbaum were certainly at Buchenwald, though the above account does not specify the date of the events described. It seems to describe the first arrival of American troops at Buchenwald, and suggests that the meeting of the council they attended occurred on the evening of April 11, and the brass band serenade on the morning of the 12th. Their description of their arrival does not mention the presence of any other American troops, however. Later in their report, Fleck and Tenenbaum recount a timeline of events at Buchenwald in the weeks leading up to the liberation that clearly was obtained from discussions with prisoners. This timeline does specifically address the 11th:

"On the morning of 11 April small arms fire was audible in the camp, announcing the imminent approach of American troops. The lead tanks of the American unit were visible from the camp at 1300. About 1430, American tanks were attacking the immediate vicinity. The SS troops began a hasty retreat, after receiving orders to move in small groups to a reassembly point at SUESSEN-BORN. At the same time the inmates brought their arms into the open and began to take control of the camp. Informants are not unanimous as to what happened then. The Communist group claims that SS troops were still on guard in the watch towers around the camp, and that these were stormed by the prisoners. Others say that there was no actual fighting between inmates and SS until the American troops had seized control of the area."[52]

It is difficult to determine from the report written by Fleck and Tenenbaum exactly when they arrived at Buchenwald, as the report blends their own recollections with material derived from discussions with prisoners in a confusing way. They represented a somewhat specialized group within Twelfth Army Group Headquarters. It is possible that information about Buchenwald was sent up the chain of command after liberation of the camp on the 11th, and Fleck and Tenenbaum arrived at Buchenwald a few days later to investigate and report back to higher headquarters.

On the other hand, the 4th Armored Division message reporting that a "PWD team" was in place at Buchenwald on the morning of the 11th suggests the possibility that Fleck and Tenenbaum were at Buchenwald on the day of liberation: they were assigned to the Psychological Warfare Section, Publicity and Psychological Warfare Team at 12th Army Group Headquarters. It is possible that they might have been in the area or detailed to 4th Armored Division when reports of the large concentration camp encountered on the 11th made their way to the 4th Armored Division, and it is possible that they might have been referred to as a "PWD team". Other aspects of their story, such as the brass band playing on the morning of the 12th, are not mentioned in other accounts and may instead suggest that they arrived at the camp some days after the liberation.

Records from the 4th Armored Division files also show that the 4th AD was active in ensuring that the 80th Infantry Division would soon arrive at Buchenwald. At 0940 on the morning of 12 April, the Commanding General of the 4th Armored Division, Major General William C. Hoge, sent a message directly to the Commanding General of the 80th Infantry Division requesting that the 80th secure Buchenwald: "To CG 80 ID (Att Mil Gov): Concentration camp BUCHENWALD (J4674) 22000 DP's uncovered. Request you take over and secure to prevent exodus. HOGE.[53]" At the same time, a message was sent to a Major Reed of 4th AD CCB referring to Hoge's 0940 message: "To CC B (Att Maj Reed): Have requested 80 Div to take over BUCHENWALD. Secure as best you can until you move. HOGE.[54]" This message was logged into CC B's G-3 log at 1019 on the 12th. These messages clearly place the 4th Armored Division at Buchenwald on April 12th, and show that 4th AD was active in coordinating relief for Buchenwald from the 80th Infantry Division. That help was on the way was confirmed to CCB at noon on the 12th: G-2 4th AD sent the following message to

---

[52] Ibid.

[53] National Archives and Records Administration, Records Group 407, Entry 427, Box 12390.

[54] National Archives and Records Administration, Records Group 407, Entry 427, Box 12419.

CCB to close the loop: "Re CONC CAMP BUCHENWALD 80 ID HAS PLAT OF CAV [platoon of cavalry - author] ON WAY TO TAKE OVER MGO [military government operations - author]55".

Liberation Day Timeline – What Happened?

Is it possible, then, to construct a timeline for the American presence at Buchenwald on April 11, 1945? Taking all of the foregoing into account, we can propose a timeline for liberation day that includes a complete list of those Americans who have the best claim to having been present at Buchenwald on April 11, 1945.

1. By 1110 on the morning of April 11, the 6th Armored Division was aware of Buchenwald, and reported that it was being administered by a PWD team of the 4th Armored Division.

2. B Company of the 37th Tank Battalion (4th Armored Division) and A Company of the 10th Armored Infantry Battalion encountered a camp containing 800-1,000 Russian and French prisoners sometime on the 11th, and liberated the prisoners. Based on the description of the prisoners and the geographic location of the unit, this must have been at Buchenwald. The presence of the 37th Tank Battalion is corroborated by the unit's After-Action Report, and coincides with the description of events that appeared in the prisoner's narrative, which became *The Buchenwald Report*.

3. Egon Fleck and 1LT Edward Tenenbaum, representatives of the Publicity and Psychological Warfare Team of 12th Corps, may have been in the camp on the morning of the 11th. Both David Hackett, in *The Buchenwald Report*, and the artifact description at the USHMM claim priority for Fleck and Tenenbaum. There is at least the possibility of corroboration in the 4th Armored Division message traffic referring to a "PWD" team at Buchenwald, but the presence of Fleck and Tenenbaum at the camp on the 11th cannot be definitely confirmed.

4. Four soldiers from the 9th Armored Infantry Battalion (6th Armored Division) (Captain Frederic Keffer, PFC James Hoyt, T/SGT Herbert Gottschalk and Sergeant Harry Ward) visited Buchenwald for a short time late in the afternoon of the 11th – most likely between 4 PM and 6 PM. This visit is documented in American records by the radio message sent by Keffer to 6th Armored Division headquarters. This visit may correspond to

---

55 National Archives and Records Administration, Records Group 407, Entry 427, Box 12365.

the prisoners' report of an "American scout car" appearing at the camp at about 4 P.M.
5. Two Free French soldiers, Sergeant Paul Bodot and LT Emmanuel Desard, who were assigned to the 4th Armored Division, are reported to have visited Buchenwald at about the same time as the Keffer party. There is a lengthy and detailed message from Desard dated April 11 describing Buchenwald in the 4th Armored Division records, and a pass issued by Desard to Hans Eiden also dated April 11 in the collection of the *Buchenwald Gedenkstätte*.
6. Two more soldiers from the 6th Armored Division (Captains Coates and Davidson) visited Buchenwald after the Keffer party. Coates is mentioned in 6th Armored Division messages as departing for the camp around 7 PM, and a report from him concerning Buchenwald was logged into 6th AD headquarters just before midnight on the 11th. Davidson composed and sent messages about Buchenwald to XX Corps headquarters the next morning.

Liberation Day Timeline – What Did Not Happen?

What is also significant for the purpose of evaluating later claims about the liberation of Buchenwald is what is missing from the records and reports. There are no reports of American tanks forcibly entering Buchenwald; no accounts of combat in or around the camp; no reports of American or enemy casualties incurred in any action in or near the camp. There are no records suggesting that American tanks crashed through any fences or blew open any gates; no suggestion that the Americans who visited the camp saw evidence of any significant combat having taken place before their arrival. No American reports mention finding any dead or wounded German soldiers at Buchenwald, only the several dozen SS guards rounded up by the inmates. None of the operational reports contain any mention of smoke pouring from the crematorium chimney, something that might well have been included in such traffic. Many later accounts that appear to be false or distorted memories of the liberation of Buchenwald do include one or more of these elements.

After Liberation

The focus of this book is squarely on the day of liberation, April 11, 1945, but what happened after the liberation is quite relevant to the issue of how liberation day has been remembered and misremembered. American troops began arriving in force on Friday, April 13. The 120th Evacuation Hospital arrived at Buchenwald late on Sunday, April 15[56], and began preparing to administer life-saving medical support to the inmates there. Many other units moved in and out of Buchenwald during the 10 weeks or so that the camp was occupied by Americans. Some of these units were there for only a short time, while others stayed longer. In addition to organized units at Buchenwald, many soldiers were sent to Buchenwald on missions of various kinds as part of small groups or detachments for a brief and specific purpose. Many others visited the camp for the sole purpose of seeing it.

Many soldiers visited Buchenwald in the weeks after liberation. This snapshot was taken June 6, 1945. Photo courtesy of Jim van Buskirk. Photograph used with permission of the United States Holocaust Memorial Museum.

Eisenhower wanted Buchenwald to be widely publicized, and very soon after liberation journalists began visiting the camp. Edward R. Murrow broadcast a report about the camp on Sunday, April 15, 1945, in which he referred several times to his visit to the camp on the previous Thursday, which would have been April 12, the day after liberation. Murrow may have been mistaken about either the date of his visit to Buchenwald or the location he visited on April 12, as he reported that he had been driving through Germany and had visited many locations. Regardless, his broadcast alerted his listeners to the existence

---

[56] McManus, John C., *Medics in Hell: Saving the Survivors of Buchenwald*, October 2017 World War II Magazine, https://www.historynet.com/medics-in-hell-buchenwald.htm, retrieved July 16, 2019

of Buchenwald, and primed them for horrific reporting and imagery that would soon begin to pour from Buchenwald.

On April 15 General George S. Patton visited Buchenwald, accompanied by photographer Margaret Bourke-White, whose iconic images of Buchenwald captured the horrors of the camp. On April 16 residents of the town of Weimar were forced to tour Buchenwald, their trip to the camp and their expressions while viewing the horrors of Buchenwald captured for both newsreel and print. Similar scenes played out at other camps, and were also given wide publicity. Nazi Germany surrendered to the Allies on May 8, 1945, and Buchenwald was occupied by Americans until early July. There was therefore a substantial period of time during which soldiers no longer engaged in combat operations could visit camps like Buchenwald after the cessation of hostilities, and indeed were encouraged to do so – and many did visit the camp.

How False Memories Are Made

It would be hard to imagine a set of circumstances more perfectly arranged to produce future memory failures than those that obtained at Buchenwald at war's end. Allied forces in the west moved very rapidly after crossing the Rhine, and units covered many miles and encountered many villages with to-them unpronounceable names, various kinds of camps, and other scenes, the significance of which they may have been unaware, every day for weeks. Later they would see images from places like Bergen-Belsen, Buchenwald, Dachau, and Ohrdruf repeated over and over again in newsreels, in newspapers and magazines, in films and books. Iconic images like the *"Arbeit Macht Frei"* signs, bulldozers pushing heaps of bodies into trenches, the table with shrunken heads and human-skin lampshade at Buchenwald, the crematory ovens, General Eisenhower surveying heaps of emaciated bodies, were sensational and everywhere.

An aspect of the post-liberation environment that is difficult to reconstruct but which must surely have had a powerful effect on subsequent recollections of Buchenwald is the nature of the informal networks of story-telling and rumor-passing that would have characterized social relations among the thousands of soldiers and others who visited or worked at the camp for various periods during the ten-week American occupation. Soldiers and survivors were exposed to some very sensational rumors and stories. For example, many soldiers and survivors relate versions of a story involving Ilse Koch, wife of the first (and ill-fated) Commandant of Buchenwald, Karl-Otto Koch, who was executed by the SS shortly before the end of the war. These stories vary in many details, but often include Ilse Koch selecting inmates with interesting tattoos from the prisoner population, often while on horseback, and then having these prisoners murdered so that their skin could be harvested and used in the production of decorative items: lampshades are the most frequently-mentioned items. That such rumors would proliferate and diversify under the circumstances is unsurprising: a lampshade reportedly made of human skin, tanned pieces of skin bearing tattoos, and shrunken heads were displayed on a table at Buchenwald for weeks after the liberation. Nevertheless, dramatic stories like the one about the lampshade, especially in the context of other titillating rumors involving the "Bitch of Buchenwald", no doubt stimulated vivid discussions and speculation. The lampshade story gained wide circulation, and lampshades were later reported in places other than Buchenwald: in *Hell Before Their Very Eyes: American Soldiers Liberate Concentration Camps in Germany, April 1945*, John C. McManus reports that a PFC Dee Eberhart was billeted in a home near Dachau, and claimed to have seen a human-skin lampshade in the house next door[57].

It is interesting that the basic story, that Ilse Koch selected inmates on the basis of their tattoos, had them killed, and then had items like lampshades produced, has never really been proven. There was a research program carried out by an SS doctor, Erich Wagner, investigating a putative relationship between tattoos and criminality, and tattooed skin apparently was harvested and retained at Buchenwald as part of this program[58]. The Kochs were investigated by the SS during WWII, but no evidence of their personal possession of such items was found. Ilse Koch was tried by an American tribunal at Dachau in 1947 and sentenced to life imprisonment. American General Lucius Clay, interim Military Governor, reduced her sentence to four years on June 8, 1948, because "there was no convincing evidence that she had selected inmates for extermination in order to secure tattooed skins, or that she possessed any articles made of human skin"[59]. Ilse Koch was also tried by a German court in 1950, but charges related to the human-skin products were dropped by the prosecution. The story lives on even today: the book *The Lampshade* relates an interesting tale involving the Buchenwald human-skin lampshade and Hurricane Katrina[60].

Alexandra Przyrembel, in a fascinating article entitled *"Transfixed by an Image: Ilse Koch, the 'Kommandeuse of Buchenwald'"*, analyzes the treatment accorded Ilse Koch after the war and the origins of the accusations leveled against

---

[57] McManus, John C. *Hell Before Their Very Eyes: American Soldiers Liberate Concentration Camps in Germany, April 1945*. (Baltimore, Johns Hopkins University Press, 2015), pp. 128-129. 3)

[58] Elsner, P. (2017). 75 years after Erich Wagner's doctoral dissertation: "A Contribution to the Issue of Tattooing" - scientific misconduct in Nazi Germany. *Journal der Deutschen Dermatologischen Gesellschaft - Journal of the German Society of Dermatology : JDDG*, (15)11, 1152-1154.

[59] Ilse Koch, Wikipedia, https://en.wikipedia.org/wiki/Ilse_Koch, retrieved 8 July 2019.

[60] Jacobsen, Mark. *The Lampshade*, (New York, Simon and Schuster, 2010).

her. Stories about Ilse Koch's atrocious behavior were widely shared and accepted among prisoners, though there were few, if any, first-hand accounts related to the lurid accusations of murdering prisoners for their tattoos. Ilse Koch was arrested in mid-1943, and left Buchenwald in early 1944, so by April of 1945 many of those in the camp could only have acquired these stories by hearsay. Indeed, such stories seem to have become a kind of camp lore that were widely believed but of very vague and uncertain origin.

Przyrembel argues persuasively that the portrayal of Ilse Koch after the war was colored by her gender, as many of the stories about her emphasized her sexuality and reported affairs with other SS officers. Przyrembel also suggests that there was a political dimension to the way Ilse Koch was portrayed and remembered, as her second trial was conducted in Augsburg, in West Germany, while the communist survivors of Buchenwald wanted the trial to be held in Weimar, in East Germany. The case of Ilse Koch illustrates that individual memories can be shaped by their social and political context, and that things everyone seems to know to be true may not, in fact, be true at all.

Soldiers visiting Buchenwald view a display of items found at the camp, including shrunken heads, preserved human skin with tattoos, and the lampshade said to have been made from human skin. Photo courtesy of Tom Morgan. The photograph is dated April, 11, 1945, on the USHMM website but must have been taken some time after the liberation. Photograph used with permission of the United States Holocaust Memorial Museum.

After the barrage of publicity about Buchenwald at the time of the camp's liberation and the occasional reminders associated with war-crimes trials in the first few years after the liberation came decades of silence about the war, and what soldiers and survivors had seen and discussed. Survivors tried to reconstruct shattered lives, while soldiers were soon returned to a different world, where they returned to or began careers, marriages, families, remote in every way from their experiences in Germany. Very quickly, it was the Cold War that came to dominate the awareness of Americans. Germany was no longer a threat: in fact, the large American troop presence there for many decades helped create strong social bonds between Germans and Americans, and the strategic realignment placed former Allies (the United States and the Soviet Union) in intense and dangerous opposition to one another. Germany (at least West Germany) was now an essential bulwark in central Europe against the possibility of complete Soviet domination of the continent. Germans were eager to move on from the horrors of the Nazi years, and America had turned its attention to the looming Soviet threat.

It was not until the 1980's and 1990's that interest in the Holocaust was rekindled. In the United States, the ABC miniseries *Holocaust* aired in 1978; *Sophie's Choice* appeared in 1982, *Schindler's List* in 1993. These films were widely discussed in American popular culture. The 20-year-olds of 1945 were 65 in 1990, retiring, renewing old friendships, reflecting on their experiences and sharing them with friends, neighbors, with children and grandchildren eager to learn about their part in the world-historical events in which the public had become more and more interested. Many had not thought or talked about their experiences for many years, but now began to do both. Dim and faded memories coexisted (and competed) with an avalanche of images from films, books, interviews, commemorations of 50th anniversaries of WWII and Holocaust-related events.

Small wonder, then, that even someone who had been at Buchenwald, where the sign at the main gate reads, "*Jedem das Seine*", might later remember seeing "*Arbeit Macht Frei*" as he approached the Buchenwald gate, as did Rabbi Herschel Schacter. General Eisenhower visited Ohrdruf on April 12, 1945, but he never visited Buchenwald: nevertheless, he is often placed there by survivors, soldiers, and even scholars. Confusions and mistakes large and small crept into the recollections of survivors, soldiers, and observers. As the moral and historical significance of being a "liberator" of the camps grew, so did the number of people who remembered, or misremembered, their role in the liberations. In this, Americans were latecomers: misremembering the liberation of Buchenwald had already been something of a national project in East Germany, as we will see shortly. Some Americans, though, rejected the heroic attributions implicitly and explicitly attached to the term, "liberator". Leonard Lubin, for example, who was among the first to arrive at Wels, a sub-camp of Mauthausen, had this to say about being hailed as a liberator:

> "It all sounds so exalted, so glamorous. But we didn't do anything to liberate anybody. It's a bunch of bull. Just a soldier, putting one foot in front of another like I was told to do, happened to be walking down that road like I was told to do, and walked into this thing. No Germans there to fight, so I didn't do anything heroic. I hate the term 'liberator'. It's a false thing"[61].

George Blackburn, a Canadian soldier who was hailed as a liberator of the Westerbork camp in Holland at the 1981 Liberator's Conference in Washington, DC, said:

> "To label me a liberator of a concentration camp is just simply not true. No one person, no single unit, no division, not even the Canadian army was capable of liberating a concentration camp. It took the full forces of the Allies crushing Germany from both directions to retake land and liberate people from those death camps and from those other horrors. I am very subdued, and I approach this all with a great sense of inferiority."[62]

"Humility" would probably have been a more apt choice of words than "inferiority". Be that as it may, the next two chapters will recite many examples of both survivors and soldiers only too eager to take credit for the liberation of Buchenwald.

---

[61] Hirsh, Michael. *The Liberators: Americas Witnesses to the Holocaust*. (New York, Penguin, 2010) p 299.

[62] Chamberlin, Brewster S., and Marcia Feldman, editors. *The Liberation of the Nazi Concentration Camps 1945: Eyewitness Accounts of the Liberators*. (Washington, DC: United States Holocaust Memorial Council, 1987). p. 26.

3 BUCHENWALD IN EAST GERMANY: THE ROLE OF COLLECTIVE MEMORY

Having established as best we can the sequence of events that unfolded at Buchenwald on April 11, 1945, we are now in a position to examine instances, both collective and individual, in which memories of those events have been distorted, forgotten, or replaced with new "memories" of events that did not happen. The first example occurred soon after the camp was liberated, in the turbulent years that saw the end of WWII, the partition of Germany, and the beginning of the Cold War between the United States and the Soviet Union. Buchenwald was located in what had been the Soviet zone of occupation and then became the Soviet-dominated *Deutsche Demokratische Republik* (DDR), or German Democratic Republic (GDR), or more commonly, "East Germany". Today the reunified Germany bears the same name as did "West Germany", the *Bundesrepublik Deutschland* (BRD), or Federal Republic of Germany (FRG). The DDR and BRD existed separately from 1949 until reunification in 1990.

American authorities immediately recognized the significance of what they had stumbled upon at Buchenwald. General Dwight D. Eisenhower visited the Buchenwald sub-camp of Ohrdruf on April 12, 1945, and was appalled by the evidence of cruelty and barbarity he encountered. While he never visited Buchenwald itself, he was quickly apprised of what had been found there and within a few days had ordered that the atrocious acts and conditions that characterized Buchenwald be widely publicized. In an effort to document the history of Buchenwald after the camp had been liberated, a report by a team of American soldiers from the Psychological Warfare Division of SHAEF[63] led by Albert G. Rosenberg[64] was commissioned. This team brought together a group

---

[63] Supreme Headquarters Allied Expeditionary Forces.
[64] Hackett, David. *The Buchenwald Report*. (Boulder, The Westview Press, 1995).

of prisoners, led by Eugen Kogon, which was provided with time, office space, and writing supplies, and encouraged to construct a history of the camp from the viewpoint of the inmates. Many of the prominent survivors of the camp leadership were, of course, German communists, and the narrative that was constructed portrayed the actions and policies of the communist-dominated prisoner hierarchy in a positive and even heroic light. The account of the day of liberation prepared by the prisoners in the weeks after liberation was lost to history for many years. Later published as *The Buchenwald Report*, it acknowledged that the camp was abandoned by the Nazis in response to the imminent arrival of American troops and tanks of the US Third Army, that prisoners stepped in to assume control of the camp, and that American forces first arrived at the camp on April 11, 1945. Kogon's classic work, *The Theory and Practice of Hell: The German Concentration Camps and the System Behind Them*[65] included some of the material developed during the writing of the report.

As time went by, however, the story of liberation day as it was presented in East Germany began to change. The new version presented the prisoners themselves as driving the Nazis from the camp by force of arms, and claimed that the Americans had only arrived two days after the liberation had already been accomplished by the prisoners themselves. This version is now referred to as the *Selbstbefreiung* (self-liberation) myth. The *Selbstbefreiung* myth soon became an important element of East German identity, and the liberation of Buchenwald would be integrated into education and popular culture in East Germany in a prominent way from shortly after the founding of the country until the Reunification. A visit to Buchenwald was a ritual in which many schoolchildren growing up in East Germany participated.

This narrative came to involve more than the events immediately surrounding the transfer of authority at Buchenwald from the Nazis to the prisoners on April 11. The role played by the prisoner functionaries in the camps during its seven years of existence as a Nazi camp came under increasing scrutiny after WWII, and some of these former prisoners were accused of criminal conduct as *kapos* or prisoners serving in other positions of authority over other prisoners. The day of liberation was a key symbolic element of the *Selbstbefreiung* myth, but the myth also encompassed the years of organization and effort by the ILK (*Internationale Lagerkomitee*, or International Camp Committee, organized and led by German communists) that had, on this account, made the self-liberation possible. The veneration and lionization of famous German anti-Nazis who died

---

[65] Kogon, Eugen. *The Theory and Practice of Hell*. (New York, Farrar, Strauss, and Giroux, 2006)..

at Buchenwald, such as Pastor Paul Schneider, and former KPD (*Kommunistische Partei Deutschlands*, or German Communist Party) leader Ernst Thälmann[66], became a standard feature of East German presentations of Buchenwald's history. The Selbstbefreiung myth also served a defensive purpose for many of the German communists and others who had served as prisoner functionaries and survived Buchenwald, some of whom had their actions later questioned and challenged as excessive and cruel, by emphasizing their positive role and contributions.

The new version of the liberation story showcased the importance of ideological solidarity in the camp and the power of international Communism in overcoming Fascism. The myth also sidestepped the potentially embarrassing fact that the Communists were actually liberated by Allied forces, in particular American forces, representing a staunchly capitalist worldview. The prisoners were gravely disappointed that they had not been liberated by the Russians, who were advancing from the east as the other Allies advanced from the west into central Europe. Christopher Burney reported that at a meeting of the German Communists at Buchenwald ten days before liberation, "it had been resolved 'that is in the highest degree regrettable that the Anglo-American capitalists should liberate us. We will do all in our power, even under them, to retain the position which we have always held'"[67].

Bill Niven's excellent book *The Buchenwald Child*[68] focuses on one fascinating element of the East German drive to rewrite the history of Buchenwald: the story of Stefan Jerzy Zweig, a Polish Jew who arrived at Buchenwald as a small boy with his father and survived the camp. The story was the basis of a novel by a Buchenwald survivor, Bruno Apitz, who distorted and sensationalized the tale to make the German communists at the camp appear heroic as they resisted the SS and saved the child. The liberation of the camp was also distorted: the novel portrayed a violent and heroic self-liberation by the prisoners themselves, led by the German communists, portraying events which simply did not occur.

The real story of Stefan Zweig was both more complicated and more morally ambiguous: Zweig was saved when the prisoner functionaries substituted a Roma boy, Willy Blum, in his place on a transport to Auschwitz, where he was murdered. The novel and films also took Zweig's father, who brought him to Buchenwald, out of the picture, effectively making the boy a ward of the communists in the camp. In reality the father was there with and for the child, and both survived

---

[66] Niven, Bill. *The Buchenwald Child: Truth, Fiction and Propaganda*. (Rochester, Camden House, 2007) p.2.
[67] Burney, Christopher. *The Dungeon Democracy*. (New York, Duell, Sloan and Pearce, 1946) p. 137.
[68] Niven, *The Buchenwald Child*.

Buchenwald. The Zweig story, which was also made into a film entitled *Naked Among Wolves*[69], helped spread and popularize the Selbstbefreiung myth in East Germany, according to Niven[70].

Niven sees the East German treatment of the role played by German Communists in Buchenwald before and during the liberation as an example of the development and nurturing of collective memory, a concept pioneered by Maurice Halbwachs. Halbwachs was a French sociologist who was an early proponent of the idea that memory is a largely social phenomenon: "…the way we remember is a function of social frameworks, which themselves serve to underpin the collective memory of any group, be this the family, a religious community, or the professional environment in which we work."[71] In Halbwachs' view, memories of the past are reshaped and reformed to serve the interests of the present. As Niven frames Halbwachs' central thesis: "…the past is being continually molded to fit the exigencies of the present[72]". It is fitting that Halbwachs' ideas help us to understand the way Buchenwald has been remembered: Maurice Halbwachs was imprisoned at Buchenwald and died in the Little Camp in 1945.

Niven also sees a direct connection between collective memory and the development of myths:

> "It would be reasonable to claim that the molding of history by collective memory identified by Maurice Halbwachs leads to myth-building – not least because what results is a tendentious and distortive version of the past. In adapting history, myth irons out its inconsistencies and contradictions, exaggerates certain of its aspects while downplaying or ignoring others, streamlines it so that it acquires a sense of shape and direction, and even adds to it entirely invented episodes"[73].

Myth-making of this sort is clearly evident in the development of the *Sebstbefreiung* story, and, as we shall see in the next Chapter, also in the story of the American film *Liberators: Fighting on Two Fronts in World War II*. The nascent Cold War and the alignment of East Germany with the Soviet Union soon produced collective and social pressure to shape and direct the Buchenwald myth in ways that would help legitimize the anti-American ideology dominant in (after October 7, 1949) East Germany. Revising the history of Buchenwald, beginning with the liberation itself, thus became a kind of national project in the DDR.

---

[69] Film refs
[70] Niven, *The Buchenwald Child*.
[71] Ibid., p. 1
[72] Ibid., p. 4
[73] Ibid., p. 5

Part of the expansive and heroic memorial structure erected at Buchenwald during the time of the DDR. The photograph is from a packet of souvenir postcards from Buchenwald sold during the time of the DDR in the author's collection.

One reason that authorities in East Germany may have felt pressured to offer a new version of the Buchenwald story is that Americans lost no time in using the testimony of a few non-German prisoners at Buchenwald to attack the International Camp Committee and paint them and their actions, clearly standing in for Communism writ large, in an extremely negative light. The report submitted by Egon Fleck and 1LT Edward Tenenbaum to the 12th Army Group Publicity and Psychological Warfare unit on 24 April 1945, less than two weeks after the liberation of the camp is a good example. The sources used by Fleck and Tenenbaum were "two Allied intelligence agents[74]" who were not part of the International Camp Committee, from which group was drawn the committee laboring under Eugen Kogon to produce the document that would eventually be published in English as *The Buchenwald Report* in 1995. The Fleck/Tenenbaum report painted a largely, though not completely, critical picture of the operations of the International Camp Committee. While acknowledging the positive impact

---

[74] Fleck and Tenenbaum, *Preliminary Report*.

of the Committee in some areas, Fleck and Tenenbaum also reported that the prisoner functionaries could be as cruel and violent as the SS, exercising as they did the power of life and death over other prisoners, and pursuing as they did the goals and aspirations of international Communism. Alfred Toombs, Chief of Intelligence for 12th Army Group, somewhat sensationally summarized the report this way:

> "Special distribution is being made of this report because preliminary evaluation indicates that it is one of the most significant accounts yet written on an aspect of life in Nazi Germany. It is NOT just another report on a concentration camp. It does not deal exclusively with the horror of life in Buchenwald, nor with the brutalities of the Nazi perverts. It is the story of wheels within wheels. It tells how the prisoners themselves organized a deadly terror within the Nazi terror. The report is obviously controversial. It has not been possible in so short a time to cross-check and weigh every detail. But independent investigation leads to the tentative conclusion that the basic story can be accepted. Later study and interrogation may lead to modification of this picture — one way or the other. But one thing is certain: There will have to be further investigation of the people of this and all concentration camps. Because the report makes it clear that in our search for decent, democratic elements which we can trust in Germany we cannot accept at face value ALL those people who were incarcerated for opposing the Nazi brand of fascism"[75].

In 1946, Donald R. Robinson published an article in *The American Mercury* based on the Fleck/Tenenbaum article entitled *Communist Atrocities at Buchenwald*[76]. The opening line of the article succinctly captures the tenor of the piece: "When the United States Army liberated the infamous Buchenwald Concentration Camp on April 11, 1945, it found that the 60,000 inmates had been dominated for three years by an underground organization composed of German Communists who used Gestapo-like tortures on their fellow prisoners in an effort to rule them"[77]. This article draws heavily on the Fleck/Tenenbaum report. Also in 1946, a remarkable book by Christopher Burney, a British officer who had been incarcerated at Buchenwald appeared: *The Dungeon Democracy*[78].

Burney, who had been at Buchenwald for fifteen months, was also a leader of prisoner resistance, but was not allied with the German communists who

---

[75] Ibid., p. 1

[76] Robinson, Donald B. Communist Atrocities at Buchenwald. *The American Mercury*, October, 1946.

[77] Ibid., p. 1

dominated the prisoners. *The Buchenwald Report* describes Burney's group as proceeding "…only on the principle of personal ability without any consideration of party affiliation" whereas the "…KPD proceeded from a position of real power in the camp. It acted out of old habits and an understandable feeling of cohesion, providing for the use of its own people almost exclusively in the takeover"[79]. Burney was quite disappointed with the inmates of Buchenwald:

> "My basic conclusion is that the vast majority of the non-Nazis of Europe, and more especially of Germany, are not material which, without careful selection and treatment, will produce a new civilized continent. There were in Buchenwald responsible representatives of almost every anti-Nazi organization. There they were, cramped in an enclosure, with an ideal opportunity to study and prove their ability to work sincerely for the common good. And they failed. They could have said: 'The Nazis have cast us brutally into the midst of horror. We will show the world by our example that our cause is just, that if we are ever freed we will be successors of whom no honest man need be afraid. We will show that we are champions at least of elementary decency and the respect of human life and liberty'. They proved the contrary. They proved that in fact they, too, were moved only by greed, ambition, or weakness.[80]"

Burney's judgment of the communists atop the prisoner hierarchy was especially harsh:

> "The Communists were merely Nazis painted red, neither better nor worse, pawning their souls and their fellows' lives for a mock abstract power – for what and over what? Power for good, when they extended the evil of their gaolers? Power over their companions to guide them to safety? It was neither, but power only as a means of expression for their thwarted, inhibited minds, power to undo all moral or material structure which kept others from joining their herd and rushing with them into anarchy. They were wholeheartedly amoral and had cast off in disgust such shreds of inherited morality as they found still clinging to them. 'Bourgeois sentimentality', they called it, but brought from the recesses of their parrot minds unpondered gilded catchwords and the twisted sayings of half-ignorant men to replace it: words of hatred and envy, apologies for murder, theft and enslavement. Some of them, it was true, were better than others, but that was a slur, and their good qualities kept them for ever below the highest places of their caste. Only the

---

[79] Hackett, *Buchenwald Report*, pp. 98-99.
[80] Burney, *The Dungeon Democracy*, pp. 142-143.

pure, the ruthless, those who had lost even the tainting shadow of a soul were fit to rule"[81].

Ouch. Burney, however, may have exercised a different standard in evaluating his own actions at Buchenwald: he portrays the transport of 8,000 inmates from Buchenwald to Theresienstadt on April 6[82], an action that he decided was one the prisoners should not resist, as a necessary compromise to benefit the larger number of remaining inmates. His characterization of some of the 8,000 as "cretins", over whom "few tears were shed" invites inquiry into the possibility of his own moral compromise, but at the moment that is neither here nor there. It is unclear whether Burney's book was well-known or discussed in Germany, but it certainly echoed the negative perception of the German communists at Buchenwald that was expressed in the Fleck/Tenenbaum report and amplified in the Robinson article. It is clear that the Robinson article was well-known and discussed in Germany: Niven reports that it was "translated into German and published in West Germany in April 1947, and then in East Germany."[83] The publicizing of this anti-Communist narrative provoked a defensive response in the east:

> "Certainly Robinson was manipulating the Fleck and Tenenbaum report in the interests of the intensifying Cold War. As for social democracies in the western zones, they had an axe to grind with the Soviet zone for its elimination of the SPD. In the face of such criticism, the communist ex-prisoners of Buchenwald set about reinforcing and expanding the myth of resistance. In the case of Kogon's 1945 report, the onus had been on preventing criticism; gradually, the focus shifted onto an aggressively marketed heroic self-image...The interest in the projection of an image of heroic communist resistance at Buchenwald was motivated not merely by the wish to establish a total counter-image to that presented by Robinson. At the same time this image was to symbolize the historical dimension to an ongoing struggle against fascism, now believed to be endemic in the west of Germany."[84]

This process of transforming the Buchenwald liberation story was soon begun in earnest. Walter Bartel was a German Communist who had been a leader of the International Camp Committee at Buchenwald. He later became a founding member of the *Sozialistiche Einheitspartei Deutschlands*, or Socialist

---

[81] Ibid., 156-157.
[82] Ibid., 129-130.
[83] Niven, *Buchenwald Child*, 54-55.
[84] Ibid., p 55.

Unity Party, in East Germany. Bartel also became active as a leader of the effort to commemorate Buchenwald. In 1948, on the third anniversary of Buchenwald's liberation, Bartel began to re-frame the liberation story by revising the Americans out of the events until two days after liberation. Manfred Overesch reports that:

> "Without burden, equipped with new self-confidence, Bartel introduced the legend of the liberation of the 11th April 1945 under the leadership of the International Camp Committee, emphasizing the use of weapons and placing the Americans on the Ettersberg two days later:
>
> 'Two days before the capture of Weimar by American troops the concentration camp Buchenwald, nine kilometers from Weimar, was in the hands of the prisoners, led by the International Camp Committee. While in Weimar the SS and the Gestapo were still in command, the prisoners atop the Ettersberg had taken matters into their own hands. In the afternoon of April 11, 1945, with the American armored spearheads nearing, the illegal, armed cadres stormed the large, iron main gate of the camp, penetrated the electrically charged fence, overwhelmed the armed-SS and hoisted a large, white cloth on the storage tower. All of the nations present in the camp set up armed protection using their most trusted comrades. Equipped with the captured weapons, 1,500 former prisoners drew a large protective chain around the camp until two days later units of the Patton army took over the camp. 21,000 prisoners from all the countries of Europe were free. The resistance and relief action was headed by the International Camp Committee made up of representatives of the nations.'"[85]

The two-day gap between liberation and the arrival of American troops created by Bartel would become an enduring feature of the liberation story as told in East Germany. *Buchenwald: Mahnung und Verplichtung*,[86] (Buchenwald: Reminder and Responsibility) first published in 1961, is a lengthy book which includes a detailed version of the liberation story. Walter Bartel, then Vice President of the International Buchenwald-Dora Committee, co-edited the book along with Klaus Trostorff, Director of the *Nationalen Mahn- und Gedenkstätte Buchenwald* (National Buchenwald Reminder and Memorial). The book contains a lengthy and detailed timeline of the events of April 11, 1945. There is an elaborate account of prisoner resistance against the SS, replete with details of different inmate units, leaders, and numbers and types of weapons employed, recounting heroic battle

---

[85] Overesch, Manfred. *Buchenwald und die DDR: oder Die Suche nach Selbst-legitimation*. (Goettingen, Vandenhoeck and Ruprecht,1995). p. 254. Translated from the German.

[86] Buchenwald: Mahnung und Verpflichtung (Dokumente und Berichte). (Berlin, VEB Deustscher Verlag der Wissenschaften, 1983).

after heroic battle as the prisoners seized the camp from the SS. American presence at the camp is part of this narrative, as US tanks are noted fighting the SS at the perimeter of the camp (even reporting that one American was wounded) and it was reported that at 3:40 PM American tanks were observed passing through the camp, but without stopping. Importantly, though, the account emphasizes that "… das Häftlingslager und seine unmittelbare Umgebung bereits fest in den Händen der aufständischen Häftlinge. Das Lager hatte sich selbst befreit"[87]. Roughly: "…the prison camp and its surroundings were already firmly in the hands of the rebellious prisoners. The camp had freed itself."

The two-day gap between the American dating of the presence of US troops at Buchenwald on the 11th and the East German dating of that arrival on the 13th is thus created because the East German account denies that any Americans stopped at the camp and made contact with any prisoners on the 11th. The East German account does assert that an American officer appeared at the camp during the night of April 12, informing the camp's military leaders that American forces were not in a position to defend the camp if German forces returned, and that the camp must defend itself. This story has the American officer describing a security-line established by American forces two kilometers from the perimeter of the camp[88], thus creating a kind of buffer both temporally and spatially between the victorious prisoners and the weak-appearing Americans.

Buchenwald: Ein Konzentrationslager (Buchenwald: A Concentration Camp), published in East Germany in 1988, also includes the 2-day gap in its timeline of Buchenwald liberation:

"April 11. At 2.30 pm, at the behest of the ILK, the head of the illegal military organization issued the order to revolt. The armed combat groups of the prisoners tear down the barbed wire fence, storm the main gate, occupy the watch towers and capture weapons. The resistance of the SS in the entire camp, command, and troop area is broken at 4 PM. At that time, no US soldier had entered the camp. 220 SS members are detained as prisoners in Block 17 and placed under strict surveillance. While the fight continues, the illegal International Camp Committee meets for its first legal session; it elects its former chairman Walter Bartel as chairman of the illegal ILK. At the same time, the Camp Elder I, Hans Eiden, was unanimously elected commander of the liberated Buchenwald camp by the ILK.

April 12. Roll call of the 21,000 survivors."

---

[87] Ibid., p. 615.
[88] Ibid., p. 617.

April 13. Takeover of the liberated camp by a unit of the 3rd US Army. The American commander orders the immediate surrender of the weapons. First legal meeting of the party organization of the KPD in Buchenwald. Meeting of the Social Democratic Group"[89].

The timing is stated precisely on page 149: "Die US-Armee traf erst am 13. April im befreiten Lager Buchenwald ein". (The US Army first arrived in the liberated camp Buchenwald on April 13.)" It appears that the East German version portrayed the period between the 11th and 13th of April as an interlude during which the area containing Weimar and Buchenwald was still being fought over: in this way, prisoners could be given responsibility for liberating the camp and running it for two days while waiting for the Americans to arrive. An English-language tour brochure from Buchenwald dated 1993, a few years after the reunification of Germany, contains a kind of hybrid timing, which retains the two days of inmate control but somehow places American troops at Buchenwald on the correct date, 11 April:

"But the resistance groups formed by the prisoners did not wait for the arrival of the liberators in a passive way. They rather used the first moments of their presence in the area still being fought over in order to occupy the watchtowers, hoist the white flag and safeguard the camp for two days. More than 21,000 people were in the camp when the first tanks of the 3rd Army arrived in camp on 11th of April"[90].

We will see in the next two chapters that here in the United States, there are many mistaken and false stories about Buchenwald that are still in widespread circulation. In Germany, the *Selbstbefreiung* myth is still sometimes encountered, as well. The German Wikipedia page entry for Hermann Pister (second Commandant of Buchenwald) contains the following text, for example: "On April 13, two days after Pister and leading camp personnel left Buchenwald, the US Army finally reached the main camp, which had about 21,000 inmates."[91]

As further evidence of American absence, *Buchenwald: Ein Konzentrationslager* reproduces this quotation from Paul Bodot, a Free French soldier who is reported by the *Buchenwald Gedenkstätte* to have visited Buchenwald at 5:10 PM on April 11 with Emmanuel Desard[92]. The quotation is under the sub-title, "Sergeant Paul

---

[89] Carlebach, Emil, Gurenewald, Paul, Roeder, Hellmuth, Schmidt, Willy, and Vielhauer, Walter. *Buchenwald: Ein Konzentrationslager*. (Berlin, Dietz Verlag, 1988) p. 187.

[90] Stein, Sabine and Harry. *Buchenwald: A Tour of the Memorial Site*. Weimar/Buchenwald, 1993. Brochure in the author's possession.

[91] Hermann Pister, Wikipedia, https://de.wikipedia.org/wiki/Hermann_Pister, retrieved September 2, 2019.

[92] The name is spelled *Desnard* in *Buchenwald: Ein Konzentrationslager, Desard* elsewhere.

Bodot, der erste Zeuge der Selbstbefreiung" (Sergeant Paul Bodot, First Witness of the Self-Liberation):

"It was April 11, 1945. As a sergeant, I was assigned to Combat Command "B" on the Military Intelligence Translator Staff, which belonged to the 4th Armored Division of the 3rd Army of General Patton ... Our mission gave us a great deal of independence, so that we had moved some distance ahead of our unit that day. In one field, we noticed a group of prisoners guarded by armed civilians.

We stopped and were received by the one who was in command. He was a Belgian who told us that a few miles away was the Buchenwald camp, in which there were about 22,000 deportees who had freed themselves by attacking the guards. They set up armed groups like his own, and are now hunting down escaped guards. He proposed to take us to the camp, and, after Lieutenant Desnard had agreed, the Belgian took his place on the hood of our jeep. He led us over fields and then through a forest to the entrance of the camp ...

Our arrival cannot be described. We were received by the officials of the liberating committee (which consisted of deportees of various nationalities). They told us that we were the first to enter the camp.

Our arrival in Buchenwald was rather coincidental. We could not stay, because we had to rejoin the unit on the main route of march as soon as possible.

To our great surprise, after a few hundred yards, we met a column of American vehicles whose drivers had no idea that they were so close to one of the notorious camps."[93]

This quotation is also reproduced in *Buchenwald: Mahnung und Verpflichtung*, and in *Buchenwald Concentration Camp 1937-1945*, published by the *Buchenwald Gedenkstätte*. The three versions are all different from one another. The version in *Buchenwald: Ein Konzentrationslager* is the only one to spell Bodot's Lieutenant's name Desnard: the other two spell it Desard, as it is spelled in the message bearing his name. This abridged version corresponds fairly closely, however, with the version in *Buchenwald: Mahnung und Verpflichtung*, which is considerably longer: 605 versus 251 words in German. These two versions both have Bodot and Desard leaving from Gotha on the morning of the 11th, identify their unit of assignment as the 4th Armored Division, note that their mission gave them a great deal of flexibility, and portray their encounter with a group of prisoners as

---

[93] Carlebach et al, *Buchenwald*, pp. 157-158

brief and accidental. Both versions also include a description of their departure from Buchenwald, which includes the observation that they had encountered a column of American vehicles and that the Americans had no idea they were in the vicinity of a concentration camp.

Buchenwald Concentration Camp 1937-1945 prefaces its presentation of the Bodot quote with the assertion that Lieutenant Desard "transferred the administration of the camp and the responsibility for the 21,000 survivors to Camp Senior One, Hans Eiden. At about the same time, a reconnaissance troop of the Sixth Armored Car Division [sic] of the Third U.S. Army was present in the camp[94]". This version of Bodot's statement alters the circumstances of Bodot and Desard's discovery of the camp by including an account of their visit to Ohrdruf (near Gotha) and making their search for Buchenwald more intentional: "After Erfurt, Lieutenant Desard and I left our line of vehicles in search of the Buchenwald camp. After we had driven about ten km, we came across a group…"[95]. This version also names the Belgian leader with whom Bodot and Desard made contact as Leopold Hansen, and does not describe their departure from the camp.

Buchenwald Concentration Camp 1937-1945 also reproduces a photograph of a pass hand-written on a US Army message form for Hans Eiden signed by Desard. As discussed in the previous Chapter, a pass was mentioned in 4th Armored Division message traffic. It seems quite clear that the visit of Bodot and Desard to Buchenwald was seen by the East Germans as an important validation of the Selbstbefreiung myth, showing both that the camp was firmly in the hands of the prisoners on April 11, and that there was no significant American presence in the camp. The fact that Bodot and Desard were Free French assigned to an American unit rather than American soldiers may have been seen as distancing the liberation from American responsibility still further: the timeline currently presented on the *Buchenwald Gedenkstätte* has Bodot and Desard arriving at 5:00 PM and the Keffer party arriving at 5:10 PM, though it is not clear where evidence for such precise timing may have originated.

These efforts to portray the events of the day of liberation in a particular way were a necessary component of the larger effort to enshrine Buchenwald as the foundation of the DDR's legitimacy. The alterations made to the liberation story in East Germany served the needs of the government at that time, and thus exemplify social memory as understood by Maurice Halbwachs: social memory

---

[94] Gedenkstaette Buchenwald (Eds.) *Buchenwald Concentration Camp 1937-1945: A Guide to the Permanent Historical Exhibition.* (Gottingen: Wallstein Verlag, 2004). p 235.

[95] Ibid., p. 235.

transforms the past in service of the present. The story of the liberation was transformed in several ways to serve the purposes of the East German regime. American forces were displaced in time, space, and importance from the act of liberation itself. The account in *Buchenwald: Mahnung und Verpflichtung* is carefully structured to keep American forces *outside* Buchenwald until the 13th.

While this book is most concerned with the story of the liberation itself, post-liberation events at Buchenwald were also subjected to significant historical revision in East Germany. The period of American occupation, from 11 April until approximately July 3, saw the arrival of the 120th Evacuation Hospital on April 15, which (along with many other units and soldiers) devoted immense effort to saving those who could be saved and treating those in need of medical aid. The security, food, and sanitation conditions at the camp were stabilized and then improved by the presence of American troops, the delivery of American food and medicine, and the work of many American soldiers. The East German account of the liberation in *Buchenwald: Mahnung und Verpflichtung* concludes by noting that when the Americans did arrive on the 13th of April, bringing medical supplies, no bond of solidarity between them and the prisoners was formed. According to a former inmate, Ernst Haberland, on the occasion of a parade of the inmate military units subsequent to the surrender of their weapons to the Americans, ordinary American soldiers looked upon their parade "mit Freude und Sympathie" (with joy and sympathy) while the officers cast "missgünstigen und scheelen Blicken" (evil and sidelong glances) at their gathering, thus activating the communist theme of class conflict by differentiating between the attitudes of common soldiers and officers. The ideological equivalence between Americans and Nazis, both fascists according to communist doctrine, was underscored by Haberland: "Die neuen Feinde der Freiheit machten sich bereits bemerkbar" (The new enemies of freedom were already apparent)[96]. As well, the five years that Buchenwald was operated as *Soviet Special Camp No. 2*, 1945-1950, and during which appalling conditions led to the deaths of some 8,000 of the 25,000 imprisoned there, were omitted from East German histories of Buchenwald.

---

[96] *Mahnung und Verpflichtung*, p. 619.

These two photos are of souvenir postcards that could be purchased in packets at Buchenwald during the existence of the DDR. These displays were set up in the cells that are found in the west wing of the building that contains the main gate to the prisoner area and clock. The postcard on the left has East German schoolchildren placing flowers at a shrine for Paul Schneider, a Protestant pastor and Nazi resister who was murdered by the Nazis in this cell. The postcard on the right memorializes Ernst Thälmann, former head of the German Communist Party who was also murdered at Buchenwald. The photographs are from a packet of souvenir postcards from Buchenwald sold during the time of the DDR in the author's collection.

A Soviet Version

The *Selbstbefreiung* myth as it evolved in East Germany prominently featured German communists as its heroes. There also appears to have been a Soviet version of the *Selbstbefreiung* legend, in which, unsurprisingly, Russians were the heroes and Americans the villains. An English-language book entitled *War Behind Barbed Wire: Reminiscences of Buchenwald Ex-Prisoners of War*, published in Moscow in 1959, provides a Soviet account through the eyes of eight Buchenwald survivors. The heroes of this colorful account of liberation day are Russians:

> "It was 3:15. The hour had struck! "Hurrah" yelled the men in striped clothes as the shots rang out and grenades exploded. Our Soviet men were to be seen where the fiercest battles were raging. The watch-towers were ablaze. Our German comrades had deenergized the fence and the prisoners cut the barbed wire. Our assault group blew up the wooden gates. The Nazis panicked; they jumped to their death from the watch-towers, fled from their bunkers, and tried to hide in the woods. Several hundred were killed and

taken prisoner. Then we made for the SS arsenal and emptied it in a minute.

The military centre, no longer underground, realized the time was not yet ripe to rejoice. According to plan, our battalions took up defensive positions around the camp to fight off any SS attempt to carry out their murderous schemes.

When the American tanks drove up we met them as free men."[97]

The Russian version of post-liberation events also diminishes and demeans the American relief efforts at the camp, substituting Russian medical personnel and supplies for the American men and women of the 120th Evacuation Hospital, and relegating ineffectual and corrupt American efforts to a sanitorium 31 miles from Buchenwald:

"We set up our general hospital in the former SS barracks. Sick and emaciated men were picked up all over the camp and carried on stretchers or in carts to the wards. Our Soviet doctors – Karnaukhov, Milstein, Suslov, Sokolov, and Dvornikov – worked day and night, helping their countrymen to regain their health. We used hundreds of quarts of blood plasma, a colossal amount of glucose, different surgical operations were performed.

The doctors of other nationalities followed our example with the result that wards were set up in fifteen SS barracks, accommodating at least 12,000 men from all the countries of Europe.

There were many patients suffering from tuberculosis. Those who had active cases, people of all nationalities, were taken to a sanitorium we had them set up in a former Nazi hospital in a picturesque spot 31 miles from Buchenwald. The U.S. Army appointed its officer as chief of the hospital.

Soon after Smirnov, one of our assistant doctors there, sent us an alarming letter in which he wrote that the patients were fed with ersatz bread made of beets and that they received neither meat, fats, nor butter. He also wrote that the sanitorium was staffed with Nazi doctors and nurses who maltreated the patients and that it was guarded by German sentries. The American officer, taken up with his own affairs, paid no attention to the patients' plight.

We left for the sanitorium at once and arrived there at dinner-time. As we entered the American officer's suite, we encountered a plump German woman carrying a tray with a sumptuous dinner and a bottle of wine for the sanitorium chief. We expressed our regret at having interrupted his meal and

---

[97] F. Solasko, (Ed.) *War Behind Barbed Wire*. (Moscow, Foreign Languages Publishing House, 1959). p. 57.

demanded of the American that he put things in order. Soon the regimen and the meals left nothing to be desired. Only a few members of the old staff were retained. The sentries preferred to leave without notice. In spite of the sanitorium chief's protests, we left our assistant doctor to keep an eye on him."[98]

The false or tendentious versions of the Buchenwald liberation story that became the officially sanctioned history of that event in East Germany and in the Soviet Union were created and sustained in a repressive police state in which dissent from the party line brought great risks. The forces that operated to ensure that the *Selbstbefreiung* myth remained the version of the Buchenwald liberation that East Germans and their Soviet patrons learned and remembered were official and overt. In the United States, public interest in the Holocaust began to grow only in the 1980's and 1990's. In East Germany, there was only one version of the Buchenwald liberation, which, however distorted, faced no competition from alternative representations. In the US the awakening of interest in the Holocaust would eventually produce many versions of the Buchenwald liberation. Some of these, like the *Selbstbefreiung* myth, were driven by collective social factors, while others, as we shall see, seem to have arisen more directly from the normal operation of human memory mechanisms that can sometimes lead individuals to distort or even create false memories of past events.

---

[98] Ibid., 154-155.

4 BUCHENWALD IN AMERICA: SOCIAL MEMORY

Remembrance of the liberation of Buchenwald in East Germany was straitjacketed into a state-sponsored deviation from the actual course of events for social and political reasons. There was no such top-down pressure to create and sustain a particular version of the Buchenwald liberation narrative in the United States, however. Insofar as there is, or was, an "official" version of the Buchenwald liberation from the American perspective, that version corresponds closely, if incompletely, with the sequence of events as detailed in Chapter Two. This version has American soldiers arriving on April 11, 1945, after the SS had fled the camp: no combat was required to "liberate" the camp, no gates or fences were violently breached. The American presence there on the 11th was brief, but resulted in the rapid initiation of a series of events that would bring substantial relief to the prisoners at Buchenwald.

Another difference between remembrance of Buchenwald in East Germany and in the United States is the timing. The *Selbstbefreiung* myth fulfilled a need that arose urgently as the DDR was founded and as the actions of prisoner functionaries at Buchenwald came under scrutiny in the years after WWII. In the United States, the Holocaust did not intrude significantly into popular culture until the 1980's and 1990's. There was a Holocaust-themed film starring Orson Welles (*The Stranger*) released in 1946, and in the 1960's Stanley Milgram's research on obedience using electric shock brought the Holocaust to awareness among psychologists, as Milgram claimed that his research explained why perpetrators had behaved as they had. But the Holocaust was not prominent in American culture until forty or fifty years after the war ended in the summer of 1945.

Adam Seipp, in his excellent article *Buchenwald Stories: Testimony, Military History, and the American Encounter with the Holocaust*[99], suggests four reasons for the dramatic increase in interest in the Holocaust in the United States in the

1980's and 1990's. First, the soldiers of WWII were nearing or entering retirement at this time, and were becoming more inclined to reflect on their military service, re-connect with old friends, and share their experiences with interested children and grandchildren. Second, the appearance of the ABC miniseries *Holocaust* in 1978, the 1981 International Liberators Conference in Washington, DC, the release of Sophie's Choice in 1982, the 1985 release of Claude Lanzmann's landmark film *Shoah*, and the 1993 release of Steven Spielberg's *Schindler's List*, which happened to coincide with the opening of the United Sates Holocaust Memorial Museum, raised public awareness of the Holocaust. Third, initiatives were undertaken to record and preserve the testimony of people who had significant life experiences related to the Holocaust. Steven Spielberg founded the USC Shoah Foundation, which has acquired and preserved a massive archive of testimony from survivors and liberators. Finally, the revolution in information technology wrought by the internet has put a staggering amount of information (and misinformation) about the Holocaust literally at the fingertips of anyone with a computer and access to the world-wide web.

There are both individual and social determinants of behavior. Sometimes what we think and do is driven mainly by the encounters and relationships we have with other people in our lives. Other times, our behavior has more to do with our own pasts, our own interpretations of our experience, our own thoughts and deliberations. With respect to the liberation of Buchenwald, both social and individual factors have operated to distort or create memories of what happened on April 11, 1945. Perhaps the earliest, and in some ways most durable, memory distortion of the Buchenwald liberation in the United States was social in nature.

How the series of events that led to what I will refer to as the "*Liberators* controversy" began is unclear to me. It is the case that two African-American veterans of WWII, Dr. Leon Bass and William A. Scott III, were active in publicly discussing their experiences at Buchenwald long before the Holocaust was widely discussed in America: certainly in the 1970's, perhaps before. In October 1981 the United States Holocaust Memorial Council sponsored an International Liberators Conference at the State Department in Washington, DC. Leon Bass, an African-American veteran of the 183rd Combat Engineer Battalion, was introduced as a liberator of Buchenwald, and Douglas Kelling, a psychiatrist who was assigned to the 45th Infantry Division was introduced as a liberator of Dachau.

---

[99] Seipp, Adam R. "Buchenwald Stories: Testimony, Military History, and the American Encounter with the Holocaust". *Journal of Military History*, **79**, 721-744.

The Conference took place long before the US Army Center for Military History had established criteria narrowly and arbitrarily defining "liberators" as those who were members of Divisions that had visited camps within 48 hours of the first arrival of American troops. Both Leon Bass and William Scott had been speaking about their experiences at Buchenwald for some years before the 1981 conference, and were often referred to as liberators by those introducing or interviewing them. This usage is consistent with the respectful treatment these veterans received as early visitors to the camp, though neither Bass nor Scott claimed to have done anything other than ride to Buchenwald in a truck and enter through the open main gate, sometime after the camp had been occupied by American forces.

Neither Bass nor Scott are especially specific in most interviews about the exact date they arrived at Buchenwald. Bass often simply referred to a day in early April. It seems clear, though, that it was a few days after Buchenwald had been discovered and occupied. William Scott, in a 1979 interview with Dr. Fred Crawford, says that he was ordered to accompany some officers and a few other soldiers to Buchenwald, and dates this occurrence to April 13, 1945, "the day that Buchenwald was overrun", a fact of which he says he had been reminded. In other interviews Scott has given the date as April 11, but evidence suggests that it was actually April 17 when Leon Bass and William Scott III visited Buchenwald.

Fred Crawford was the Director of the Center for Research and Social Change at Emory University who managed a project called "Witness to the Holocaust". Crawford conducted interviews with several soldiers who had experienced the camps at the end of the war. These transcripts are maintained at Georgia Tech and Emory University, but many are available on the internet. An interview with Dr. Leo Pine conducted on September 7, 1978 is available here[100]. Leo Pine was the white, Jewish, German-speaking commander of the all-African-American unit to which Leon Bass and William A. Scott belonged, the 183rd Combat Engineers. Dr. Pine was clearly struggling with his memory during the interview, but he does make clear that that he and the truckload of African-American soldiers who visited Buchenwald (which would have included Scott and Bass) did not do so on the day of liberation, but, he says, two or three days later. He says (on page 3) "liberated is not the right word" to use describe their arrival at the camp.

Leo Pine's recollections seem to be significantly affected by post-event information: he remembers the sign over the gate, for example, as "Arbeit Macht

---

[100] Dr. Leo Pine interview, https://witness.digitalscholarship.emory.edu/items/show/81, retrieved October 7, 2019.

Frei" and also another reading "All those who pass through here leave hope behind". Neither of these signs were at Buchenwald, and Pine self-consciously examines his own memory in the transcript to ask if he may have heard this elsewhere. Pine also remembered seeing lampshades with tattoos, and a wallet made from a woman's breasts with the nipples still evident. He heard that Ilse Koch conducted experiments where she tied the legs of women delivering children together to kill them both. He discusses gas chambers in a confusing way, seeming at one point to remember them, but at other points in his narrative seeming to remember only being told about them. Interestingly, he mentions a film about a child protected by the prisoners at Buchenwald (this must have been the 1963 German version of *Näckt unter Wolfen*, "Naked Among Wolves", telling Bruno Apitz' story of Stefan Jerzy Zweig) and reports that he met the child (who he called "*Yankela*") and was encouraged by the prisoners to take the child with him when he left. In Pine's remembering the child was born in the camp, the child's mother was murdered by the Nazis the day after giving birth, and the prisoners somehow protected the infant for three years.

Pine's memories also bear some similarities to stories heard from others. For example, he remembers a place where German prisoners were being held, and that a white American soldier went into the prisoners' cell and beat a former Nazi guard. He says he gave permission for one of his African-American soldiers to do likewise, which he did. After the beatings, the German was provided a rope with which he obligingly hanged himself. This sounds a bit like the story related by Harry Herder, Jr., (see Chapter 5) who was at Buchenwald around the same time as Pine. Neither Herder nor Pine claim to have seen these events with their own eyes.

Fred Crawford's *Witness to the Holocaust* program also produced some television programs featuring liberators. One such program was produced on June 4, 1979, and was later transcribed as part of the 1981 Holocaust Memorial Council Liberator's Conference. This program may be found on the website of the United States Holocaust Memorial Museum here,[101] though the USHMM website incorrectly dates the interview to October, 1981. The three WWII veterans (John Glustrom, Leo Pine, and Dennis Wile) remembered their experiences at Buchenwald. Leo Pine's testimony in this interview is quite consistent with the interview he had provided to Dr. Crawford a year earlier. John Glustrom's testimony contains several questionable memories: for example, he remembers seeing human-skin lampshades with tattoos lit and in use in the administration

---

[101] United States Holocaust Memorial Museum, Oral history interview with John Glustrom, Leo Pine, and Dennis Wile, https://collections.ushmm.org/search/catalog/irn513307, retrieved October 7, 2019.

building. He describes gas chambers with spigots in the ceiling that spewed poison gas instead of water, equipped with heavy metal doors. Gassed victims were then dropped down a chute to the crematorium, according to Glustrom. He also reports that the furnaces were still burning when he arrived at Buchenwald. There were no gas chambers at Buchenwald, and the crematorium had ceased operation for lack of fuel long before the liberation.

The story of the *Liberators* controversy may have begun with an article by John Tagliabue ("At Buchenwald, Ceremony of Bitter Memory") that appeared in the *New York Times* on April 14, 1985, a few days after the fortieth anniversary of the liberation of Buchenwald[102]. Tagliabue's article reported on the anniversary celebration that had taken place at Buchenwald a few days earlier. Tagliabue's brief description of the liberation itself was apparently derived from the East German version, and repeated the false story of the *Selbstbefreiung*. The article focused more extensively on the anti-American rhetoric that dominated the remembrance of the liberation of Buchenwald in East Germany, which included the not-so-subtle equation of Americans and Nazis that was a staple of East German discussions of World War II and the Holocaust.

A week later, on April 22, 1985, a letter to the editor ("I Was Liberated at Buchenwald on April 11, 1945") authored by Holocaust survivor Benjamin Bender was published as a response to Tagliabue's article. Bender took issue with the portrayal of the liberation as resulting from the actions of the inmates themselves, and credited American forces instead:

"The survivors of Buchenwald owe their lives to the American people and not to the "resistance fighters." The short resistance uprising took place hours before the American forces entered Buchenwald. The German SS guards, sensing the approaching defeat, escaped en masse on bikes, on horses or just running. Credit for the liberation belongs totally and unequivocally to the American people, and not to cheap propaganda trying to erase the shameful memories."[103]

Bender's description of the American liberators included the detail that they were Black:

"I was liberated at the Nazi concentration camp of Buchenwald on April 11, 1945. For me it was a glorious day, full of sunshine, an instant awakening of life after long darkness.

---

[102] *New York Times*, At Buchenwald, Ceremony of Bitter Memory, https://www.nytimes.com/1985/04/14/world/at-buchenwald-ceremony-of-bitter-memory.html, retrieved October 6, 2019.

[103] *New York Times*, I was Liberated at Buchenwald on April 11 1945, https://www.nytimes.com/1985/04/22/opinion/l-i-was-liberated-at-buchenwald-on-april-11-1945-180220.html, retrieved October 6, 2019.

The recollections are still vivid - black soldiers of the Third Army, tall and strong, crying like babies, carrying the emaciated bodies of the liberated prisoners."[104]

Bender published a memoir in 1995, the fiftieth anniversary of the liberation of Buchenwald, entitled *Glimpses: Through Holocaust and Liberation*[105]. Bender's description of his first encounter with Americans is quite vivid:

"I stood ten or fifteen yards from the main gate. The huge roll call square was full of American soldiers, General Patton's best, tall black men, six footers, with colorful scarves around their necks. I had never seen black men before. They were unreal to me. The soldiers were trying to help, carrying inmates on stretchers, some dead, some dying and stretching out their hands and saying, "Brother, I'm dying, give me your hand.". The soldiers were in shock, crying like babies. They gave them their hands."[106]

Bender is convinced that this encounter occurred on April 11, though there does seem to be some possible confusion in his memory of the event. In a USC Shoah Foundation interview[107], he says that he was released from the camp hospital on April 11. He provided a timeline of events throughout the day, which has the African-American soldiers ("tall slender beautiful giants") arriving around 3:00 or 3:15 in the afternoon. Bender seems to recognize a difficulty in his story, as he repeatedly refers to returning to Block 62 from the main gate area. Block 62 was in the Little Camp, which was separated from the main camp by a barbed-wire fence. He resolves this by reporting that a *kapo* had transferred him to the main camp hospital sometime after he had been admitted to the hospital in the Little Camp, though he persists in saying that he returned to Block 62 to find it deserted. He says that a friend refreshed his memory recently about the transfer. It is possible that Bender's recollection here is confused as to exactly when the events he reports as having occurred on April 11 actually occurred.

Bender's interview also includes the observation that in the days before liberation, American forces were only three miles from the camp but the Germans evacuated Jews from the camp on death marches "under their noses", though he says he is not accusing anyone (Tape 4, 23:30); he also repeatedly describes the

---

[104] Ibid.

[105] Bender, Benjamin. *Glimpses: Through Holocaust and Liberation*. (Berkeley, North Atlantic Books, 1995).

[106] Ibid., 161-162.

[107] USC Shoah Foundation interview, reviewed onsite at the United States Holocaust Memorial Museum. Bender's discussion of these events occurs on Tape 4, 25:39, https://collections.ushmm.org/search/catalog/irn505590.

triangles worn by criminal prisoners as purple, though criminals wore a green triangle – purple was the color for Jehovah's Witnesses (Tape 4, 5:53).

In an epilogue to *Glimpses*, Bender explains how he came to be involved in the film *Liberators: Fighting on Two Fronts in WWII*[108]. This film, narrated by Denzel Washington, was produced with support from WNET, a public television station in New York, as part of *The American Experience* series, and was nominated for an Academy Award for Best Documentary Feature. Bender's 1985 letter to the *New York Times* had apparently come to the attention of William Miles and Nina Rosenblum, who contacted him in 1988 about a documentary film project. Their project dealt with the role of African-American soldiers in WWII, in particular the 761st Tank Battalion, and they had noticed Bender's assertion that "tall black men" had liberated Buchenwald on April 11, 1945. Bender became a significant contributor to the project, and traveled to Buchenwald to take part in the filming in 1991.

Liberators: Fighting on Two Fronts in WWII, initially released on November 11, 1992, was screened on December 17, 1992, at the Apollo Theater in Harlem. In attendance were then-New York Mayor David Dinkins, former Presidential candidate Jesse Jackson, and Representative Charles Rangel. The film told the story of the 761st Tank Battalion and the 183rd Combat Engineers, both all-black units that had served extensively and honorably in combat in Europe in WWII. The film made the claim that Buchenwald and Dachau were both liberated by African-American soldiers from these units.

Relations between the African-American and Jewish communities in the United States have been characterized by tension and misunderstanding at various times in our nation's history[109]. *Liberators* presented a narrative that could symbolically bridge the gulf that divided the two minority groups, uniting them in a moment of delivery from oppression. Mark Schulte, grandson of a Sixth Armored Division veteran of WWII, has written extensively about the liberation of Buchenwald, and has been exposing erroneous claims about the events of April 11, 1945 for decades.[110] Schulte cites two articles published in the *New*

---

[108] Potter, Lou. *Liberators: Fighting on Two Fronts in World War II*. (New York, Harcourt-Brace Jovanovich, 1992).

[109] See, for example, Greenberg, Cheryl Lynn. *Troubling the Waters*. (Princeton, Princeton University Press, 2006).

[110] Schulte, Mark. Buchenwald Liberation Myths: 1945-2013. https://blogs.timesofisrael.com/buchenwald-liberation-myths-1945-2013/, retrieved July 7 2019.

York Times in 1988[111] in which Jesse Jackson, then running for the Democratic Presidential nomination against Michael Dukakis, cited two African-American soldiers in an "Appeal for Black-Jewish Ties" and a "Bridge Between Jackson and Dukakis". The social and political value of this narrative of African-American and Jewish solidarity made it an appealing story, so appealing, perhaps, that it was not approached with an appropriate level of journalistic rigor or scrutiny.

The historical accuracy of *Liberators* was publicly questioned soon after it began to air on public television. The film was investigated by Kenneth Stern of the American Jewish Committee[112], and by Morton Silverstein, a well-known documentary film-maker. Both investigations determined that the film's central claims could not be substantiated, and that there was a considerable body of evidence to suggest that the African-American soldiers who were, indeed, at Buchenwald were most likely there a few days after the April 11, 1945 liberation. Both of these investigators concluded that the film departed so significantly from accepted journalistic standards that without significant changes, the film should be withdrawn from further public presentation, which it soon was.

The producers' response to the challenges to the accuracy of *Liberators* suggests that the version of the Buchenwald liberation presented therein had been or had become embedded in a larger social and political discourse. Kenneth Stern, who authored one of the reports documenting problems with the film, described the reaction of Nina Rosenblum, one of the film's producers:

> "In all her conversations with me, and in quotes in various articles, Ms Rosenblum has deflected criticism of the film by charging prejudice. In a conference call with me and two members of the 761st, she continually encouraged the veterans to blame any challenge of the film's veracity on bigotry (despite the fact that some of the loudest critics are black veterans of the 761st). Ms. Rosenblum, when told that the commander of the 761st said that he had not even "heard of the names Dachau and Buchenwald until after the war," asked whether the questioner was "willing to believe a white commander and [not the black] soldiers." Ms. Rosenblum has said that those who challenge the film's accuracy "are of the same mentality that says the

---

[111] Bernard Weinraub, *New York Times*, Jackson Makes Appeal for Black Jewish Ties; https://www.nytimes.com/1988/05/31/us/jackson-makes-appeal-for-black-jewish-ties.html; *New York Times*, Black Ex-GI a Bridge Between Jackson and Dukakis, https://www.nytimes.com/1988/06/03/us/black-ex-gi-a-bridge-between-jackson-and-dukakis.html; Mark Schulte, Chuck Schumer, NY Times, Fake World War II News, https://dailycaller.com/2017/05/05/chuck-schumer-ny-times-fake-world-war-ii-news/; Current, Karen Everhart, https://current.org/1993/09/review-finds-factual-flaws-in-the-liberators/. All retrieved October 6, 2019.

[112] The American Jewish Committee describes itself as "the leading global Jewish advocacy organization." www.ajc.org, retrieved July 7, 2019.

Holocaust didn't happen." But the question is not whether societal prejudice diminished the recognition of the accomplishments of blacks in the military (it did), but of historical accuracy. Prejudice does not explain why essential documents were not examined, nor why inconsistencies about the locus of heroic acts were ignored."[113]

Writing in *The New Republic* in 1993, shortly before public airing of the film was stopped, Jeffrey Goldberg cites the reaction of Peggy Tishman, "former president of the JCRC [Jewish Community Relations Council] and a co-host of the evening at the Apollo"[114]. Goldberg characterized Tishman's comments this way:

"Why would anybody want to exploit the idea that this is a fraud?" she says. "What we're trying to do is make New York a better place for you and me to live." She claims that the accuracy of the film is not the issue. What is important is the way it can bring Jews and blacks into "dialogue". "There are a lot of truths that are very necessary," Tishman says. "This is not a truth that's necessary."[115]

This indifference or hostility to historical accuracy coupled with a passionate and determined commitment to an appealing narrative seems to fit well with the concept of social or collective memory, and parallels the development of the *Selbstbefreiung* myth in East Germany. The process through which this myth was created in East Germany was overtly political, and publicizing and perpetuating this myth was accomplished by the repressive authoritarian regime in East Germany. I cannot trace the full history of the events that led to the *Liberators* fiasco, but the process seems to have been organic and even opportunistic. Memories of individuals, perhaps in this case the memories of Benjamin Bender or the vague but suggestive memories of Leon Bass (Bass was not certain exactly when he had visited Buchenwald) and William A. Scott were recruited into an enterprise with an explicit social and political agenda, and that agenda soon came to drive, control, and push the narrative from above, as it were. The important difference between the *Selbstbefreiung* myth and the *Liberators* case was that they occurred in societies with very different social and political climates: the *Selbstbefreiung* myth could not be challenged in East Germany because to do so would be to invite the wrath of the State, whereas in American society such challenges are part and parcel of public discourse.

---

[113] Stern, Kenneth S. *Liberators: A Background Report.* The American Jewish Committee, Institute of Human Relations, 165 E. 56th Street, NY 10022. Feb. 10, 1993. p. 14.

[114] Goldberg, Jeffrey. The Exaggerators. *The New Republic*, **208**, (2003), p. 14.

[115] Ibid., p. 214.

Indeed, the consensus that the *Liberators* film was deeply flawed continues to be challenged to this day in the United States. Asa R. Gordon, Executive Director of the Douglass Institute of Government, has been a persistent and consistent critic of those who reject the claim that the liberation of Buchenwald was accomplished by African-American soldiers. A link on Gordon's website to his webpage entitled "Liberators Under Fire" makes clear that the conflation of the Buchenwald liberation story with larger issues of race and social justice continues: "Censorship by Public TV has consigned the documentary film on African American soldiers to an historical purgatory by joining Holocaust and racial revisionist history."[116]

The controversy over the *Liberators* film also touched Kareem Abdul-Jabbar. Abdul-Jabbar's father, F.L. Alcindor, was acquainted with one of the 761st Tank Battalion veterans, Leonard Smith. Abdul-Jabbar attended a screening of *Liberators* in 1992 at the Lincoln Center, and encountered Smith there. Abdul-Jabbar later published a history of the 761st Tank Battalion titled, *"Brothers in Arms: The Epic Story of the 761st Tank Battalion, WWII's Forgotten Heroes"*. In the preface to the 2004 work, Abdul-Jabbar referred to the *Liberators* controversy:

> "Unfortunately, some of the events referred to in the documentary I saw that night, *Liberators: Fighting on two Fronts in WWII*, had not been adequately researched. The film was produced with the best of intentions, but crucial facts were incorrect or transposed. The resulting controversy tarnished the record of one of the most highly decorated and courageous combat units in the war, and made me aware of the need to tell the 761st's story in a way that would attempt, insofar as possible after almost sixty years, to set the record straight."[117]

Abdul-Jabbar's account of the 761st's encounter with concentration camps does set the record straight, as he does not place the 761st at Buchenwald. He identifies the camps visited by the 761st as sub-camps of Mauthausen. *Gunskirchen Lager* was such a camp, and Abdul-Jabbar describes a visit to the camp by members of the 761st Tank Battalion. While Abdul-Jabbar's book did clarify the role of the 761st Tank Battalion as not having liberated Buchenwald, later statements made subsequent to a trip to Israel unfortunately continued to muddy the waters with respect to the role of African-American soldiers in liberating the camps. Responding to a reporter's question in an ESPN interview on June 20,

---

[116] Asa Gordon, Green Party Speakers Bureau, http://asagordon.byethost10.com/, retrieved 4/6/2019.

[117] Abdul-Jabbar, Kareem. *Brothers in Arms: The Epic Story of the 761st Tank Battalion, WWII's Forgotten Heroes*. (New York, Harlem Moon, 2005) p. xiv.

2011, Abdul-Jabbar mistakenly claimed that the 761st Tank Battalion liberated Dachau, and that the 183rd Combat Engineer Battalion liberated Buchenwald:

"I have heard this amazing tale about your dad and a boy he helped liberate from a concentration camp at the end of World War II. Would you mind recounting briefly the story of Rabbi Lau and your dad?

That story — people have gotten that all mixed up. There was a reporter in Israel who put my father into the tank battalion that liberated Dachau.

My dad was a police officer in New York.

One of the guys that he was a police officer with was in a tank battalion that liberated Dachau. Rabbi Lau was a boy in Buchenwald, which was also liberated by black troops, but it was a totally different group than the one that my dad's friend was in.

The group that helped liberate Buchenwald was the 183rd Combat Engineers, an all-black unit.

And that's who you wrote the book about?

No, I wrote the book about the 761st Tank Batallion [sic]. That was the unit my dad's friend was in. They liberated Dachau. The reporter in Israel mixed all of the facts up, and got it all conflated. People were thinking my dad was a lieutenant in the 761st Tank Battalion. My dad was a lieutenant in the New York City Transit Police!"[118]

This exchange is a somewhat eye-popping reminder of how quickly and how dramatically facts can get distorted and confused when there is a good story to be told. While Kareem Abdul-Jabbar was fortunately able to correct the errors made by the reporter, he unfortunately repeated two other errors, the placing of the 761st at Dachau and the 183rd at Buchenwald at the liberation of these two camps. The emotion that was and to some extent remains attached to the question of whether African-American soldiers liberated Buchenwald or Dachau is clearly the result of the symbolic transformation of the event into a proxy for the entire record of enslavement and abuse of African-Americans in the United States. Seen against the staggering weight of that record, quibbling over documents and inconsistencies in testimony to question this version of the liberation can seem to some like a continuing victimization of African-Americans. Phyllis Klotman, in *Struggles for Representation* explains the divergent interpretations of the liberation stories this way:

---

[118] ESPN True Hoop, Henry Abbott, *Kareem Abdul-Jabbar on Youth, LeBron*, http://www.espn.com/blog/truehoop/post/_/id/30461/kareem-abdul-jabbar-on-youth-lebron, retrieved 4/6/2019.

"Responding to *Liberators*, film scholar/critic Annette Insdorf wrote in the *Washington Post*: 'In 1993, we don't seem to be in danger of forgetting the Holocaust. But we are in danger of forgetting that all films – even documentaries – have a point of view, and that truth will always be partial.' Insdorf added that *Liberators* is "certainly not the first – and probably not the last – Holocaust film to provoke heated discussion about the sanctity of the subject and the limitations not only of individual memory but of official records."

If film theory offers useful insight into the way documentary presents a structured point of view, then critical race theory may provide a larger context for understanding the way that differing views of reality have contributed to the *Liberators* controversy. Critical race theory has emerged out of the desire of minority scholars in legal studies to construct an alternative way of explaining racial issues. In an attempt to attack racial subordination, some have developed a multiconsciousness analysis of phenomena that rejects efforts to harmonize diverse understandings. In fact, some scholars question whether objective reality matters when institutional structures, including the justice system, are designed to reflect the values of the dominant culture, ignoring or suppressing the perspectives of minorities.

Multiconsciousness analysis focuses on differences, not commonalities, in comprehending a given phenomenon. It posits competing versions of reality in part because our understanding of reality is based on different underlying assumptions and different belief systems. Many critical race theorists 'consider that a principal obstacle to racial reform is majoritarian mindset – the bundle of presuppositions, received wisdoms, and shared cultural understandings persons in the dominant group bring to discussions of race. To analyze and challenge these power-laden beliefs, some writers employ counterstories, parables, chronicles and anecdotes aimed at revealing their contingency, cruelty, and self-serving nature'.

The controversy surrounding Liberators may invite analysis based on critical race theory that can help us understand the difficulties of reconciling such different views of reality. It is important to remember that, whatever its successes and failures, Liberators as a counterstory of World War II provides the privileged view of black soldiers and Jewish survivors themselves – one that should not be disregarded. The intense debate over truth and factual accuracy may tell us a lot about institutional and alternative ways of constructing history, but should not overwhelm the legitimate values of the film."[119]

---

[118] Klotman, Phyllis R., and Cutler, Janet K. *Struggles for Representation: African American Film and Video.* (Bloomington, Indiana University Press, 1999) pp. 61-62.

It seems unfortunate that Leon Bass and William Scott and Leonard Smith and so many others became entangled in this controversy over whether their experience fit the arbitrary and narrow definition of "liberator" now endorsed by the United States Holocaust Memorial Museum and the US Army Center for Military History. Both Bass and Scott appear in a temporary exhibit at the United States Holocaust Memorial Museum entitled "American Witnesses" (summer 2019) and both are identified as soldiers who visited Buchenwald in the days after liberation. Bass and Scott engaged in considerable civic outreach, speaking to student and other groups on many occasions. Some of these events were recorded, and the eloquent testimony of Leon Bass about his experiences in the Jim Crow south, as a soldier in a segregated unit, and as a human being encountering the horrors of Buchenwald mindful of the racist theories of the Nazis and the common ground they shared with the racism with which he had grown up is very powerful and moving. Leon Bass used his time at Buchenwald as a basis on which to engage others in a positive dialogue about difficult and important issues. Are his tireless and inspiring efforts to teach the lessons of Buchenwald somehow diminished by the fact that he was probably at Buchenwald on April 17, 1945, rather than April 11? Of course not.

If tendentious and misleading arguments have been forwarded to place soldiers like Leon Bass and William Scott at Buchenwald within the time-window that would accord them official "liberator" status, the real shame is that such value was placed on being accorded this status in the first place. Conflicting documentary evidence only adds to the confusion: the Georgia Commission on the Holocaust and the United States Holocaust Memorial Museum both host on their websites a photograph of Generals Patton, Bradley, and Middleton taken on April 12, 1945 at Ohrdruf, a sub-camp of Buchenwald which was visited by a group of dignitaries including General Eisenhower on that day. The photo credit on both sites is to William A. Scott III, who does not mention Ohrdruf in any of the interviews I have seen or read, and whose testimony would seem to preclude his having been there on that date. The *Buchenwald Gedenkstätte* website also hosts this same photograph, but credits it to William A. Newhouse, an Army photographer who took a well-known series of photographs at Ohrdruf on April 12, to which this photograph appears to belong. The Newhouse attribution is apparently correct, but the attribution of this photograph to Scott by two well-known Holocaust organizations could easily encourage continuing, but unnecessary and misplaced controversy over Scott's whereabouts on that day: according to Scott, he was at Eisenach, where he would be ordered to Buchenwald the next day.

Generals Patton, Bradley, and Middleton at Ohrdruf, April 12, 1945. Photo by William A. Newhouse, US Army Signal Corps. Photo credit on USHMM website is to William A. Scott III. Photograph used with permission of the United States Holocaust Memorial Museum.

Many hundreds, perhaps thousands of American soldiers visited Buchenwald from April 11 to July 3, 1945. Some, even some who fit the definition of "liberators", did little more than drive into the camp, remain for a few minutes or hours, and leave. Some, including many medical personnel who do not fit the official criteria as "liberators", remained in the camp for weeks, experiencing the horrible legacy of Nazi barbarism day after day, doing their best to serve the needs of the survivors. Dr. Leon Bass and William A. Scott III reflected on their time at Buchenwald and worked hard to use their experience to help others see the camp through their eyes and to think through the lessons the experience had taught them, conditioned as they had been by their own backgrounds to appreciate those lessons. In the great scheme of things, are their contributions diminished because they do not fit the technical definition of "liberator" as adopted by USHMM and USACMH? I don't think it matters so much exactly which days or how many days these American soldiers spent at Buchenwald: what matters a great deal more is how they spent the days that remained to them after having visited the camp passing on the lessons of their time on the Ettersberg to others.

Survivor's Memories of Black Liberators

Rabbi Lau

The *Liberators* story was not solely based on the claims of soldiers: survivors seemingly corroborated the presence of African-American soldiers at Buchenwald on April 11, 1945. Rabbi Israel Meir Lau (through his brother Naphtali), Benjamin Bender, Elie Wiesel, Alex Gross, and Dr. Henry Oster are all survivors who have claimed to have seen African-American soldiers at Buchenwald on the day of or the day after liberation. The fact that several Holocaust survivors have reported seeing African-American soldiers at Buchenwald has lent credibility to the claims of those who insist that Black soldiers were first on the scene. The public prominence of two of these survivors, Rabbi Israel Meir Lau and Elie Wiesel, has been especially significant.

Lau's memories of seeing black soldiers are actually second-hand repetitions of reports from his brother, Naphtali:

"We all stared at the six soldiers, one of whom was black. We knew they were the saviors we had been awaiting for such a long time....

I was just under eight years old. Many of the events of that day I do not remember directly, but rather through the words of others who described them for me decades later."[120]

Naphtali's recollection was of seeing six soldiers arrive in two jeeps on the afternoon of the 11th. Only one of these six soldiers were black. These soldiers remained in the camp only a short time, and Naphtali reports that later in the afternoon, a convoy of ten vehicles, led by two tanks, entered Buchenwald. An officer addressed the inmates on a megaphone, and Naphtali was soon taken away to receive medical treatment, and therefore missed much of what went on over the next few days.

Naphtali was infected with typhus, and was "fighting fever and suffering hallucinations and nightmares"[121]. Rabbi Lau's memories of the liberation of Buchenwald cannot be considered very authoritative, as he was only a young child and admits that much of what he "remembers" about the liberation really came from things he learned only later. Lau did have a very dramatic way of discussing his experiences in the Holocaust, though accuracy and consistency

---

[120] Lau, Israel Meir. *Out of the Depths: The Story of a Child of Buchenwald Who Returned Home at Last*. (New York: Sterling, 2005). pp. 65-66.

[121] Ibid., p.151.

were not hallmarks of his presentations. For example, in his book *Out of the Depths* Lau related a story involving an American soldier:

> "After the liberation of the camp, I stayed in Buchenwald for a while. Buchenwald was in the suburbs of the city of Weimar, the home of Goethe and Schiller. Ironically, the concentration camp was just a ten-minute walk from the German national theater, a bastion of German culture…
>
> I was wandering around the camp, free and fearless, when I saw the Weimar residents, mostly women and elderly men. Suddenly, a command car stopped next to me, and a giant American soldier lifted me. Gripping my heels in one hand and my shoulder with the other, he raised me high in the air, and shouted in German to the Weimar residents: "Do you see this little boy? This is who you have been fighting for the past six years. Because of him you started a world war. He is the enemy of National Socialism, the Nazis' archenemy. A little Polish boy! You murdered his father and mother, and you almost murdered him as well! You followed the Fuehrer – for this? You followed him in blind faith – for this?!"[122]

It is worth noting that the distance from Weimar to Buchenwald is actually about seven miles: the camp was not located in the "suburbs" of Weimar, and is about a fifteen-minute drive from the camp, far more than a "ten-minute walk". The soldier in this story is described as a "giant", but not as Black.

Lau then relates a conversation he had with Kareem Abdul-Jabbar, in which Abdul-Jabbar seems to identify the soldier who picked him up that day as Leonard "Smitty" Smith, the soldier in the 761st Tank Battalion who was the friend of Kareem Abdul-Jabbar's father, F.L. Alcindor:

> "He [Abdul-Jabbar] explained that one of his father's close friends had been among the American soldiers who liberated Buchenwald. This friend [of my father's], said the basketball player, "was a giant, like me. He lifted a little boy in his arms and showed him to the Germans, rebuking them for considering this little boy their enemy, and for fighting against him with merciless cruelty." For fifty years, Abdul-Jabbar recounted, he and his father followed the path of this little boy, and they learned that he had become a very important rabbi in Israel. "My father", he told the American reporters, "is a very religious Christian, but he cannot visit the Holy Land due to health reasons. When he heard that on this trip I would be stopping in Israel, he asked me to go the rabbi and ask for his blessing." The famous basketball player remained

---

[122] Lau, Depths, pp 71-72..

faithful to his word, and paid me an emotionally charged visit at the office of the chief rabbinate of Israel."[123]

Lau's description of the event a few paragraphs earlier has the soldier speaking to the civilians of Weimar in German. It is certainly possible that Leonard Smith spoke German, or learned enough to make this statement, but a more significant difficulty with this story arises in view of a footnote on the next page of Lau's book, in which he says: "A documentary film broadcast in the States in 1992 claims that Battalion 761 also liberated Buchenwald, but Abdul-Jabbar explained in his book that this was erroneous, and that it was a different black unit that liberated Buchenwald". Leonard Smith was assigned to the 761st Tank Battalion, and so, according to Lau's (and Abdul-Jabbar's) reckoning, couldn't have been at Buchenwald, and so couldn't have been the giant who lifted up the little Polish boy in one hand.

To complicate matters further, Lau later related another version of this same story in a speech May 15, 2014 at Young Israel Beth El Of Borough Park, Brooklyn[124]. On this occasion, however, he unambiguously identified the person who lifted him up and made this speech: it was General George S. Patton himself. Patton did speak some German (he spoke French quite well) and was at Buchenwald on April 15, 1945, and while there was accompanied by many reporters and photographers. None reported any incident of the sort described by Rabbi Lau.

Benjamin Bender

Benjamin Bender's descriptions of the soldiers he saw in Buchenwald in 1985 in his letter to the Editor of the *New York Times* and in his 1995 book both included the details that they were tall, strong, black men crying like babies. The 1995 description added the detail that these black men wore colorful scarves. Eli Wiesel did not mention the skin color of his liberators in his statement at the 1981 liberators conference: I do not know when he first identified his liberators as African-Americans, but in a 1989 article in the *New York Times*, Henry Kamm quotes Wiesel as saying:

> "The most moving moment of my life was the day the Americans arrived, a few hours after the SS had fled", he recalled in a telephone interview from his home in New York. "It was the morning of April 11",

[123] Youtube, Holocaust Survivors and Heroes Honored at Day of Remembrance, https://www.youtube.com/watch?v=SkJZtKARYe4, retrieved October 6, 2019.

"I will always remember with love a big black soldier", he went on. "He was crying like a child – tears of all the pain in the world and all the rage. Every one who was there that day will forever feel a sentiment of gratitude to the American soldiers who liberated us."[125]

Both of the details included by Wiesel, that the black soldiers were unusually big men and that they were weeping, appeared in Bender's letter to the *New York Times* four years earlier. These two details appear and reappear in many survivor accounts.

Alex Gross

Alex Gross is another Holocaust survivor who has supported the claim that Buchenwald was liberated by African-American soldiers. An interview with Gross recorded on August 7, 1983 may be found in the archives of the United States Holocaust Memorial Museum. In this interview Gross recalls that five or six years before the interview he had been contacted by Fred Crawford of Emory University, who invited him to participate in a Holocaust-related program at the school. Gross reports that when he arrived at the studio for the program, Crawford told him that he had a surprise for him and that he would meet one of the soldiers who had participated in the liberation of Buchenwald. Gross then saw a "black gentleman" sitting in the studio, and immediately recognized him as a soldier who had arrived in a tank at Buchenwald, and blown a hole in the electrified fence[126]. Other sources indicate that the veteran Gross met was William A. Scott[127]. Gross says that he viewed this soldier as an angel, and concluded that all angels must be black.

William A. Scott had been a member of the 183rd Combat Engineer Battalion, an all-black unit from which some soldiers did visit Buchenwald, though most agree that the visit occurred on April 17, 1945, six days after the liberation. In an interview with Fred Crawford transcribed on April 9, 1979 in the offices of the *Atlanta Daily World* (perhaps this interview coincided with the program at which Scott and Gross met?) Scott reported that he was with his battalion near "Eisenauf", Germany (it was actually Eisenach) when Buchenwald was overrun on April 13 (it was first visited by American troops on April 11). He was then

---

[125] *New York Times*, Henry Kamm, *No Mention of Jews at Buchenwald*. thttps://www.nytimes.com/1989/03/25/world/no-mention-of-jews-at-buchenwald.html, retrieved October 6, 2019.

[126] United States Holocaust Memorial Museum, Oral history interview with Alex Gross, https://collections.ushmm.org/search/catalog/irn508092, retrieved October 6, 2019.

[127] W.A. Scott III, "United States Holocaust Memorial Council," *Georgia Journeys*, accessed October 6, 2019

ordered to go to Buchenwald and after some difficulty locating the camp, arrived and offered his impressions of what he saw.

While Gross identifies William Scott as a soldier he saw at Buchenwald on April 11, Scott himself said in his interview with Crawford that he was only ordered to go to Buchenwald on April 13. Scott was a photographer in an Engineer unit, not a tanker, and his account does not include any mention of tanks or firing at a fence. Alex Gross wrote a book in 2001 entitled *Yankele*, in which he offered a somewhat more detailed account of the liberation than that provided in the 1983 USHMM interview. The USHMM transcript includes Gross' recollection that an American tank had breached the fence at Buchenwald by firing explosive shells at it. In his book, Gross adds the detail that the firing caused "sparks and explosions …like fireworks, brighter than the mid-morning sun"[128]. This seems to suggest that the fence was still electrified, though Gross also says that his brother Bill had joined other prisoners in disabling the electric fence on April 10 or 11, escaping through a hole they cut and searching for Allied help, so according to Gross, the fence should not have been electrified when the Americans arrived. Gross' memories are surprisingly vivid considering his physical condition: in *Yankele*, he says that he was unsure of the outcome of his brother Bill's mission to cut the fence. "I don't know just how long it took them; I was comatose, too weak to grasp what was going on. Because of my semi-conscious state, many of the details of that day and the next remain a blur."[129] In a USC Shoah Foundation interview, Gross says that his brother Bill participated in a revolt against the SS, climbed a guard tower and overpowered guards, and assisted the "partisans"[130].

Gross' account of the liberation shares some common ground with the myth of the *Selbstbefreiung*, including the story of prisoners storming the watchtowers, overcoming the guards on duty, and taking their weapons. Gross is, as far as I know, alone in saying that the American tanks fired at the fence to blow a hole in it, or that the revolt was assisted by partisans. There are other liberator and survivor accounts (which are also problematic) that claim that tanks burst through the fence, but Gross' claim to have seen tanks fire at the fence may be unique.

Gross' book *Yankele* also contains a number of factual errors, mistakes of timing or location, or conflation of various events unrelated to the liberation of

---

[128] Gross, Alex. *Yankele*. (Lanham, MD, University Press of America, 2001) pp 79-80

[126] Ibid.

[127] USC Shoah Foundation interview with Alex Gross, reviewed onsite at the United States Holocaust Memorial Museum. The reference to his brother Bill occurs on Tape 3 at 12:29. https://collections.ushmm.org/search/catalog/vha11272.

Buchenwald. In fact, the editors of *Yankele* felt compelled to add several footnotes pointing out the potential problems with Gross' recollections[131]. Gross repeated a story he had heard after the war that there was a daily goal of killing twenty thousand Jews at Auschwitz, for example, and that officers were incentivized to achieve the goal and so distorted the criteria for selection for extermination.

Gross also appears to have conflated stories about Ilse Koch at Buchenwald with Auschwitz. In both the USHMM interview and his book, Gross tells a story about the "Bitch of Auschwitz" who inspected prisoner's arms on the *Appelplatz* at Auschwitz, searching for boys with skin just the right color. Those with desirable skin would have their arms chopped off on the spot, left to bleed to death in view of the others. This memory is also very vivid to Gross: "Once she picked boys in front of me, to my side, and behind me. Somehow I was spared; I'll never know why."[132] There is also a USC Shoah Foundation interview in the USHMM collection, and Gross repeats the story about the "Bitch of Auschwitz" in that interview. He also reports that the SS soldiers ordered prisoners to throw boys in the air, and would then impale them on their bayonets. He further reports that SS soldiers would randomly shoot boys through the head, betting which of their eyes they would shoot out.[133]

Gross was clearly aware that there was a "Bitch of Buchenwald" named Ilse Koch, as he mentions her on page 71 of his book, but he also insists that the "Bitch of Auschwitz" was real, though I have been unable to find any other reports of incidents anything like those described by Gross on the *Appelplatz* at Auschwitz[134]. Gross' description of his arrival at Buchenwald also mistakes the sign at the camp gate (it reads *"Jedem das Seine"*, not *Arbeit macht frei"*) but he also embeds this error in a vivid, elaborate, personal memory:

"Once again I saw the familiar electrified barbed-wire, the watch towers looming over the camp, and the iron sign at the entrance stating "Arbeit macht frei" ("Work Makes One Free") – just as in all the other camps that had imprisoned me. I wondered how many more times I would have to pass through those gates and experience the irony of that message before "freedom" became completely meaningless."

---

[131] Gross, *Yankele*, 261-262.

[132] Ibid., 51.

[133] USC Shoah Foundation interview with Alex Gross, reviewed onsite at the United States Holocaust Memorial Museum. The references to impaling boys and shooting them through the eye appear on Tape 2, 18:04. The "Bitch of Auschwitz" is mentioned a bit later, at 18:25.

Henry Oster

Dr. Henry Oster has also been a very visible figure, and numerous examples of speeches, school visits, and media stories about him are readily available on the internet. His account of the liberation of Buchenwald usually includes a story about seeing an American tank emblazoned with a Star of David arrive on the day of the liberation. I am not aware of any other testimony or evidence to support that claim. In his 2014 book *The Kindness of the Hangman*[136] Oster also includes Black soldiers in his story of the Buchenwald liberation. Oster's book appears to be an amalgam of first-person recollections and material he has encountered in the years and decades since liberation. Oster identifies Captain Frederic Keffer and Technical Sergeant Herbert Gottschalk as the first Americans to enter the camp. Oster's description of the liberation has African-American soldiers arriving at Buchenwald on April 12, offering the generalization that Black soldiers were compassionate and caring, while white soldiers were cold and distant. Oster describes "a huge, muscular black man, standing in the middle of this barbed-wire prison, with tears streaming down his face."[137] Oster also activates the theme of African-American/Jewish solidarity in the face of oppression and suffering.

Oster appears to have included events from several time periods in this passage. Oster's description also includes the elements that we can trace back through Wiesel and Lau to Bender's original description: black soldiers as huge, muscular, and weeping. Oster says that black and white American soldiers were never seen together, an assertion contradicted by any number of WWII photographs. In fact, the April 17 photograph of African-American soldiers at Buchenwald depicts them standing in a group that appears to include two or perhaps three white soldiers[138.] There does not appear to be a significant disparity in the average height of the black and white soldiers in this photograph, which respects the statistical reality that black and white men are not significantly different in average height.

....

[134] There is an assertion here http://www.auschwitz.dk/Women/Grese.htm (retrieved 10 July 2019) that three lampshades made from human skin were found in the hut of Irma Grese, a notorious female SS guard at Auschwitz who was hanged by the British after the war.

[135] Gross, *Yankele*, 69.

[136] Oster, Henry, and Ford, Dexter. *The Kindness of the Hangman: Even in Hell, There is Hope*. (Manhattan Beach, CA, Higgins Bay Press, 2014).

[137] Oster, *Kindness*, 143-144.

[138] United States Holocaust Memorial Museum, American troops, including African-American soldiers from the Headquarters and Service Company of the 183rd Engineer Combat Battalion, 8th Corps, U.S. 3rd Army, view corpses stacked behind the crematorium during an inspection tour of the Buchenwald concentration camp, https://collections.ushmm.org/search/catalog/pa13316, retrieved October 6, 2019.

This photograph was taken by William A. Scott III at Buchenwald on April 17, 1945, according to the photo credit on the United States Holocaust Memorial Museum website. Used with permission.

The descriptions of the African-American soldiers as "tall", "muscular", "huge", "giants", and "crying like babies" may be evidence of the influence of both suggestion and the operation of common stereotypes about African-American men in these survivor recollections. A 2017 psychological study[139] showed that young Black men are judged as bigger and more muscular than young white men, and accordingly as more threatening. Minority groups are also often stereotyped as infantile or childlike: this raises the possibility that if young African-American men were inserted into a liberation memory by suggestion or other means, the memory might then be constructed or shaped based on common stereotypes of African-American men. That might help explain why nearly all the descriptions of black liberators are of unusually tall, muscular men crying like babies.

Oster's book contains a considerable amount of historical analysis and background explaining the origins of the Holocaust, but contains no citations or references, so it is difficult to sort out reliable, documented material from Oster's own memories, attitudes, and ideas. Oster's website[140] contains a list of his many outreach presentations, and several video clips, including some attacking

---

[139] Wilson, J. P., Hugenberg, K., & Rule, N. O. (2017). Racial bias in judgments of physical size and formidability: From size to threat. *Journal of Personality and Social Psychology*, 113(1), 59-80.

[140] The Kindness of the Hangman, https://www.thekindnessofthehangman.com/, retrieved 10 July 2019.

Donald Trump by comparing him to Hitler and the Nazis. Oster also criticizes "right-wing pundits" in his book.[141]"

Oster also claimed that American propaganda leaflets used racist images of African-American soldiers to demoralize German soldiers. Oster reported that American psychologists working for General George Patton had decided to use images of African-American soldiers castrating Nazi soldiers as a way of demoralizing the enemy. According to Oster, a demeaning caricature of a black American soldier with a knife in one hand and a white penis and testicles in the other was intended to terrorize German soldiers into surrendering to white American soldiers."[142]

It is easier to show that something did exist than that it did not, but I have not been able to locate images of any WWII American propaganda leaflets, or references to them, that match Oster's graphic description. Oster makes numerous other questionable claims in his book, and many that are known to be in error. On page 102 he claims that human fat from murdered Jews was rendered into soap, for example, a myth that circulated widely during the war[143]. He describes a "Pflaume feur", a punishment he says was commonly visited on Jewish women by the SS at Auschwitz in which their genitals would be doused with gasoline and ignited; on pages 38 and 41 he refers to wearing the Jewish star on his clothes in Cologne in 1938 and 1939, but wearing the star in Germany was not required until September 1, 1941[144]. Oster's Shoah Foundation interview contains the claim that children were murdered in gas vans at Auschwitz as they were moved from Auschwitz-Birkenau to Auschwitz I and that Ilse Koch would ride her horse through the camp at Buchenwald, though he only arrived at Buchenwald in January 1945, long after Ilse Koch had left[145].

Oster also describes the mass burial of corpses at Buchenwald in terms that suggest that he may have conflated images of Bergen-Belsen with Buchenwald. Oster reports that American soldiers using bulldozers "carved out a trench in a nearby field" and "pushed in the bodies in one great, tumbling heap"[146]. This

---

[141] Oster, Kindness, 15.

[142] Ibid., 126-7.

[143] There was a small-scale research program, but no industrial-scale activities of this kind.

[144] United States Holocaust Memorial Museum, German Government Forces Jews to Wear Yellow Stars, https://newspapers.ushmm.org/events/german-government-forces-jews-to-wear-yellow-stars, retrieved October 6, 2019.

[145] USC Shoah Foundation testimony of Henry Oster, reviewed onsite at the United States Holocaust Memorial Museum. The reference to gas vans occurs on Tape 3 at 25:55; the reference to Ilse Koch may be found on Tape 4 at 12:45. https://collections.ushmm.org/search/catalog/vha4284.

[146] Oster, Kindness, 154-55.

accurately describes footage of mass burials at Bergen-Belsen, which is contained in many films about the Holocaust[147], but bulldozers were not needed or used at Buchenwald. On the south slope of the Ettersberg there were natural depressions in the earth that were used to bury bodies when coal for the crematoria was short. SS and local civilians were later required to dis-inter and re-inter the bodies.[148]

Oster's historical sketch at the beginning of his book describes American eugenics programs at some length[149], but rather myopically, leaving the clear impression that Nazi racial policies were mainly and specifically inspired by and drew support from American eugenics programs. There was, of course, significant opposition to the eugenics movement in America, and the United States was only one of many countries that adopted eugenics policies in the early twentieth century: the United Kingdom was also a thought and policy leader in this area. Moreover, the racial theories on which Nazi racial policies were based had significant European roots.

Later in the book Oster returns to the theme of eugenics, claiming that he was denied admission to the University of Southern California School of Dentistry because of anti-Semitism. Oster reports that he had sent an expensive new television set to the Chair of the Admissions Committee, one Dr. Rutherford, as an apparent bribe to gain admission. Rutherford had told Oster that few students were admitted the first time they applied, and that he should re-apply the next year. Oster did not submit an application the next year (he says he did not realize this was necessary) and so was not admitted. Oster linked his rejection from the school to Rutherford's anti-Semitism and the eugenic beliefs of a former USC President, Rufus Bernhard von KleinSmid[150].

The Trouble with Testimony

Survivor testimony is often treated as "socially privileged" material: we are loath to question or challenge survivor testimony (or liberator testimony, for that matter) because to do so seems disrespectful. But survivor and liberator testimonies are still human memory: we sometimes seem to act as if the scale and importance of certain events somehow exempts memories of them from the normal operation of human memory processes, which may produce flawed recollections. Lucy

---

[147] Such as the film *Todesmuehlen*
[148] Personal communication, Bernd Schmidt.
[149] Oster, *Kindness*, 16-17.
[150] Ibid., 204.

Dawidowicz, who spent time in Displaced Persons camps after the war working with refugees, observed:

> "...besides, the survivor's memory is often distorted by hate, sentimentality, and the passage of time. His perspective on external events is often skewed by the limits of his personal experience. Survivor accounts of critical events are typical of all testimony, that is, they are full of discrepancies. About matters both trivial and significant, the evidence is nearly always in dispute. In part the unreliability of these accounts derives from imperfect observation and flawed memory, but in larger part from the circumstance that they are not constructed exclusively on the basis of firsthand experience. In order to present a coherent narrative, the author has likely included a large measure of hearsay, gossip, rumor, assumption, speculation, and hypothesis."[151]

I've discussed the East German *Selbstbefreiung* myth and the case of the *Liberators* in the US as examples of social or collective memory in action. In both cases the distortion of the facts was ultimately shaped in a particular direction by forces operating above the level of the individual: Communist ideology on the one hand, a societal history of racial tension on the other. But both individual and social factors play a role even when the ultimate direction taken by memory distortions seems to be influenced mainly by collective considerations.

There is, perhaps, a useful analogy to epidemiology here: just as we may sometimes be able to trace the origins of an epidemic to a "patient zero", an individual source of infection, we may be able to pinpoint the origins of a mistaken memory to a single person. Once that individual memory is communicated to others, it becomes subject to social mechanisms of transmission and amplification: as it spreads among a population, others with vague recollections who encounter it may find that it gives form to their own memory. Mutual reinforcement, apparent validation, and gradual embellishment can turn a single mistaken memory into what appears to be a self-validating network of interlocking memories rich in vivid detail. Memories sometimes contain distinct or unusual content or modes of expression that can serve as tags to help us trace their passage through a population. The description of black liberators as unusually large, muscular, and childlike may be such a tag.

Two human memory processes, suggestibility and misattribution, can help explain how a distorted or incorrect memory can begin to spread in this way. Daniel Schacter's book *The Seven Sins of Memory*[152] offers several examples of

---

[151] Dawidowicz, Lucy S. *A Holocaust Reader*. (Springfield, NJ; Behrman House, 1976) p. 11.
[152] Schacter, Daniel L. *The Seven Sins of Memory*. (Boston, Houghton Mifflin, 2001).

the role suggestion can play in shaping our recollections of the past. If a friend or relative recounts a memory of a past event to us in a certain way, we may accept that memory as true, even if we ourselves do not have a specific recollection of that same event. Later, we might misattribute the suggested memory to our own experience, not that of the person who shared their memory with us. One can see quite readily how minor details of past events might be altered in our memories in this way, but can such processes really explain memories of dramatic, traumatic, major life events, like the liberation of a concentration camp?

The answer is: "Yes, absolutely." Schacter provides several examples of just such occurrences. People have, for example, mistakenly confessed to murder and other serious crimes based on suggestion. There was a spate of notorious criminal cases in which children recalled sexual and other abuses at the hands of caregivers that were lurid in details of Satanic rituals and the like: suggestion was later shown to have been the source of these stories. That suggestion and misattribution may have played a role in spreading a memory of "big, black soldiers" "crying like babies" on the day of the liberation of Buchenwald among survivors and soldiers is well within the realm of possibility.

Of course, it is also possible that there were unusually tall African-American men weeping at the horrific scenes at Buchenwald on April 11 or April 12, 1945. We noted in Chapter 2 that there appear to have been soldiers at Buchenwald, such as those with Major Reed of the 4th Armored Division, or the cavalry platoon from the 80th Infantry Division that arrived on the 12th, whose precise identities are unknown to us at this time. Might some of them have been African-American? Perhaps. We can be reasonably confident that the soldiers of the 761st Tank Battalion and 183rd Combat Engineers were not at Buchenwald until several days after the liberation, but we cannot say with absolute certainty that no African-American soldiers were there during the 48-hour period specified by the US Army Center for Military History.

5 BUCHENWALD IN AMERICA: INDIVIDUAL MEMORY AND PUBLIC OUTREACH

I consider the *Liberators* controversy to be at least partly a phenomenon rooted in collective or social memory. Larger social issues, especially the long history of American racism against African-Americans and the tensions between the Jewish and African-American minorities in the United States came to shape the way individual memories were interpreted, and raised the stakes in evaluating the truth of these memories well beyond the level that would apply to an individual memory unentwined with these vexing social issues. We will now turn to just such individual memories: recollections of survivors and soldiers whose memories appear to be mistaken, but which have not been integrated into a larger social or political framework.

American schoolchildren may encounter a book titled "*Eyewitness to the Liberation of Buchenwald*"[153]. The first chapter of this book begins as follows:

"On April 11, 1945, the forests in central Germany were quiet. Troops and vehicles of the U.S. Third Army were traveling through the trees. Private Harry J. Herder was on alert. His division had been told to investigate Buchenwald, a German war camp. However, most of the men knew little about their assignment.

At the time, Germany was controlled by the **Nazi Party**. The country was part of a group of nations called the Axis Powers. They had been at war with the Allied Powers since 1939. The Allied Powers included Britain, the United States, and the Soviet Union.

---

[153] Sherman, Jill. *Eyewitness to the Liberation of Buchenwald*. (Mankato, MN; The Child's World, 2016).

The American troops neared the camp. Their tanks slowed down but did not stop. They crashed through barbed-wire fences. Soldiers jumped to the ground. They prepared to meet enemy troops. But no attack came.

Something wasn't right. The camp was eerily quiet. A pillar of foul-smelling black smoke poured from a chimney. Soldiers examined the buildings around them. They looked for people nearby."[154]

Attentive readers will doubtless have noted that there are several aspects of this story that are inconsistent with contemporary and historical accounts of the liberation of Buchenwald. (And perhaps also that two of the three Allied Powers mentioned did not go to war with Germany until 1941). First, Americans did not arrive at Buchenwald by crashing through fences in tanks: they drove through an open gate or a hole in the fence. Second, American troops were not looking for the camp, they happened upon it. Third, there could not possibly have been a "pillar of foul-smelling black smoke" pouring from a chimney (presumably that of the crematorium) because the supply of coal used to fuel the Buchenwald crematorium had been exhausted weeks before[155]. This is why there was a stack of unburned corpses outside the crematorium when Buchenwald was liberated, a stack which was left in place for weeks and photographed countless times.

Harry Herder, Jr.

Harry J. Herder, Jr. was a soldier in the 5th Ranger Battalion. Herder's complete account appears in several places on the internet: the citation in *Eyewitness to the Liberation of Buchenwald* is to this site[156]. Herder's elaborate liberation story appears to be inconsistent with the facts as they are known. The 5th Ranger Battalion was at Buchenwald, but not until several days after the liberation. According to Robert W. Black *in Rangers in WWII*, "April 15 was proof that the war was coming to a close: On the 15th, the 5th Rangers were ordered to guard a signal dump at Lehesten. Many Germans were denying the horrors of the concentration camps. To burn the memory of this evil into the German brain, General Patton directed that German civilians be given a tour of the camps. On the 16th of April, the 5th Rangers escorted one thousand German civilians to Buchenwald"[157]. Lehesten is about fifty miles south of Buchenwald. Bill Justis, a

---

[154] Ibid., p. 5.

[155] Gros, Louis. *Survivor of Buchenwald: My Personal Odyssey Through Hell.* (Brule, Wisconsin; Cable Publishing, 2012). p. 106.

[156] Liberation of Buchenwald by Harry Herder, http://remember.org/witness/herder, retrieved July 10, 2019.

[157] Black, Robert W. *Rangers in WWII.* (New York, Ballantine Books, 1992).

friend of Herder's, remembers (or perhaps his memory is a result of suggestion from Herder) crashing through the gates of Buchenwald, but he fixes the date as April 15, four days after the liberation[158]. Herder and Justis were most likely at Buchenwald four or five days after the liberation. Herder's account of liberating Buchenwald appears to be an amalgam of memories from his time at the camp several days after liberation with stories and images encountered later, and some imagination.

Herder's full story contains numerous errors of detail that suggest that his memories have been influenced by information to which he was exposed after the fact. For example, the account cited in *Eyewitness to the Liberation of Buchenwald* mistakenly describes the sign at the main gate this way: "High up above the opening for the gate was a heavy wooden beam with words carved into it in German script, Arbeit Macht Frei." The gate at Buchenwald contains the motto *Jedem das Seine* as part of the wrought-iron: the motto *Arbeit macht frei* was part of the wrought-iron gates at Auschwitz and some other camps, images of which were and are very common in Holocaust-related material, but not at Buchenwald. But there was indeed a carved wooden sign above the gate at Buchenwald (it is no longer there) with the motto *Recht oder unrecht – mein Vaterland* (My country, right or wrong).

The electrification of the fences at Buchenwald figures into several survivor and liberator accounts. Herder's full account includes the following description of his entry into the camp: "We hit those fences with enough speed so that it was unclear to me whether it was the first level, or the second, or the third, but at least one of those levels was hot with electricity. We hit the fences, blew through them, and shorted out whichever it was on the damp ground." Electricity to the fences had been turned off before the arrival of the Americans, and there is no evidence of any tanks having crashed through fences at Buchenwald.

Herder reports that he and a comrade were assigned to perform guard duty during the night at one of the watchtowers at Buchenwald during his unit's stay there. While walking to the tower, he heard voices behind him and discovered two prisoners, who were eastern European professors, conversing. These professors said that they had been at Buchenwald for four years. He invited the two into the tower, and Herder and his comrade listened to stories about Buchenwald from the two professors for the duration of their guard shift that night. The stories Herder remembers hearing from these professors concerned medical research projects conducted at Buchenwald. The professors described medical experiments

---

[158] O'Donnell, Patrick. Beyond Valor (New York, Touchstone, 2001) p. 324.

related to infectious diseases, according to Herder. Typhus was a serious problem at Buchenwald and elsewhere, and there was such research conducted at Buchenwald. Herder also reports that the professors described experiments at Buchenwald related to re-warming people who had been subjected to freezing temperatures. Herder specifically described an experiment in which prisoners who had undergone exposure to severe cold were introduced into a bed with naked women to test the efficacy of human warmth as a re-warming treatment.

Freezing and re-warming experiments of the sort Herder says the two professors described to him as having taken place at Buchenwald are not known to have been conducted at the camp. Such experiments were conducted at Dachau, however, and were widely publicized after the war. It is likely that Herder became aware of these experiments later and wove them into the fabric of his recollections of Buchenwald.

An example of how soldiers acquired some of their knowledge and memories of places like Buchenwald appears in Herder's full account. He describes an incident in which a Sergeant Blowers told him and some other soldiers about Ilse Koch's selection of prisoners with tattoos, how they would be taken to the hospital to be skinned for their tattoos which would then be pieced together for lampshades. Herder makes the claim that there were originally three such lampshades at Buchenwald, but that the "history books" mention only two. One disappeared after they arrived, according to Herder[159].

Sergeant Blowers was Herder's Platoon Sergeant. There are countless versions of Ilse Koch-human skin tattoo stories, which differ in many details. Controversy continues over the human-skin lampshades at Buchenwald[160], though the lampshade visible in the display set up by American soldiers on the 16th of April for the visit of Weimar civilians does not appear to include any tattoos. Rumors, gossip, stories, and myths were rampant among soldiers in WWII, as they probably have been in armies throughout history. These myths and rumors form part of the raw material that are a source of potential misattributions as soldiers begin to think about their experiences decades later. Such myths and rumors can even be given new life when they are inadvertently validated in the course of gathering personal testimony: the United States Holocaust Memorial Museum

---

[159] Liberation of Buchenwald by Harry Herder, http://remember.org/witness/herder, retrieved July 10, 2019

[160] Jacobsen, Mark. *The Lampshade: A Holocaust detective Story from Buchenwald to New Orleans*. (New York, Simon and Schuster, 2010).

[161] Oral History Interview with Harry J. Herder Jr., USHMM, https://collections.ushmm.org/search/catalog/irn80099, retrieved 8 July 2019.

[162] Ibid., 26:37-27:15

has in its collection a recording of an interview with Harry Herder conducted in 1994[161]. This interview contains the following remarkable exchange between the interviewer and Harry Herder[162]:

> Interviewer: "Did you see the gas chamber at Buchenwald?"
>
> Herder: "Did I see…?
>
> Interviewer: "Mm hmm. The gas chamber at Buchenwald."
>
> Herder: "No. In fact I thought of it later. Well in fact at that time we didn't even know there was such a thing as a gas chamber."
>
> Interviewer: "I see."
>
> Herder: "Yeah…and it was a room next to the furnace but we never thought to go in there and it was only after we got home and heard all the nonsense that we thought well my God, there must have been one there someplace."

This is an excellent example of the way suggestion can introduce inaccuracies into the testimonies of survivors or soldiers. This passage is noteworthy because there was no gas chamber at Buchenwald. By asking the question as she did, the interviewer makes clear to Herder that she believes there was a gas chamber at Buchenwald, and Herder responds by immediately shaping a memory to fit the false narrative of the gas chamber. He mentions a room next to the crematorium as a potential location for the gas chamber, and adds that after the war he learned that there must have been a gas chamber at Buchenwald, though of course no such facility existed at that camp. This unfortunate exchange in the context of a formal historical interview certainly created and perpetuated a false narrative about the existence of a gas chamber at Buchenwald in the mind of Harry Herder. When we consider how many conversations survivors and liberators have with others who may not have either broad historical knowledge of the events or adequate interviewing skills, it should not be at all surprising to discover that many survivor and liberator accounts contain inaccuracies of just this sort.

The interview in the USHMM archive also contains a detailed description of an event that we know did not happen, "turning off" the crematoria ovens:

> Herder: "When we broke into the place, the crematorium furnace was still going. The black smoke was still pouring out of the chimney."
>
> Interviewer: "Do you know what that black smoke was?"
>
> Herder: "No, not right away, but we knew it very shortly. Uh, our company commander and our platoon officer and our platoon sergeant all roamed around and they finally found a way to turn the crematorium off."[163]

---

[163] Ibid., 6:44.

Herder's apparently false recollection was not questioned or challenged by the interviewer, who apparently did not know very much about Buchenwald or its liberation. Both survivor accounts and contemporary American reports are quite consistent in describing the crematorium at Buchenwald as out of fuel and not functioning at the time of the liberation.

Herder recounts a disturbing tale about a young (approximately 18 years old) German guard having been captured by prisoners in a nearby village and returned to the camp. Herder's narrative places this event soon after the visit of German civilians to the camp on the 16th. Herder says that he and some fellow soldiers followed a group of prisoners into a cell, where this young German was being tortured. The prisoners then forced their captive to tie a hangman's noose, with the appropriate thirteen-turn coil, and climb onto a table. The noose was placed on his neck and he jumped off the table, but was caught by the prisoners before his neck could be broken. He was then placed back on the table and eased off the edge by the prisoners so that he would strangle slowly. Herder and his comrades, who were armed and capable of intervening, watched the entire episode without taking any action. Herder reports that he had agonized over the moral implications of his (and the others') inaction after the war.

The Camp Committee had asserted firm control over the prisoners early on the 11th, as soon as the Nazis had left the camp. That relative order prevailed in the camp even as early as the 11th was remarked upon in American radio traffic, as we saw in Chapter 2. The 80th Infantry Division began arriving in force on the 12th, General Patton visited the camp on the 15th, and elements of the 120th Evacuation Hospital began arriving that evening, so the American presence at Buchenwald was quite significant by April 16, 1945. The inmates themselves were also determined to demonstrate their commitment to good order and discipline, so it seems unlikely that this sort of vigilante justice would have been permitted. There are, nevertheless, several reports of prisoners killing former guards: whether they represent actual memories or recollections of rumors or stories passed on by others is unclear.

An aspect of Holocaust literature illuminated by Herder's account of his experiences is how widely and deeply such accounts can spread via the internet. *Eyewitness to the Liberation of Buchenwald* is a book specifically intended to be placed in schools and to be used by children learning about the Holocaust. The book does provide a generally accurate picture of the camp and the context in which it existed, but its reliance on Harry Herder as "eyewitness to liberation" is troubling in a couple of ways. First, his account is presented as if it is a credible one, but it should now be clear that Harry Herder, Jr., who was a soldier who served honorably in both World War II and in Korea, where he was seriously wounded by a land mine, was probably not an "eyewitness to liberation", at least not the liberation of Buchenwald. The mere fact that Herder's story has spread so widely and is found quoted and mentioned in so many other places seems to bestow on it a level of credibility that an unverified, uncorroborated first-person account filled with deviations from the existing historical consensus does not deserve. Herder is even mentioned in Dan Stone's book *The Liberation of the Camps: The End of the Holocaust and its Aftermath*, a scholarly book published by Yale University Press, with a citation to the same webpage used in *Eyewitness to the Liberation of Buchenwald*. The presence of such sources in scholarly works without qualification or explanation gives them an immediate imprimatur of credibility.

In this connection, it is especially troubling that *Eyewitness to the Liberation of Buchenwald* cites an article published in the *Journal of Historical Review*, the journal of the Institute for Historical Review, an organization that has been branded a Hate Group by the Southern Poverty Law Center for the Institute's statements and publications promoting Holocaust denial[164]. Teachers or children seeking further information about the Holocaust might well consult the list of references at the end of the book: what should they make of the presence of this citation?

One last point to raise before discussing another individual with a popular but apparently false story of the liberation of Buchenwald concerns the existence of so many transcripts and recordings of individual testimonies. The archives of the United States Holocaust Memorial Museum, the USC Shoah Foundation, Yad Vashem, and other repositories contain staggering amounts of such information. These testimonies have been collected and stored as a way of ensuring that as much of this material is preserved for posterity as possible. A great deal of this information is now available online, to anyone who would take the trouble to read or listen to it.

These testimonies are generally not vetted in any way: to attempt to assess the accuracy of every statement in them would be impossibly difficult and time consuming. It is appropriately left to those who access them to perform their own due diligence, determining where these accounts are consistent with known facts, and where there may be inaccuracies or distortions. As it happens, though, even reputable Holocaust-related institutions sometimes accept personal testimonies at face value and publicize them without much or any critical review, and present a flawed version of history to the public as a result, as both the previous and the following examples illustrate.

---

[164] "Institute for Historical Review", Southern Poverty law Center, https://www.splcenter.org/fighting-hate/extremist-files/group/institute-historical-review, retrieved 8 July 2019.

Leo D. Hymas

If you type "Leo Hymas Holocaust" into an internet search engine, you will get pages of hits. Hymas was a prolific and tireless participant in Holocaust outreach events, speaking to countless schools, Army units, conferences, and remembrance events over the course of many years. Hymas believed he had been a liberator of Buchenwald. This is his story of the liberation:

> "About the first part of April – I know now that it was about the 8th or 9th of April we were on a hillside overlooking a beautiful green valley – it didn't look like a war was going on, there was a pretty little town down below with a church and our forces were all gathered on this hill and we knew the enemy was there…there were heavy artillery shells going over and we could see where they were landing around the town in various places. There were a lot of trees, it was very wooded and our objective that day was to be that town, which I learned the name of the town was Weimar in southern Germany. And by this time my machine gun squad consisted of only four men…As I told you, we came to the town of Weimar and the assignment I received from my commanding officer was you four guys uh the machine gun was mounted on the jeep in a mount where we would put the windshield down and it could fire so I was carrying my carbine as well as my pistol and my four guys…the jeep was going to come later. As we moved down this valley into this town and began the attack we can see in the glasses through the trees there's some barbed wire looks like a deserted prison camp of some sort. There isn't any activity that we can tell – check it out, it may be something where prisoners of war are held, our own men.
>
> So we said OK and so we grabbed a couple of bangalore torpedoes out of the trailer to take along with us. A bangalore torpedo is a tube of metal about six feet long and has threads on the end and its use is its filled with explosives – its about 2 inches in diameter, you screw them together and you push them under barbed wire entanglements and when you set them off the sharp shreds of metal cut the wire and give you a pathway to go through a barbed wire entanglement and we grabbed a couple of these as we went. And we very stealthily were going through the trees, keeping out of sight, made our way to this barbed wire fence. I could see immediately that it had insulators that the wire was electrified. It was tall twelve feet high and there were two sections of it and there were more wires on the ground behind and I thought to myself this is no prison camp its so big. There are dozens of big brown buildings and over here is this square funny looking chimney. But I couldn't see anybody there was a guard house in our sight but I couldn't tell if anyone was in there or not.

Interviewer: How big? When you say big? How many acres?

Hymas: It looked as big as a tennis court to me at that time. It was much bigger than that I found out but that's what it looked like. A tennis court, or a park, I thought. There weren't any green grass, it was all gravel inside. On our farm we used to put up an electric fence to keep the cattle and horses in their proper place and I knew exactly what those insulators were.

So we didn't touch anything. We pushed this torpedo underneath the wire and set it off. And then we received fire from around the corner of one of the barracks building and from the tower. And one of my friends, not Arbazu, was wounded in the shoulder. But we went through quickly and we just ran every place shooting and uh some surrendered my best recollection is that there were fourteen guards. I know that they were all officers, there was not a single enlisted man. I know by their uniforms and they were all SS officers every single one of them.

Interviewer: How could you tell that?

Hymas: Because they wore black uniforms and they had the lightning on their collars and they had the death head on their caps and they told us our uniforms were not very pretty, but theirs were. We had the steel helmets, and the olive drab and no insignias and they wore all their insignias and everything into battle. We killed or captured all of those men. I can't tell you how many were killed and how many were captured but there were a total of fourteen. And I ran and my friends ran to each of these barracks to see if there were other guards. No guard would go in there. I didn't believe what I saw."[165]

This account, like Herder's, appears to be inconsistent with the facts as they are known. First, there is no controversy as to the date of the liberation: American troops arrived at Buchenwald not on April 8 or 9, but on April 11. Second, the town of Weimar was not occupied by the Allies until April 12, 1945, and was never shelled or attacked. Third, Hymas' description of the fourteen SS officers he claims his group killed or captured describes their uniforms as black, but in 1945 the SS units administering the camps wore field-gray or green uniforms, not black ones. Fourth, as far as I can determine, there are no survivor accounts of American soldiers breaching a Buchenwald fence in this way at any time.

Moreover, Hymas' unit was nearly 200 miles west of Buchenwald on the day Buchenwald was liberated. Hymas was assigned to H Company, 2nd Battalion, 303rd Infantry Regiment, 97th Infantry Division. At the time Buchenwald was

---

[165] United States Holocaust Memorial Museum, USC Shoah Foundation Testimony of Leo Hymas, https://collections.ushmm.org/search/catalog/vha35983 retrieved 8 July 2019, 1:18:48 – 1:22:50.

liberated, Hymas' unit was heavily engaged in Siegburg, at the battle for the Ruhr Pocket, having just crossed the Rhine River from west to east and then the Sieg river from south to north. We can probably pinpoint where H Company was on the 11th of April: the 303rd Infantry Regiment Journal for April 10 -11 1945 contains the following entry for the transmission of a message: "2435 H Co Prerson (619454) Bdg, Dutch, Fr, Russian and political Germans who are mostly criminal. 250 cases of typhus. Guards are Germans. Some prisoners are armed. Emplacements across river in front of H. We have prisoners where are the trucks"[166]. "2435" refers to the time the message was sent: 12:35 AM on the morning of the 11th. "Prerson" apparently is "prison", because the grid coordinates given specify a location in Siegburg, Germany, where the Siegburg Prison still stands today[167]. So on or about the time Buchenwald was being liberated, it is quite possible that Hymas' unit was indeed at a prison, one which contained prisoners of much the same sort that were imprisoned at Buchenwald, but that prison was Siegburg Prison, not Buchenwald. The 97th Infantry Division was also at Flossenburg shortly after the liberation of that camp on April 23, 1945. While the 97th Division is not credited as a liberating Division by the USHMM, there are memorial plaques to both the 90th and the 97th Infantry Divisions at Flossenburg today.

Memorial plaque at Flossenburg Concentration Camp. There is another to the 90th Infantry Division.
Author's photograph.

---

[166] National Archives and Records Administration, Records Group 407, Entry 427, Box 11583.

[167] National Archives and Records Administration, Record Group 407, Entry 427, Box 11583, 303rd Infantry Regiment Journal File.

Hymas' account further establishes that he was with his unit at Siegburg at this time by referencing a specific incident which is known to have occurred on a particular date. An important and traumatic event to which Hymas devotes considerable attention in his accounts of his wartime experiences was the death of his friend and fellow machine-gun crewmember, PFC James V. DeMarco. Hymas' description of that event includes graphic and disturbing detail:

> Hymas: And the order came for Jimmy and I to move. I carried the machine gun barrel and receiver and he had the tripod with the cradle that holds it over his shoulder. When the order came to go over I hesitated. DeMarco stood up and was hit by a 20mm explosive shell. He was totally destroyed and so was the machine gun cradle. We'd been in combat twenty minutes and he lost his life. And I never looked back. I don't know where his body is buried. I don't know anything about his family. He was my friend for a little more than two months.
>
> Interviewer: How did you cope with that loss?
>
> Hymas: He taught me courage. That young man was the epitome of courageous action. Following orders under fire and I resolved to do likewise in his memory[168].

Leo Hymas makes it clear that he was with PFC James V. DeMarco when DeMarco was killed in action. Army records show that PFC James V. DeMarco was killed near Siegburg, Germany (the exact location is unclear) on April 12, 1945. Hymas' account thus places him in two different locations, nearly 200 miles apart, at the same time: Buchenwald and Siegburg. He could not have been in both places at the same time, and there can be little doubt that he was in Siegburg with his unit and PFC DeMarco, not at Buchenwald.

Aside from these basic facts, other aspects of Hymas' story diminish its credibility. Hymas shared his story widely, and there are some discrepancies that crop up among different versions of the story. A transcript of a lengthy interview with Hymas may be found here[169], with a credit to Bristol Productions. In this version of the story, Hymas dates his liberation of Buchenwald to April 5, and specifies that the events took place in the early morning hours:

> "I know now that it was a Wednesday. I know that it was April the, I think 5th. It was overcast. It had been raining. We were on a hill. We were preparing to

---

[168] USC Shoah, Hymas, 56:55.

[169] Bristol Productions, Education/Research: Transcripts: Europe (Army), http://www.wwiihistoryclass.com/education/transcripts_europe_army.html, retrieved October 6, 2019.

attack the town of Weimar... So we went sneaking down through these bushes and trees very still. It was quite a ways. It must have been about 10 o'clock in the morning perhaps. 9:30, I'm not sure."

April 5, 1945, was a Thursday. April 11, the correct date for the liberation, was a Wednesday. Hymas also describes some post-liberation events:

"We were ordered to go into Weimar and march all the civilians out to see what had happened, and we did it at the point of a gun or a bayonet. They went with their hands behind their heads saying, Mir nicht Nazi, Mir nicht Nazi. When we got them all out there, we made them pick up and carry all of these dead, rotting bodies to place them, to dump them into a large burial pit that the engineers had dug. There was an inspection team that came from allied high command and from our own congress. General Eisenhower came, General Bradley came, General Patton came. We called him blood and guts. General Patton threw up when he saw what we had found. Most of the evidence that was used in the Nuremberg War Crime Trials after the war was gathered at that time. At Buchenwald Concentration Camp, just outside of Weimar."

There are also factual errors here: there are films of the citizens of Weimar marching to Buchenwald, and none of them show them with their hands behind their heads. Bodies were not buried on that day by civilians (April 16, 1945). General Eisenhower never visited Buchenwald, and General Patton is reported to have vomited when he visited Ohrdruf on April 12, not when he visited Buchenwald on April 15. At the time of day reported by Hymas for the explosion and firefight as they breached the camp (assuming that he has merely confused the date), survivor accounts instead have the camp commander making a general announcement over the camp loudspeaker ordering the SS to leave the camp, and the Camp Committee asserting control over the camp. The Holocaust was not the primary focus of the Nuremberg Tribunals, and Buchenwald did not play a central role in the prosecutions.

Hymas describes his entry into combat as a contested crossing of the Rhine at Remagen, where the capture of the Ludendorff Bridge a few weeks earlier was later made famous in the film *The Bridge at Remagen*[170]. The 97th Infantry Division did cross the Rhine near Bonn on April 3, and the Remagen bridge is near Bonn, so it is possible that this was where Hymas crossed the Rhine. The Division also crossed the Sieg River a few days later. In the version provided in the interview with the USC Shoah Foundation, Hymas crosses the bridge in a truck:

---

[170] The Bridge at Remagen, https://www.imdb.com/title/tt0064110/, retrieved 10 July 2019.

"They loaded us aboard the trucks, the shells began to come the bullets began to fly and we were loaded in the trucks and we passed over this bridge at night under fire. I still remember the tracers as they came over the convoy as we went across. Some of them were hit, our truck was not."[171]

In the Bristol version, Hymas is in the front seat of a jeep, and does not mention resistance:

"So when the order came to attack, the engineers had built a floating bridge across the river and the trucks and the tanks and the halftracks and the jeep with me in it with the machine gun sitting on the dashboard. I sat in the front seat beside the driver. We went across."

There are many other suggestions in Hymas' testimony that his recollections are confused and inaccurate. He says that the Little Camp at Buchenwald was for children, for example, and says that all the inhabitants of the Little Camp were between approximately the ages of four and fourteen years, which is simply not true[172]. There were children in the Little Camp, but the Little Camp was not exclusively for children, it was the place in which the desperate survivors of transports and death marches from camps farther east were dumped at Buchenwald at this phase of the war. Hymas also says that all the prisoners at Buchenwald were in desperate straits[173], but many of the inhabitants of the Main Camp were in quite good condition, in marked contrast to those in the Little Camp. Hymas frequently gives impossible dates: the date of the liberation of Buchenwald, April 11, 1945, is widely known and reported but Hymas erred in both the USC Shoah interview and in the Bristol transcript, reporting it as 8-9 April and 5 April respectively. He related a story in the USC Shoah interview about a little Dutch girl giving him a one-guilder note as he was moving toward the front on a train. Hymas' unit moved to the front in late March, 1945. When asked by the interviewer when this event occurred, Hymas first says May, 1944, and then corrects himself to say October 1944, still off by approximately six months. Hymas frequently errs in the timing of his combat in Europe, always extending the experience much farther into the past. He describes the cathedral at Cologne silhouetted against the flames from an Allied bombing raid, and dates this to late 1944 or early 1945; around the holidays, he suggests.[174] Hymas

---

[171] USC Shoah, Hymas, 56;00.
[172] USC Shoah, Hymas, 1:38:11.
[173] USC Shoah, Hymas, 1:40.
[174] USC Shoah, Hymas, 1:00:24.

unit did not arrive in Europe until March, 1945; the last Allied bombing raid on Cologne had occurred before the unit's arrival[175].

In discussing and explaining some artifacts he brought back from the war in the USC Shoah interview[176], Hymas offers some quite misleading interpretations. Displaying a German 8x57 mm small-arms cartridge with a wooden bullet, Hymas claims that the wooden bullet was a result of late-war material shortages, and that the bullets were dipped in some kind of biological agent to complicate wounds with infectious diseases. There were many erroneous GI myths circulating in the Army in WWII, of which this is an example. These cartridges were simply blanks, not intended or practical for anti-personnel use. Hymas displays an armband that he says belonged to an Army officer, though it is an SS armband. He also displays a Hitler Youth knife, and implies that the Hitler Youth was a kind of direct elite pipeline into the SS, but of course it was nothing of the kind: all German boys were required to participate in the Hitler Youth after 1938.

Hymas also took it upon himself to apologize for the timing of the liberation of Buchenwald, though as a Private First Class, Hymas would not have had much say in the operations of the Third U.S. Army, which in any case never undertook to liberate Buchenwald at any time, having merely stumbled upon it. Rabbi Lau had encountered Hymas in Seattle, and described Hymas' apology to Lau for arriving at Buchenwald too late:

> "I was in a very small Holocaust Museum, one room. At the front stood a Brigadier General, an old man, very handsome, uniform with all the medals of the United States. He welcomed me with tears in his eyes. He knew that I am a Holocaust survivor a child from Buchenwald. He shook my hand and said "Rabbi, I was one of the liberators of Buchenwald, I served with General Patton. When I heard that you are coming to Seattle I asked for permission to meet with you. Before I give back my soul to the Lord of the universe, me Leo Hymas am asking from you forgiveness… for being late, we came too late. I saw what we have seen, I understand we were late, forgive me." I told him, "67 years you have in your heart, in your consciousness this worry that you have to ask forgiveness, you must be a great man."[177]

---

[175] Bombing of Cologne, Wikipedia, https://en.wikipedia.org/wiki/Bombing_of_Cologne_in_World_War_II, retrieved 11 July 2019.

[176] USC Shoah, Hymas, 2:44:00.

[177] Don't Be Too Late, https://mikereport.wordpress.com/2013/03/22/rabbi-lau-references-seattle-visit-tells-president-obama-dont-be-too-late/, retrieved 10 july 2019. The video can be seen here https://www.youtube.com/watch?feature=player_embedded&v=4WIKvOjJv1A, retrieved 8 July 2019.

(Rabbi Lau, whose credibility on matters of detail has been shown to be wanting, identifies Private First Class Hymas as Brigadier General Hymas here.) Careful consideration of the entire body of Hymas' statements about Buchenwald can only lead to one conclusion: it is highly unlikely that he was at Buchenwald at or near the time of the liberation. What is most surprising about this is (1) How easy it is to make that determination, given the ready availability of relevant information on the internet and (2) That Hymas engaged in countless outreach efforts until the end of his long life, was mentioned by Rabbi Lau in 2013 in the presence of President Barrack Obama at Yad Vashem in Israel, has had his story told in countless articles and stories, and yet his story, so easy to disprove, was never challenged. How can this be?

But it was challenged: Eric Schulte called it out at the time of Lau's mistaken identification of Hymas as a Brigadier General and Buchenwald liberator at Yad Vashem, in his *Times of Israel* blog[178]. The Holocaust Center for Humanity, an institution located in Seattle that sponsored Hymas' outreach efforts for many years, continued to present Leo Hymas as a liberator of Buchenwald on their website until the late summer of 2019, when their website was substantially remodeled for the institution's 30th anniversary. Questions about Hymas' credibility have surfaced from time to time; after years of promoting Hymas as a liberator of Buchenwald, the Holocaust Center for Humanity seems to have removed references to him from their website. Before the remodeling Hymas was prominently featured on the website: his biography and photo were presented in several places, as were links to video testimony and transcripts. As of this writing I have found only a few stray references to him, such as the one here[179].

Harry Herder's apparently mistaken account also continues to exist and even spread on the internet, as more people find references to it, incorporate it into reference lists, classes, programs. We will encounter several more such instances in the pages ahead. Why does there appear to be so little interest in vetting these accounts, and correcting the record when necessary?

Perhaps part of the reason may be that our vocabulary for discussing issues like this is too limited. If a story is not true, then what is it? The opposite of true is false. So, if a Holocaust survivor or witness or liberator tells us a story that is false, is it a lie? I think it is our unwillingness to call such people liars that is partly

---

[178] Buchenwald Liberation Myths, 1945-2013, https://blogs.timesofisrael.com/buchenwald-liberation-myths-1945-2013/, retrieved 8 July 2019.

[179] Holocaust Center for Humanity, "These Were Not Nameless People", https://www.holocaustcenterseattle.org/about-us/in-the-media/379-these-were-not-nameless-people-being-killed-by-the-nazis, retrieved August 9, 2019.

responsible for our culturally pervasive whistling-past-the-graveyard approach to glaring errors in this kind of testimony. Absent a readily-articulable alternative explanation in cases of testimony that is telling us something we know or suspect to be false that might permit us to honor the truth while simultaneously still honoring the teller, for sound psychological and emotional reasons we simply choose to not look too closely at whether such testimony is true or false. Certain memories are socially privileged, exempted by unspoken agreement from too much scrutiny because the only two categories into which we can place them is truth or lies, and we are not eager to call survivors or liberators liars.

One purpose of this book is to suggest and perhaps begin to describe a readily articulable alternative explanation for survivors telling false stories that does not involve lying. I don't believe that either Harry Herder or Leo Hymas were lying. I am convinced that they both believed the stories they told, just as did the relative whose experience I described in the Introduction to this book, but that they were mistaken about what happened to them, as was she. In the next Chapter we will delve more deeply into the psychological study of memory and see if it can help us understand how people like Harry Herder and Leo Hymas can be wrong but not be liars. First, though, there are several more claimants to the status of Buchenwald liberators to discuss, and then we must return to survivor testimonies to see how accurate such works are outside the narrow issues raised by the *Liberators* controversy.

Rick Carrier

The *Holocaust Encyclopedia* on the website of the United States Holocaust Memorial Museum contains a page entitled "Recognition of US Liberating Army Units"[180]. As of this writing (November 2019) the banner at the top of the page has a background photograph of a much-bemedaled white-haired WWII veteran saluting. Over that photograph is this explanatory material: "The United States Holocaust Memorial Museum and the US Army's Center of Military History have worked together to define, recognize, and honor all the US Army divisions that took part in the liberation of prisoners from Nazi concentration camps and other sites of incarceration". The soldier in the photograph is a World War II veteran named Frederick Goss Carrier, who went by the nickname "Rick". Mr. Carrier died in 2016.

---

[180] US Holocaust Memorial Museum, https://encyclopedia.ushmm.org/content/en/article/us-army-units, retrieved 6 October 2019.

Photo and screenshot used with permission of the United States Holocaust Memorial Museum.

Like Leo Hymas, Rick Carrier has a very large internet footprint. Type "Rick Carrier Buchenwald" into an internet search engine and you will find news stories[181], YouTube videos[182], even a CNN interview[183] telling Rick Carrier's story. Carrier breakfasted with Mayor Bill DeBlasio before a New York City Veteran's Day parade, was lauded by Dan Rather, participated in the 2012 March of the Living at Auschwitz (where Rabbi Lau, about whom we have heard in connection with Leo Hymas, introduced the liberators), shared the stage at the Krakow Opera House with Irving Roth, a Buchenwald survivor[184], and was awarded the Chevalier of the Legion of Honour, the lowest grade of the highest civilian award in France in 2014.

---

[181] Rick Carrier, 91, Blazed Through the 20th Century as a Renaissance Man, https://www.thevillager.com/2016/12/rick-carrier-91-blazed-through-the-20th-century-as-a-renaissance-man/, retrieved 8 July 2019.

[182] Rick Carrier Buchenwald Story, retrieved 8 July 2019.https://www.youtube.com/watch?v=bbzbmsRKhAY

[183] WWII Veteran Recalls Liberation of Buchenwald, https://www.youtube.com/watch?v=5PwPAGwUqNg, retrieved 8 July 2019.

[184] Irving Roth was a child survivor of Buchenwald who was in the Little Camp at the time of liberation. He remembers his first encounter with liberators as being with two American soldiers, one white and one black.

Carrier was a combat engineer in WWII, whose duties, he said, were to scout for useful construction materials behind the retreating Germans that could be obtained for use by American forces. Carrier says that he was engaged on this mission near Weimar on April 10, 1945, when he decided to enter a church and ask some questions, as he had frequently had success in obtaining information about useful materials in this way.

Carrier reports that a local priest suggested he visit the quarry and lumber yard at Buchenwald, and agreed (along with an escaped Russian prisoner and the Gauleiter's assistant) to travel there in Carrier's jeep on the afternoon of the 10th. Carrier reports arriving at the camp and describes arriving at the wrought-iron gate with the *Jedem das Seine* motto, which he asked his companions to translate. He saw many emaciated prisoners clinging to the fence, and used his pliers to cut an oval hole in the fence. Suddenly there was a burst of machine-gun fire as the SS guards and the prisoner leaders engaged in combat, in the course of which gunfire struck the iconic clock at the main gate, stopping it at 3:15. Carrier decamped hastily back to Weimar.

Once there, he radioed his commander, telling him what had happened, and his commander contacted SHAEF headquarters and General Patton's forces. Carrier was instructed to return to the camp the following morning (April 11) and escort tanks into the camp. He did so, and blew open the gate by wrapping explosive cord around the padlock, opening the gate without damaging the wrought iron. A prisoner grabbed the padlock as a souvenir. Within hours of this entry at 8:00 AM on April 11, according to Carrier, thousands of Allied troops had arrived at Buchenwald and begun to provide relief to the inmates[185].

Carrier's account, like Hymas', appears to be an elaborate false memory. There are some important contradictions between Carrier's story and the sequence of events related by both survivors and the available documentary record. Carrier reports that he hastily abandoned Buchenwald because there was a firefight taking place between SS guards and prisoners late on Tuesday, April 10, 1945. Even those who claim, in the context of the Selbstbefreiung, that there was fighting between guards and prisoners unanimously date that fighting to the next day, Wednesday, April 11. The accepted consensus now, however, is that no such fighting occurred on either day. The clock was not stopped by gunfire on the 10th, or the 11th, or on any other day: there are many post-liberation photos showing the clock keeping time. It was deliberately permanently set at 3:15 years after the liberation, when the site was developed as a memorial.

---

[185] Rick Carrier Buchenwald Story,.https://www.youtube.com/watch?v=bbzbmsRKhAY, retrieved October 6, 2019.

Carrier's claims about his visit to the camp the next morning, April 11, are also problematic. Survivors are unanimous that no one had to force the gate open, much less use explosives to open it, because the camp had been abandoned by the Nazis sometime on the morning of the 11th. If a commotion involving the blowing open of the gate, followed by an American tank and then thousands more Americans pouring into Buchenwald had occurred beginning around 8:30 AM, it seems likely that the prisoners would have noticed, but again, prisoner reports are clear that no such events occurred. The Nazi evacuation of the camp was not completed until around mid-day.

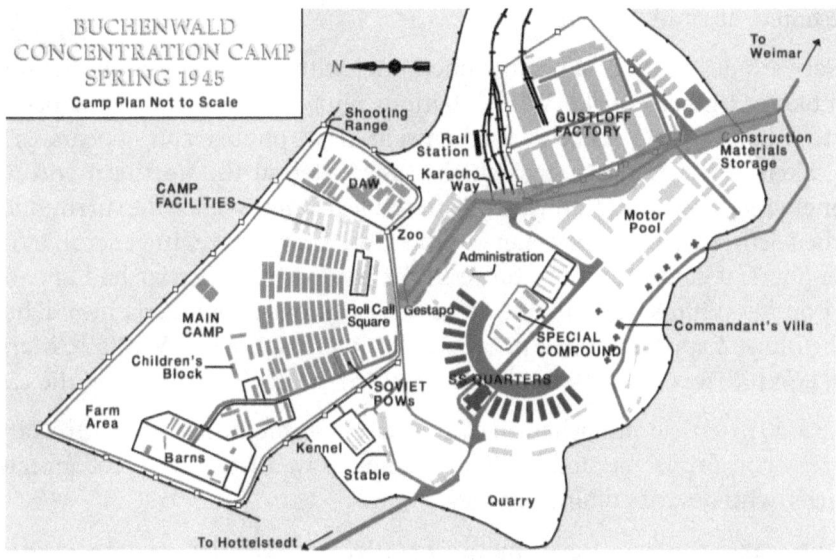

The thick line shows the path Carrier would have had to travel from Weimar to arrive at the "Jedem das seine" gate. Map used with permission from the United States Holocaust Memorial Museum.

At least three other circumstances should invite skepticism about Carrier's story. First, Carrier's description of the sequence of events makes it sound as though one would encounter the *Jedem das seine* gate upon arriving at the perimeter of the camp, but a quick look at a map of the camp shows otherwise. Buchenwald had several separate perimeters: one surrounding the entire camp, one within that perimeter surrounding the prisoner area (which is where the gate in question is located), yet another perimeter within that one defining the Little Camp, and also perimeters around the Gustloff works and the DAW compound. Traveling along the road from Weimar, Carrier couldn't have gotten to the *Jedem das seine* gate without having first penetrated the outer sentry-line of the camp, which was patrolled by SS guards, passing the area where construction materials were stored (which was what he was looking for), passing the Gustloff Werke, which had been heavily damaged in the August 24, 1944 bombing, and crossing through the main SS area of the camp. The iconic gate is not on any edge of the Buchenwald camp, it is in the center of the grounds. Second, Weimar was in Nazi hands until it was occupied by the 80th Infantry Division on Thursday, April 12. The armored units in the area had simply bypassed it so that they could forge ahead, securing the entrances and exits to the town as they moved through. Third, Carrier claims that the Gauleiter's assistant accompanied him on his foraging expedition to Buchenwald, but as the assistant to a Nazi Party official, it seems odd that she would have been so willing to help an American soldier, who represented, after all, the enemy.

Carrier's description of his first encounter with inmates paints a picture that resembles Margaret Bourke-White's famous photograph of emaciated prisoners behind a barbed-wire fence at Buchenwald. That photograph appears to have been taken at the Little Camp, which was located at the northern end of the prisoner area, a few hundred yards from the *Jedem das seine gate*, surrounded by a barbed-wire fence. The prisoners in the Little Camp were, in general, in much worse physical condition than those in the main camp. Carrier had apparently seen Bourke-White's work: in one of his presentations about Buchenwald, he says that he himself appears in two photographs taken by Bourke-White[186]. Margaret Bourke-White was at Buchenwald on April 15, the day Patton visited the camp.

In a 2016 article published in *The Villager* on the occasion of Mr. Carrier's passing, Scott Stiffler quoted William Daniel Grey, a friend and collaborator of Carrier's, who described him this way:

> "the craziest person I ever met in my life, and take that in a good way. His mind just worked differently than most people's. He would explore these fantastical realms," recalled Grey, citing how Carrier generated ideas for everything from decreasing our dependency on fossil fuels to an epic opera written in collaboration with Grey, focusing on how immigrants came to influence various forms of American music."[187]

Grey also recalled that Carrier had not begun talking about his wartime experiences until about ten years before his death. Stiffler notes that Carrier's life partner, Lynn Ramsey, also recalled that his memories of being a liberator were of recent origin: "Tracing his newfound willingness to speak about the

---

[186] Survivor and Liberator, Two Accounts from the Holocaust, https://www.torahcafe.com/mr-irving-roth/survivor-and-liberator-two-accounts-from-the-holocaust-video_51f296f6c.html, retrieved September 5, 2019.

[187] Rick Carrier, 91, Blazed Through the 20th Century as a Renaissance Man

war back to their 2012 trip to Poland, Ramsey noted the emotional impact that meeting other concentration camp liberators had on Carrier. Prior to that, she said, "he was interviewed a few times about the war, typically around Veterans Day, but he never mentioned Buchenwald."[188] Interestingly, Carrier did submit an unsolicited story to the US Army Center for Military History entitled "A Teenager's Experience in the First Wave Assault onto Utah Beach" in 1994[189].

Carrier's 70-page submission to the Army Center for Military History in 1994 concerning his D-Day experiences offers some potentially valuable clues about the origins of his Buchenwald story. In this version of events, Carrier and some buddies encounter General Theodore Roosevelt on the ship transporting them all to Utah beach, the USS Barnett (APA 5)[190]. Roosevelt was drinking out of a bottle of Old Overholt rye whiskey, so one of Carrier's buddies asked the general to share his whiskey. The general passed the bottle to the soldiers, who finished it and through the empty bottle into the sea[191]. Carrier's detailed account of D-Day does not include any mention of meeting General Roosevelt on the beach.

Carrier also described his D-Day experiences elsewhere[192]. In this later version of the story, he recalls meeting up with Brigadier General Theodore Roosevelt on Utah beach, who he says followed him in the second assault wave after Carrier had landed with the first wave. In this story General Roosevelt gulped Old Overholt whiskey from Carrier's canteen, after which Corporal Carrier and General Roosevelt spent considerable time together as Carrier unraveled the pattern of German mines in a minefield and determined a path for Roosevelt's troops to advance.

Carrier was a colorful, even flamboyant figure, who lived a remarkably rich and active life. His wartime recollections also included participation in the Battle of the Bulge and the battle for the famous Ludendorff bridge at Remagen. He wrote three columns for *The Villager* describing some of his exploits: in one column he described an incident on March 7, 1945 in which he was observing the Ludendorff Bridge from the west bank of the Rhine when a German *Kubelwagen* (a small wheeled vehicle rather like an American jeep) with two drunk Germans

---

[188] Ibid.

[189] A Teenager's Experience in the First Wave Assault onto Utah Beach, https://history.army.mil/reference/hrc2.htm, retrieved 12 September 2019.

[190] Carrier refers to the ship as the "PA Barnett". USS Barnett had an extensive WWII history, including landing the 2nd Battalion, 8th Infantry Regiment, 4th Infantry Division at Utah Beach on D-Day. USS Barnett, https://en.wikipedia.org/wiki/USS_Barnett_(APA-5), retrieved October 3, 2019.

[191] A Teenager's Experience in the First Wave Assault Onto Utah Beach, Frederick Goss Carrier, April 25, 1994, pp. 39-40.

[192] Rick Carrier, https://www.youtube.com/watch?v=vDGliq363d4, retrieved September 14, 2019.

happened upon his position. His pliers came in handy in this instance as they would in his stories about D-Day and Buchenwald, as he says he crept under the vehicle, cut the brake cable with them, and sent the vehicle and its occupants crashing over a cliff onto the rocks below, though Carrier says he did not report the incident to his superiors. One difficulty with this story is that the terrain on the west side of the Ludendorff Bridge is relatively flat: there really aren't any cliffs of the sort Carrier describes close to the bridge on the west side of the river, though the Erpeler Ley does rise as a steep and forbidding basalt cliff on the east (far) side of the river where the Ludendorff Bridge stood.

Two views of the site of the Ludendorff Bridge at Remagen today. The left photo shows the west towers of the bridge as seen from a point just south of the site of the bridge. Rick Carrier's reported experience with the Kubelwagen happened on the west side of the river. On the right is a more expansive view of the west bank of the Rhine in this area – the east tower of the bridge can just be seen in the far right of this photo. Author's photographs.

His other two columns concern his time at Andernach, a village about 15 miles south of Remagen. Carrier was there to take measurements of the water level in the river each day and radio them to headquarters, he says. He recounts jeeps trips to Cologne to buy cases of beer, target practice with a captured German sniper rifle on floating debris in the river, and his liaison with "The Rhine Maiden", a comely OSS spy who was, according to Carrier, a frequent guest at Hitler's long-winded dinners. After killing an American MP who she claimed had attempted to rape her, she bedded down with Carrier for five days in Andernach, after which she used Carrier's radio to contact her OSS handler. Carrier then escorted Rhine Maiden to meet General Patton as he crossed the Rhine[193], and placed her (wearing his uniform) into the car of her OSS handler. Carrier says he wrote a 2,400-page report on their "pillow talk". This would amount to one page for every three minutes Carrier says he spent with Rhine

---

[193] Patton crossed the Rhine at Oppenheim, about 75 miles southeast of Andernach, on March 24, 1945.

Maiden over the course of five days and nights, though I have been unable to locate any other reference to such a report. Carrier's column also alludes to a new kind of night flashlight of his own invention remarked upon by Rhine Maiden[194].

These later recollections are especially interesting in light of the concluding paragraph of Carrier's 1994 submission to the Center for Military History:

"Before I returned to the States, I would have a pretty Normandy girl friend, get to Paris on pass, move to Fort Eben Emael Belgium just in time for the Battle of the Bulge, come face to face with Nazi Sturmbannfuhrer Otto Skorzeny's troopers disguised as American soldiers, survive V-1 and V2 close blasts, get shot at while on a Rhine River detail, have an affair with a German Countess concert pianist, discover a cave full of Nazi silver and silk, study fine arts at the Beaux Arts in Paris, have an incredible affair with a French widow who owned my hotel in Paris, and returned home a happy, healthy, twenty-year-old Amphibious Combat Engineer."[195]

A certain skepticism may be in order on some of these specifics, but what is most striking about the conclusion of Carrier's 1994 telling of his wartime experiences is that his list of significant exploits between D-Day and returning to the States makes no mention whatever of the liberation of Buchenwald, an event he later portrayed as a defining event of his wartime service. This 1994 summary likewise omits any mention of the "Rhine Maiden" or the Remagen bridge. Apparently, Carrier did not begin talking about Buchenwald or the stories told in his *Villager* columns until nearly twenty years after submitting the paper to the Center for Military History. It is possible that Carrier had these memories and was aware of them in 1994, but chose not to include them in his story, but that seems unlikely. It is far more likely that these are false memories that arose in the later years of his life through suggestion, misattribution, or other such mechanisms.

There is evidence that some units associated with the 1st Engineer Special Brigade visited Buchenwald. Saul "Pete" Pryor, a soldier assigned to the First Engineer Special Brigade, penned a letter on March 6, 2002, describing his service in the unit from D-Day onward which may be found here.[196] Pryor recounted his memory of Buchenwald:

---

[194] Securing the Remagen Bridge, https://www.thevillager.com/2015/05/securing-the-remagen-ludendorff-bridge/, retrieved 10 September, 2019; Andernach and the Rhine Maiden, https://www.thevillager.com/2015/05/andernach-and-the-rhine-maiden/, retrieved September 10, 2019; Rhine Maiden Tells All, https://www.thevillager.com/2015/06/rhine-maiden-tells-all/, retrieved September 10, 2019.

[195] Carrier, *A Teenager's Experiences*, p. 70.

[196] 20th Engineers, "letter from a soldier", http://www.20thengineers.com/ww2-caffey.html, retrieved September 10, 2019.

"We kept moving east and south, into Belgium (at St. Vith, during the Battle of the Bulge) and into Germany at Trier, where, as we came into town, the MPs told us that there was an operating brewery nearby, so you can guess that we got pretty sloshed that night. We kept moving east in Germany until we came to Weimar, close to the Buchenwald concentration camp. I am sure you remember my telling you the story of how we transported townspeople from Weimar into the Buchenwald camp, where the cadavers were still piled up and where the commandant's wife, the infamous Ilse Koch, had made a lampshade out of the tatoos [sic] on the skin of inmates, and all of the townspeople pretended to be shocked – shocked (like Claude Rains in Casablanca) that such horrible deeds had taken place so close to them and they had not had the slightest inkling, etc.. Of course, they were lying through their teeth."

Pryor was a well-known entertainment attorney in the Denver, Colorado area, who died in 2008. An obituary released by his law firm and written by Pryor's partner included the following: "Pryor also participated in the liberation of the Buchenwald concentration camp and convinced his commanding officer to force the neighboring villagers to visit the camp which they had denied existed"[197]. Rick Carrier, like Saul "Pete" Pryor, may well have visited Buchenwald soon after the liberation – if the visit of civilians mentioned by Pryor was the one ordered by Patton, it took place on April 16, five days after the liberation.

There are two memoirs of WWII service in the 531st in print[198]. Both memoirs have the 531st landing at Utah Beach on D-Day, and remaining in place until sometime in November, 1944. The brigade then travelled to Belgium and was indeed billeted at Fort Eben Emael. Elements of the 531st (the unit was disbanded sometime in 1944, and the troops assigned to the 1186th Combat Engineer Group as three Combat Engineer Battalions, the 3051st, 3052nd, and 3053rd) were ordered to return to Le Havre, France in January, 1945 to embark on transports that would return them to the United States in preparation for redeployment to the Pacific theater. Before departing for France, the brigade crossed the German border to visit the town of Aachen. The brigade turned in their equipment, packed and returned to Le Havre in mid-January, only to have their orders to return to the US cancelled and be ordered instead to return to Belgium on the way to Germany,

---

[197] Pryor Cashman Founder Saul "Pete" Pryor Passes Away, https://www.pryorcashman.com/news-and-insights/pryor-cashman-founder-saul-pete-pryor-passes-away.html, retrieved September 10, 2019.

[198] These are: Kenneth H. Garn, "*Storming Ashore: One Soldier's Adventures in the First Engineer Special Brigade 1942-1945 Including D-Day*", (Huntington, WV, University Editions, 1998), and Kathleen Shelby Boyett, "*Cannon Fodder on Utah Beach*", (Charlotte, NC, Searching Mink Publications, 2018). This summary is taken from these two books.

a trip which two of the battalions began in February. The troops remained in Belgium for a few weeks, then moved into Germany in the vicinity of the Ruhr Pocket in late March after the process of obtaining new equipment and weapons to replace those that had been turned in was completed, and moved eastward after the Rhine was crossed in late March. Some of the troops encountered the Nordhausen concentration camp, a horrific sub-camp of the Dora-Mittelbau complex, not far from Buchenwald.

Taken as a whole, Corporal Rick Carrier's memories of his experiences during the Second World War raise significant questions. It seems quite clear to me that Carrier's Buchenwald liberation story is not true. But did this corporal really confer with Theodore Roosevelt's eldest son on the best way to breach a minefield on Utah beach, sharing Old Overholt rye whiskey from Carrier's canteen? Did he really cut the brake cable on a Nazi Kubelwagen on the west bank of the Rhine overlooking the Ludendorff bridge, causing two German soldiers to plummet to their deaths, when the terrain makes such a scenario unlikely? Did he really shack up with a triple-spy confidante of Hitler named after a character in a Wagnerian opera for five days, drinking beer and eating pretzels? Did he really meet with General George Patton as he delivered the Rhine Maiden to her handler? Did he have torrid affairs with German countess-concert-pianists and Parisian hotel-owners? Perhaps all this is true. It is quite difficult to fact-check claims like these, because, unlike the Buchenwald liberation, there is little documentary or photographic evidence to examine to assess them. I have to confess that I am more than a bit skeptical.

J. Ray Clark

A WWII veteran of B Company, First Battalion, 317th Infantry Regiment, 80th Infantry Division, J. Ray Clark wrote a book in 1996 titled: *Journey to Hell: The Fiery Furnaces of Buchenwald*[199]. Clark was apparently active locally (Indiana) in historical societies and VFW activities, but his work does not have the extensive internet presence and consequent notoriety of the previous three WWII vets. Clark's book is filled with inaccuracies large and small, however, along with some unfounded conspiracy theories[200] and much garbled history. Speaking of the town of "Weiner"[201], by which he clearly means "Weimar", Clark says:

---

[199] Clark, J. Ray. Journey to Hell: The Fiery Furnaces of Buchenwald. (USA, Pentland Press, 1996).

[200] Ibid., pp 96-99. Clark paints the Dulles brothers as German collaborators who influenced Nuremberg trials for von Papen.

[201] Ibid., p. 96

"We jumped off early on 10 April 1945 and advanced north of the city, engaging in two or three fire fights as we encountered pockets of resistance. Then we lost contact with the enemy. About 10:00 AM, we approached what appeared to be another slave labor camp. The machine gun guard towers did not return our fire and as we got closer, we could see prisoners at the fences. It was obvious that the German troops had fled. On entering this camp, we received the shock of our lives.

We had liberated the infamous Buchenwald Concentration Camp. Inside the camp, we found a cadre of slave laborers, who were killing and burning other prisoners. Later, we learned that they had been threatened by the departing Nazis, 'If you quit burning them, we will come back and burn you'...

This camp was commanded by a woman, Ilsa [sic] Koch, 'the Bitch of Buchenwald'. In her office, we found polished skulls of various (adult and children) sizes used as paperweights, and lamp shades made of tattooed human skin on every desk. Also some tattooed skin had been stretched over boards and was used as wall hangings. You could almost see your reflection in the shiny skulls, and the skin looked and felt like parchment."[202]

The date, April 10, is inconsistent with what we know about the liberation, and there are no reports of American troops firing on the guard towers. Neither are there any reports that inmates of Buchenwald were killing other inmates on the orders of departed Nazis, and tattooed human-skin lampshades were certainly not to be found on "every desk". Reports from both Buchenwald prisoners and arriving American troops agree that the prisoner organization at the camp quickly imposed order on the camp as the Germans fled. Clark, on the other hand, reports that American troops were forced to shoot some of the prisoners to stop them from killing and burning other prisoners."[203] There is no record or even suggestion of which I am aware that American troops were compelled to use force against the inmates of Buchenwald. Clark also claims that on April 12, Generals Eisenhower and Patton brought a group of US Senators and Congressmen to tour Buchenwald.[204] We know that Eisenhower never visited Buchenwald; that General Patton did visit Buchenwald, but not until April 15; and that Senators and Congressmen visited Buchenwald weeks after the camp was liberated, not on April 12: the camp was only discovered the previous day, and it would have been impossible for them to have crossed the Atlantic and arrived in the middle of a war zone so quickly. Ilse Koch was never "commandant" of Buchenwald, and had

---

[203] Ibid., p. 101.
[204] Ibid., p 103.

not been a public presence at the camp since her arrest by the SS in mid-1943. Such stories are given credibility by their inclusion in the memoirs of a WWII veteran, and unfortunately are often uncritically accepted and spread further by readers unfamiliar with the real story.

Others

The cases of Herder, Hymas, and Carrier are worthy of extended discussion because the stories of these three men have spread extensively on the internet. Hymas and Carrier both gave many public appearances and speeches, and have a substantial internet presence. Herder's detailed description of his recollections of Buchenwald have been cited and discussed in many places, both electronic and print. Clark's book does not seem to be known as widely as the others. There are many other examples of veterans who are described as, or claim to be, "liberators" of Buchenwald that may easily be found on the internet. In some cases, this reflects only a colloquial use of the term "liberator". The definition adopted by the Center for Military History and the United States Holocaust Memorial Museum is quite arbitrary, and it is not surprising that many are unfamiliar with this narrow and technical definition and use the word more loosely. Many of these instances do not represent either a failure of memory or deliberate embellishment, but rather a more generous application of the term "liberator" than is consistent with the "official" definition. In some cases, though, there are apparent confusions in veterans' recollections of their wartime experience. A list of others mentioned on the internet as Buchenwald liberators I have run across may be found in the Appendix, with URL's to the websites that mention them.

Survivor Memoirs

I discussed several survivor memoirs at length in the last Chapter because they were relevant to the controversy over the *Liberators* film. There are many other survivor memoirs of Buchenwald, and many of them contain inaccuracies and inconsistencies just as do liberator accounts. As with the liberators, there are some elaborate but apparently false stories of the liberation from the survivor viewpoint, and many minor discrepancies between their accounts and the historical consensus.

Jack Werber

Jack Werber's book *Saving Children: Diary of a Buchenwald Survivor and Rescuer* was first published in 1996, and re-issued in 2014. Werber was at Buchenwald for almost the entirety of the camp's existence under the Nazis, and appears to identify strongly with the Camp Committee. Twice in the book (page xvi and page 111) Werber specifically reminds readers that the inmates themselves liberated Buchenwald: "It is important to stress that, contrary to popular opinion, it was the Underground, and not the U.S. Army that liberated the camp.[205]" Alex Gross described how his brother Bill had cut the electrified fence, but Werber provides another version of the story, claiming that he and a fellow inmate used "scissors wrapped with ropes" to cut the fence and avoid electrocution, after which inmates attacked the SS barracks.[206]

Werber also offers a detailed description of Ilse Koch's behavior at the camp. He says that Ilse Koch would sit astride a white horse by the camp gate each morning, and note the prisoner number of any individuals with tattoos she fancied. These numbers would then be called out at evening roll-call, and these prisoners would disappear. Werber specifically describes the case of Hans, a German prisoner with whom he worked side by side. Hans had a tattoo on his chest (in the USC Shoah Foundation interview cited below Werber identifies the tattoos as a boat and the German phrase "Ich liebe dich" [I love you]) and Werber claims that Koch recorded Hans' prisoner number. In the USC Shoah Foundation interview, Werber dates this first encounter to the time they were building brick buildings at the Gustloff Werke[207]. According to Werber, Hans was later executed and his skin prepared for use in a lampshade. Werber also claims that three Jehovah's Witnesses who refused to prepare the skin were hanged by the Nazis."[208] A bit later, Werber completes the story. Buchenwald was bombed by the US Army Air Corps on August 24, 1944, at which time significant damage was inflicted on the industrial works and the SS barracks:

> "As a bricklayer, I volunteered to go out and help repair the damage. I was motivated by curiosity about Ilse Koch's home. I wanted to see the lampshade that had been made from Hans' skin, the fellow who had worked with me on the scaffold.
>
> Well, I got to see it with my own eyes. It was all the more shocking to look at it since I had known the man it belonged to so well when he was alive.

---

[205] Werber, Jack. *Saving Children: Diary of a Buchenwald Survivor and Rescuer*. (New Brunswick, NJ: Transaction Publishers, 2014). p 111.

[206] Ibid., pp. 108-109.

[207] USC Shoah Foundation interview, reviewed onsite at the United States Holocaust Memorial Museum, Tape 6, 20:50. His description of the tattoos occurs at 21:36. https://www.ushmm.org/online/hsv/person_view.php?PersonId=4975215.

[208] Werber, *Saving Children*, p. 75.

Underneath the lampshade was a stand made from pieces of human bone and, as a decorative item, a shrunken human skull. The parchment-like material looked like a Torah scroll. You could see the tiny holes where the hair once was. There was also a shrunken head that served as a handle for one of her riding whips. To this day, whenever I think about it, I close my eyes and the lampshade with Hans' tattoos is right there. It's a horrific vision that has always remained with me."[209]

This story is apparently false. The Kochs were arrested by the SS for corruption in August 1943, and were imprisoned in Weimar until their trial in late 1943. Karl Koch was convicted, but Ilse Koch was acquitted. She moved to Ludwigsburg in early 1944 to be with relatives, and was not living in "Haus Buchenwald" (the Koch villa) at the time of the raid. Heinrich Nett, an SS investigator, and Georg Konrad Morgen, an SS lawyer and judge, both signed depositions in 1947 attesting to the fact that they had searched the Koch home as part of their investigation and had found no objects made of human skin or body parts[210].

Werber relates other stories that are difficult to credit. For example, he reports that just before liberation, the prisoners "laid out earthenware white plates on a tar roof background, in a pattern spelling out the letters S-O-S. After the liberation, American fliers told us they had indeed seen the signal.[211]" There are other stories like this that give prisoners an important role in bringing the Americans to Buchenwald, though all evidence suggests that American forces stumbled upon Buchenwald, as they did most of the camps. Werber also says that the clock over the main gate was stopped at 3:15 to denote the ending of the battle between the Nazis and the prisoners, an event that happened much later[212]. Werber reports that food given to Buchenwald prisoners contained ground glass, and that the coffee was poisoned[213]. He also says that the soap given to inmates was made from the body fat of Jews[214], and that it was the inmates, not the Americans, who forced the people of Weimar to view the camp[215]. He somewhat cryptically challenged the veracity of Rabbi Hershel Schacter during the USC

---

[209] Ibid., p 87.

[210] Whitlock, Flint. Buchenwald: Hell on a Hilltop. (Brule, Wisconsin:, Cable Publishing, 2014). p. 142, footnote 15.

[211] Werber, Saving Children, p 104.

[212] Ibid., p. 109.

[213] Ibid., p. 34.

[214] Ibid., p. 41.

[215] Ibid., p 111.

Shoah Foundation interview (Tape 8, 17:34) suggesting that "he tells stories that aren't true", and also reports that Ilse Koch wielded the real power in Buchenwald even after her husband was transferred out and the new commandant took over.

Werber also claims that the Germans planned to use German airplanes disguised as American aircraft to destroy Buchenwald at the end[216], and that a Nazi flame-throwing unit ordered to destroy the camp as the SS fled was beaten off by the prisoners, with several Nazis killed and wounded[217]. Werber is quite insistent that Americans do not deserve credit for liberating Buchenwald, specifically stating that it was the prisoners who did battle with SS and liberated the camp in two places in his book[218]. Given the discrepancies between Werber's account and the accepted historical narrative, the following passage from Werber's book is especially interesting:

> "Over the years I wrote notes about my life in Buchenwald, without any specific purpose in mind. I never planned to write a book. I even wondered if perhaps too many personal accounts of the Holocaust had already been published…The rise of revisionism requires that all of the survivors who can, should preserve their stories. Each survivor had a different experience. By presenting a chorus of different voices we disprove the theories of the Holocaust deniers."[219]

Other Discrepancies

How many ovens?

There are many factual errors contained in the many survivor and liberator testimonies about Buchenwald that have been published. Many of these are relatively minor: for example, the number of furnaces/ovens in the crematorium is often mistaken. There were six ovens at the Buchenwald crematorium. Leo Hymas described the crematorium as having four ovens[220]; Harry Herder described a bank of ovens three high and at least ten long[221]; Gerald Myers, a

---

[216] Ibid., p. 105.

[217] Ibid., p. 109.

[218] Ibid., pp. Xvi, 111.

[219] Ibid., p 3.

47 McManus, John C. *Hell Before Their Very Eyes: American Soldiers Liberate Concentration Camps in Germany, April 1945*, (Baltimore, Johns Hopkins University Press, 2015) p 128.

[220] USC Shoah, Hymas, 1:28:21.

[221] Liberation of Buchenwald by Harry Herder, http://remember.org/witness/herder, retrieved 8 July 2019.

[222] Hirsch, *Liberators*, p 53.

soldier with the 80th Infantry Division who was probably at Buchenwald on April 12, remembered four "crematories"[222]. Eugene Weinstock, in *Beyond the last Path: A Buchenwald Survivor's Story*, provided this vivid but inaccurate description of crematorium operations:

> "Mass executions took place in a large room designed for that purpose in the crematorium. The method of execution was amazingly like that used to dispose of cattle in the Chicago stockyards. Prisoners did not walk into this room. They were thrust down a dark chute which opened on the chamber, and as each victim reached the bottom of this Kelly-slide, a crematorium employee struck him violently over the head with a blunt instrument. In a brief time the room would be filled with dead, half-dead, or insensate people who were then placed on a moving belt which brought their bodies into the cremating hall where attendants stripped them of their clothes and their dental gold. If the person had neither gold nor platinum in his mouth he was immediately thrust, still warm, into one of the ovens. Eight furnaces, each with two ovens, were constantly blazing. The rules of the crematorium allowed twelve minutes for each body to be reduced to ashes."[223]

The two banks of three crematory ovens at Buchenwald. Photograph used with permission of the Buchenwald Gedenkstaette.

Arbeit macht frei or Jedem das seine?

Confusing the "Jedem das Seine" inscription on the main gate into the prisoner area at Buchenwald with the "Arbeit macht frei" inscription seen on the gate at Auschwitz and other camps is also a common error. We have already noted

---

[223] Weinstock, Eugene. *Beyond the Last Path.: A Buchenwald Survivor's Story*. (New York, Boni and Gaer, 1946). p 6.

that Harry Herder and Hershel Schacter mistakenly remembered seeing "Arbeit macht frei" on the Buchenwald gate. Another such confusion appears in Michael Hirsh's excellent book *The Liberators*:

> "At about three in the afternoon of April 11, the day the fourteen-year-old Menachem Lipshitz was watching American tanks approach the main camp, [Buchenwald - author] Staff Sergeant Robert Burrows and his driver, Ben, were in their jeep, scouting ahead of the 2nd Battalion, 317th Infantry Regiment, of the 80th Infantry Division. It was a lightly overcast day, and they were driving through the slight rolling hills. To their right was a grassy meadow, but on the rise to the left they could see a camp, fenced with barbed wire, with a building right next to the gate. 'This gate was here,' he says, gesturing with his hands, 'and these fellows were standing to the left. Two POWs in their striped uniforms. Just standing there, watching me. They didn't move. Just had their hands on the wire like they were resting, just like this. Both of 'em. And I thought it was strange, but I didn't want to be bothered, to be honest with you. I had things on my mind. I was supposed to be out scouting ahead of the battalion, and if I run into anything to let 'em know [by radio]. But I went up to the front of this office building – it had a walk-in-door – here. I didn't go in the gate. The gate was closed. It was on the left side of the administration building. It said, '*Arbeit macht frei*'". (The phrase, loosely translated as "Work will make you free" or "Work will liberate you," was displayed on or above the entryway of many of the Nazi concentration camps.)"[224]

This account is also complicated by the geography of Buchenwald. The main gate at Buchenwald, the one with "*Jedem das seine*" in the wrought iron, is the main gate to the prisoner area of the camp, which was separated from the area of the camp reserved for the guard barracks, administrative facilities, and the industrial concerns located at the camp. This gate is really located near the center of the camp, and in order to reach it one would have had to penetrate the outer perimeter of the camp and, if coming along the road from Weimar, cross through a significant portion of the camp itself before reaching the gate. Adam Seipp recounts several more examples of soldiers mis-remembering the gate inscription as *Arbeit macht frei*[225]. It is also worth noting that the *Arbeit macht frei* gates are meant to be read from the outside, while the *Jedem das Seine* gate is meant to be read from the inside of the camp, looking out.

---

[224] Hirsh, Michael. *The Liberators: America's Witnesses to the Holocaust*. (New York, Bantam Books, 2010). p. 44.
[225] Seipp, Adam R. Buchenwald Stories: Testimony, Military History, and the American Encounter with the Holocaust. *Journal of Military History*, **79**, 739.[222] Hirsh, *Liberators*, p 53.

The main gate to the prisoner area at Buchenwald. Note that this view is from the inside looking out: the building visible outside the gate is part of the Commandant's command headquarters. Author's photograph.

Eisenhower at Buchenwald

Perhaps the most commonly misremembered fact about the liberation of Buchenwald is the non-visit of General Dwight D. Eisenhower to the camp. A great many liberator accounts include a visit by Eisenhower[226], and even scholarly works, such as Adam Seipp's article on remembering Buchenwald perpetuate this error:

> "The next day, a delegation of senior American officers, including General of the Army Dwight D. Eisenhower, visited Buchenwald. The day before, they had seen Ohrdruf, where Eisenhower had remarked, 'We are told the American soldier does not know what he is fighting for. Now, at least, he knows what he is fighting against.'"[227]

Eisenhower never visited Buchenwald, though he did indeed visit Ohrdruf on April 12, 1945. If he had visited Buchenwald the day after visiting Ohrdruf, the visit would have taken place on the 13th. *The Buchenwald Report*, which is considered authoritative on many subjects, gets this wrong as well: "On April 13, less than forty-eight hours after its liberation, Eisenhower, along with Bradley and Patton, toured Buchenwald camp.[228]".

The confusion that places Eisenhower at Buchenwald is one more example of the same mechanisms that have led to so many other errors in remembering the liberation of Buchenwald. Eisenhower did make a well-publicized visit to

---

[226] Moser, Joseph F., and Baron, Gerald R. *A Fighter Pilot in Buchenwald: The Joe Moser Story*. (All Clear Publications, 2009).

[227] Seipp, *Buchenwald Stories*, p. 732.

[228] Hackett, *Buchenwald Report*, p 10.

Ohrdruf on April 12, and soon after, Buchenwald (at Eisenhower's urging) became a much-visited destination. Soldiers remembered their impactful visits to Buchenwald, remembered photos of Ike at a concentration camp, and associated the two events. Once these mistaken associations began to appear in public statements or in publications, many who heard or read them assumed they were true and integrated them into their own internal narrative about Buchenwald.

General Dwight D. Eisenhower and General Troy Middleton at Ohrdruf, April 12, 1945. Photograph used with permission from the United States Holocaust Memorial Museum.

Radio calls?

Some survivors have reported communicating with the Allies before liberation by radio. There appears to have been at least one, and perhaps more than one clandestine home-made radio receiver in the possession of Buchenwald inmates, and there is also a report of a clandestine transmitter built in the camp theater[229]. The communication story seems to have originated as part of the *Selbstbefreiung* myth, as this gives prisoners the active role in getting the Allies to the camp. Hermann Langbein relates a detailed account of this radio communication in his book *Against All Hope: Resistance in the Nazi Concentration camps 1938-1945*[230].

---

[229] Radiomuseum, Radio built in Buchenwald concentration camp near Weimar, https://www.radiomuseum.org/forum/empfaengerbau_im_kz_buchenwald_bei_weimar.html, retrieved October 6, 2019.

[230] Langbein, Hermann. *Against all Hope: Resistance in the Nazi Concentration Camps.* (St. Paul, MN: Paragon House, 2009) p. 502.

The following message was said to have been transmitted in Morse code from Buchenwald at mid-day on April 8 in several languages: "To the Allies. To the army of General Patton. This is the Buchenwald concentration camp. SOS. We request help. They want to evacuate us. The SS wants to destroy us." A few minutes after the last transmission, this message was said to have been received: "KZ Bu. Hold out. Rushing to your aid. Staff of Third Army." Flint Whitlock, in *Buchenwald: Hell on a Hilltop*[231] offers the assessment of "Red Triangle", an alias for Pierre C.T. Verhaye, a Belgian who was imprisoned at Buchenwald, on the veracity of this story. Verhaye is quite doubtful of the tale, for several reasons. While the exact range of the transmitter (if a functional unit did exist) is unknown, it seems unlikely that any transmission would reach its intended recipient. Third Army Headquarters was in Frankfurt at the time, and the 4th and 6th Armored Divisions were both more than twenty miles from Buchenwald. The abbreviation "KZ Bu" is a Nazi construction, and it again seems unlikely to have been used in an American response. Furthermore, if the Third Army was made aware of the need to rush to Buchenwald, one wonders why none of the units that arrived there on the 11th and 12th had any advance knowledge that the camp even existed. Lastly, there are no known records of the receipt of such a message in Army files, though an exhaustive search for such a record has probably not been performed.

There are many, many more instances of claims by liberators and survivors that do not appear to be consistent with what we know or suspect to be true about the liberation of Buchenwald. Eugene Weinstock reports that 60 Nazi sappers arrived in trucks full of explosives to blow Buchenwald up just as the white flag was raised on April 11[232]; Benjamin Bender claims that SS soldiers were drowned in the excrement pits at Buchenwald at 11 AM on April 11[233]; Jack Werber says that a unit of Nazis equipped with flame-throwers arrived on the 11th to destroy the camp but were repulsed by the inmates[234]. What are we to make of this massively complicated memory picture? Many of the inconsistent reports are "orphan memories", incidents recalled by only one person: Leo Hymas' story is a good example. Others, though, such as the Ilse Koch stories, are shared by many people. In the next and last chapter, I'll take a systematic look at how our psychological understanding of memory can help us understand the many ways the liberation of Buchenwald has been remembered and misremembered.

---

[231] Whitlock, *Hilltop*, pp 235-236.

[232] Weinstock, *Beyond*, p 161.

[233] Bender, *Glimpses*, 161.

[234] Werber, *Saving Children*, 109.

EPILOGUE

Sometimes in historical research we unearth stories within stories, and cannot resist the temptation to dig deeper. That happened to me while writing this book. The interior story in this case is the story of Private First Class James V. DeMarco. PFC DeMarco was the soldier killed while serving with Leo Hymas somewhere near Siegburg, Germany on April 12, 1945. Hymas' insistence that he was with PFC DeMarco when he was killed is one of the ways we can be reasonably sure that Hymas was not at Buchenwald at or near the time of the liberation of that camp. Hymas, who referred to PFC DeMarco as "Jimmy", described his death quite graphically. Hymas said that PFC DeMarco was struck in the chest by an explosive 20 mm anti-aircraft projectile, and that his body was completely destroyed, blown to bits, along with the tripod for the machine gun they crewed together. Hymas also remarked that he did not know where PFC DeMarco had been buried, or anything about his family.

I obtained PFC DeMarco's Individual Deceased Personnel File from the National Archives and Records Administration, and, through the efforts of my friend and research associate Max Cameron, made contact with a close relative of PFC DeMarco. The DeMarco family was unaware that Leo Hymas had had anything to say publicly about PFC DeMarco, and his surviving relatives were quite surprised and somewhat puzzled by Hymas' remarks.

PFC DeMarco was born January 4, 1926, and was known as "Vince-e" to his family, not "Jimmy". In fact, PFC DeMarco is listed as "Vincent DeMarco" in the 1940 census records. One DeMarco family member remembers his first and middle names having been reversed to "James Vincent" by the Army, and "Vince-e" simply became accustomed to being called "Jimmy" in the Army. His mother chose to memorialize him as he was known in the Army. Vince-e was the oldest of six children, four boys and two girls. He was nineteen when he was killed in action in the battle to eliminate the "Ruhr Pocket".

The story of Vince-e's death remembered by the family differs significantly from that told by Leo Hymas. Army records list PFC DeMarco's cause of death as a gunshot wound to the back: the two burial documents in PFC DeMarco's file both list the cause of death as "GSW back". After the war, members of PFC Demarco's unit who were with him when he was killed came to visit the DeMarco family, and a surviving relative remembers the family becoming quite close to one of them and driving quite a long distance to visit him. According to the family's recollection of events as related by his comrades, soldiers from PFC DeMarco's unit were pinned down by enemy fire, and all the leaders were killed or wounded. PFC DeMarco took the initiative to lead the remaining soldiers back from their vulnerable location, and was rendering aid to a wounded comrade when he was shot in the back and killed by a German soldier hiding in the bushes, who was subsequently killed by PFC DeMarco's comrades.

The chain of events that followed PFC DeMarco's death is disturbing to read, as the twists and turns of government bureaucracy did not make the loss of PFC DeMarco any easier for the family. There are two Reports of Burial in PFC DeMarco's file. The first describes his burial at Ittenbach, Germany, on April 18, 1945. This form lists his date of death as April 10 (estimated), which is corrected with pen-and-ink to April 12, 1945. The form lists his place of death as one-half mile northwest of Driesch, Germany. The remains of PFC DeMarco were disinterred and reburied in Margraten, The Netherlands, on September 7, 1945. The second Report of Burial describes this interment, though the place of death on this form is recorded as one and one-half miles northwest of Driesch, rather than one-half mile.

The cemetery for German war dead at Ittenbach where PFC DeMarco was buried from April 18 – September 7, 1945. Author's photograph.

Despite the fact that PFC DeMarco had been buried on April 18 in Ittenbach, for some reason he was listed as missing in action until May 1, 1945. On April 30, a telegram was sent to the family informing them that PFC DeMarco had been listed as missing in action since April 11, 1945. He was declared killed in action the very next day, and the family was apparently notified of his death on or about May 12, 1945. Germany surrendered to the Allies on May 8, 1945. VJ Day, the day the Empire of Japan formally surrendered to the Allies ending World War II, was August 14, 1945. As she listened to the sounds of celebration in the streets that evening, PFC DeMarco's mother, Mrs. Mary DeMarco, composed a heartbreaking, handwritten eight-page letter to President Harry Truman, which is still in PFC DeMarco's IDPF. The letter is tear-stained in places. Mrs. DeMarco was writing to request that her son's remains be repatriated to the United States for burial in the family cemetery. These are some of her words, telling President Truman about her son:

> "He was part of a heavy machine gun platoon that captured a very important objective. He had an important job to do in this action and fulfilled it with highest devotion to duty. He was courageous and fought valiantly in a supreme hour of his country's need so peace and liberty would be preserved on earth. That letter of confirmation we received from his commanding officer will always be kept and cherished for it really means a lot and is very important in both my husband's eyes and mine. And this is one part dear President Truman that really made his parents in a way feel very good and real proud of their beloved soldier son. This is the part – As James Vincent's company commander, I knew him very well. His excellent traits of character set a good example for the men of this organization. He was very devoted and loyal to his company and strived to make it the best in the regiment. With the passing of your son we have lost a true friend, a loyal American and a fine soldier."

The Netherlands American Cemetery in Margraten, The Netherlands. PFC DeMarco was buried here from September 7, 1945, until his remains were repatriated to the United States in late 1948. A Dutch family cared for his grave during that time. Approximately 60% of the soldiers buried here during WWII were eventually repatriated to the US. Author's photograph.

Mrs. DeMarco received a reply to her letter (not from President Truman) on September 25, 1945. That letter informed her that burials of American soldiers were being consolidated at cemeteries not on German soil, and that the family would be notified when PFC DeMarco's remains were moved. The second Report of Burial shows that this had in fact already occurred, as the re-interment at Margraten had taken place at 1 PM on Friday, September 7, 1945. The notification that PFC DeMarco's remains had been moved was sent to the family, but not until December 17, 1946, more than 13 months after the event.

A few days later (December 20, 1946) Mrs. DeMarco inquired again about the repatriation of her son's remains, and expressed surprise that she had not been notified that her son's remains had been moved. In her letter she mentioned that the notification had included the name and address of a Dutch family that had adopted and cared for PFC DeMarco's grave. Surviving family members remember that Vince-e's parents were very grateful to the Dutch family that had adopted and cared for his grave, and sent them "care packages" containing flour and sugar, as food was in short supply in Holland at the time. In return, the Dutch family sent wooden shoes to the DeMarcos.

On January 27, 1947, Mrs. DeMarco received a letter from the Army saying that she would receive a definitive reply to her recent letter soon. On February 6, 1947, that reply arrived, informing the family that a letter would be sent when the government was ready to begin the repatriation process. That notification arrived December 5, 1947. The DeMarco's signed the necessary forms on December 10, 1947. On April 15, 1948, the disinterment directive for PFC DeMarco's remains was issued. The disinterment took place on September 21, 1948. The remains were described as complete but in a state of advanced decomposition. The casket was boxed and marked on November 20, 1948. At 4:45 PM on Monday, January 10, 1949, Mrs. Mary DeMarco's wish was finally granted: PFC James Vincent DeMarco's remains arrived at South Station in Boston.

PFC James Vincent DeMarco's grave in Malden, Massachussetts.

James Vincent (or Vincent James) DeMarco was the oldest child of Mary and Anthony DeMarco, of Revere, Massachusetts. He died on April 12, 1945 in the service of his country, the same day that Franklin Delano Roosevelt died, a coincidence noted by Mrs. DeMarco in her letter to President Truman. He was the apple of his mother's eye, a cheerful and good-natured young man, by all accounts. He had been a great swimmer, and was known for saving several lives in his hometown of Revere, Massachusetts, which is a beach town. Vince-e quit school after the 8th grade to help support his family. He worked on a farm, dug clams, delivered ice, and delivered oil to help make ends meet. He was training to be a boxer when he was drafted in 1944. His three younger brothers were Vince-e's "little men", who adored him. Vince-e took his brother Anthony to his first baseball game, and bought him ice cream with the little money he had.

I think that PFC DeMarco deserves to be remembered in his own right, not just in Leo Hymas' confused narrative of their time together, even though that narrative respects and honors him in its own way. I visited each step along PFC James V. DeMarco's journey from somewhere northwest of Driesch, Germany, to the Holy Cross Cemetery in Malden, Massachusetts, and paid our (Max's and mine) respects. Mrs. DeMarco proudly described the headstone she had picked out for her son in her letter to President Truman: she had lovingly and carefully chosen it for her boy. The photograph of him in the oval near the top was missing when I visited the cemetery in Malden, but the face of Mary and

Anthony DeMarco's fallen hero, resting near his boyhood home after a long and winding journey, was clear in my mind's eye.

6 MEMORY AND HISTORY

Documentary evidence is one of the mainstays of professional historical research. In Chapter 2 I tried to establish as best I could what the documentary evidence tells us about the liberation of Buchenwald. Three obvious limitations of documentary evidence were apparent in this effort. First, we sometimes lack documents that might help us establish what did happen at a particular time and place. We might like to know if Egon Fleck and Edward Tenenbaum were at Buchenwald on April 11, 1945, for example, but as yet no documents have come to light that unequivocally verify their presence there on that day. So, we have to use other available evidence to make a best guess. But we can be reasonably sure that the Keffer party from the 6th Armored Division and elements of the 4th Armored Division did visit Buchenwald and make contact with inmates on April 11, 1945, because there are records to verify these events.

Second, documentary evidence can be misunderstood, falsified, purposely or inadvertently distorted, or de-contextualized in ways that are misleading. The photograph taken at Ohrdruf on April 12, 1945, and incorrectly credited to William A. Scott III on the USHMM website is an example. Third, documentary evidence may not be much help in determining what did not happen. Some military records that might help us determine the whereabouts of the 761st Tank Battalion or 183rd Combat Engineer Battalion on April 11, 1945, for example, are missing, having been destroyed by a fire at a US Army records facility in the 1970s. The absence of these records creates a documentary lacuna: where were these units on the dates of interest? To some, this shifts the burden of proof onto those who maintain that these units did not participate in the liberation. But documenting a negative (these units were not at Buchenwald on certain dates) is difficult: normally this would be done by documenting that the units were somewhere else on those dates (as can be done in the case of Leo Hymas) but those records are no longer available for these units. Thus, a few remain convinced that African-American soldiers from the 183rd Combat Engineers were present at the liberation of Buchenwald.

Another important resource for historical research is personal testimony. Such testimony can fill in the gaps where documentary records are absent.

Like documentary evidence, personal testimony may be true or false, accurate or inaccurate. One important difference between personal testimony and documentary evidence is that documentary evidence sometimes contains within it features that allow us to determine its validity. Contextual attributes of the document may enable historians to determine whether the document can be accepted at face value, or requires more investigation and interpretation.

Personal testimony is different. There are very good reasons that "lie detectors" are not admissible evidence in most courts: memories themselves contain no telltale markers that allow us to judge their veracity. Our only recourse is to consider all the evidence available, and make an informed and reasonable judgment. Personal testimony is only one element of a pattern of converging evidence that must be consulted to help us establish the truth.

The below Venn diagram is my simple attempt to outline the task confronting us if we hope to make sense of the past using documentary evidence and/or personal testimony. We begin with the set of everything that might have happened. This universe of possibilities contains things that might have happened, but didn't: e.g., Leo Hymas might have been at Buchenwald on April 11, 1945, but wasn't, and things that might have happened, and did, such as the fact that Captain Frederic Keffer might have been at Buchenwald on April 11, 1945, and was. These two sets of possible and actual events are represented by the concentric outer and inner ovals, respectively.

As we have noted, it is possible to find documentary evidence of things that did not happen (falsified or misleading documents or faulty interpretations) and documentary evidence of things that did happen (valid documents or interpretations). These two cases are represented by the interior oval offset to the right. The same is true of personal testimony: some testifies to events that did happen, while some is mistaken: unknowingly wrong or deliberately false. These possibilities are represented in the interior oval offset to the left.

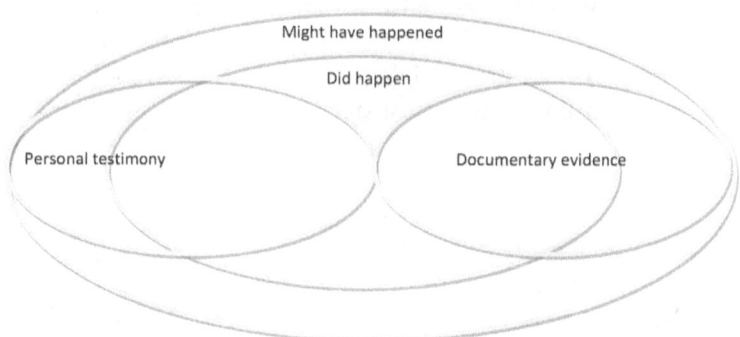

Historians are compelled to work with all the sources of information and all the truth-possibilities in these diagrams. Historians have skills to deal with documentary evidence: to find it, evaluate it, and interpret it, that are generally not part of a psychologist's training or background. Historians also deal with personal testimony as a matter of course, and have developed methods, procedures, and standards for working with such material.

Holocaust historians have, to some extent, grappled with the likelihood that some survivor testimony may include inaccuracies. High-profile cases like that of Binjamin Wilkomirski, whose Oprah-lauded book *Fragments*[235] was shown to be a fabrication or false memory, have raised public awareness of the issue, but Holocaust historians have long known that personal testimony can be problematic. Twenty years ago, Mark Roseman presented a detailed accounting of errors in the personal testimony of Marianne Ellenbogen, a Holocaust survivor whose memories could be and were compared to an unusually complete documentary record. Roseman found that there were significant disparities between Ellenbogen's current memories and accounts from her own diaries and from existing records. Roseman speculated that the disparities were not random, but rather reflected an instrumental process of modifying memories as a way of making sense of her experience[236].

Many historians cross-check personal testimony against other sources and treat this material in more or less the same way that any historical data might be treated: with an appropriate and respectful skepticism. Many historians exhibit an intuitive appreciation for the vagaries of human memory, and while they may not employ the same vernacular psychologists favor, they nevertheless are sensitive to the possibilities of inaccuracy or distortion. But it appears to me that historiographical epistemological standards with respect to personal testimony are somewhat diverse and sometimes loosely applied: different historians treat such material differently. This is also true in psychology, insofar as the experimental and clinical sides of my discipline fought the so-called "memory wars" over certain kinds of personal testimony: experimentalists are generally more skeptical of certain kinds of memory claims (recovered memories of trauma, for example) than are clinicians. Most of the psychologists who have contributed meaningfully to Holocaust studies have been clinicians.

---

[235] See, for example, *The Guardian*, Fragments of a Fraud, https://www.theguardian.com/theguardian/1999/oct/15/features11.g24, retrieved 19 August 2019

[236] Roseman, Mark. (1999). "Surviving testimony: Truth and Inaccuracy in Holocaust Testimony". *The Journal of Holocaust Education*, **8(1)**, 1-20.

It seems to me, then, that experimental psychology might have something meaningful to contribute to the left side of this diagram: we have studied and understand memory, which is the basis of personal testimony, in a particular way that may be helpful in sorting out historical evidence. What we can do is explain memory as psychological research has shown it to be, and apply our understanding to specific cases to illustrate how these mechanisms operate. The determinations that I have made about the accuracy of much of the testimony discussed above are not psychological in nature: I have made these determinations based on documentary evidence that conflicts directly with remembered accounts. My thinking about *how* these survivors and liberators may have arrived at their mistaken beliefs about the past is psychological, though: more on that below.

Finding the Truth

Anyone who tells you that it is possible to determine the correspondence between an individual memory and ground truth based solely on an examination of that memory is wrong. No amount of experience, or technology, or knowledge can tell you whether a given memory is real or false without recourse to sources of validation beyond the memory itself. Christopher Browning, a distinguished Holocaust historian, proposed a four-part test to help assess the validity of memories, which I have discussed at length elsewhere[237]. Briefly, that test is (1) Does the memory work against the individual's self- interest? (2) Is the memory vivid? (3) Is it possible that the memory is true? (4) Is it probable that the memory is true?[238]

The last two elements of the test, possibility and probability, are exactly the old-fashioned hard work of the sort I did in evaluating the liberation claims discussed above. Is it possible, for example, that Leo Hymas might somehow been taken from a great battle at Siegburg and transported nearly two hundred miles to Weimar, appeared at Buchenwald, participated in a pitched battle with fourteen SS officers dressed in the wrong uniforms, violently liberated Buchenwald using explosives without the awareness or knowledge of any of the prisoners, and then been returned to his unit somewhere near Siegburg to be with James V. DeMarco when he was killed the next day? Well, I suppose it is possible, but it is not very probable. Could Rick Carrier somehow have gotten to

---

[237] Mastroianni, George. *Of Mind and Murder: Toward a More Comprehensive Psychology of the Holocaust.* (New York, Oxford University press, 2018).

[238] Browning, Christopher.*Collected Memories: Holocaust History and Post-War Testimony.* (Madison, WI; University of Wisconsin Press, 2003).

the main gate at the prisoner area of Buchenwald on the afternoon of April 10, 1945, without encountering any SS guards or other German personnel? Possible, but highly unlikely.

The first two elements of Browning's test, self-interest and vividness, smuggle a kind of fudge-factor into the business of testing memories against the facts. These really represent nothing more than intuition or judgment, as there is no real evidence to support their inclusion in a memory test. False memories can be as vivid as real ones, and self-interest is an unreliable gauge of the accuracy of a memory. People might deliberately recall a memory that puts them in a bad light on one point as a way of establishing credibility on other, more important points.

I will say that I have great respect for historical study, scholarship, experience and the expertise and intuition these can bring. Historians who have steeped themselves in their subject matter develop special insights into the subjects of their historical research. In cases in which no evidence to definitively adjudicate a question of historical fact is available, I would give more credence to the judgment of an historian who is expert in his/her area than I would to someone not so experienced and prepared, though I would bear in mind that a judgment made by an historian is still, at the end of the day, a judgment.

So, neither historians nor psychologists have a fool-proof way of examining a memory or piece of personal testimony and determining whether or not it is true, apart from doing the same kind of shoe-leather detective work that is necessary to evaluate the truth of any claim: we look at the evidence. There are, however, some features or aspects of memories that, when considered in conjunction with our psychological understanding of memory mechanisms, can help us make educated guesses about the probable origin of some memories. First, let's delve into the mechanisms, and then we'll apply our understanding of them to some of the survivor and liberator accounts.

Memory

Psychologists use the terms encoding, storage, and retrieval to describe three stages of remembering. Encoding is the process of converting our experiences into representations in our brains, welding together a representation of environmental energy (sights and sounds) and internal psychological states (feelings. emotions) and turning them into patterns of neural activity and structure. Storage is the process of maintaining that representation in a stable way over a period of time. Retrieval is recalling that memory to our conscious mind. Retrieval sometimes occurs spontaneously, sometimes as an act of intention or will.

Analogies between human memory and computer memory can be useful, but are fraught with potential mischief, because there are important, fundamental differences between human and computer memory. But at this stage, we can appreciate that encoding is like the typing I am now doing on this keyboard: I push keys, those keypresses result in information from the outside world (my keyboard inputs) being transferred to the inner workings of the computer. Those inputs may or may not be saved: if I close this document without hitting "Save", then they will not be stored in the computer, they will be lost. If I do save them, then those inputs will be placed in a memory location somewhere on a storage medium and maintained. Computers are quite good at maintaining stored information intact over a long period of time: the file I saved a year or a month ago is no less accurately stored than the one I saved five minutes ago.

Retrieval is a more deliberate process in the computer than in human memory. Many memories come to us humans unbidden, rising to consciousness as we wade through the constant stream of stimuli we experience and responses we generate as we go through our daily lives, sometimes mystifying us as to why a particular memory comes to mind at a particular time. Sometimes we find ourselves wracking our brains to remember something (a computer password, for example), but much of our remembering is routine. All retrieval on a computer is deliberate, and if we tag a file in a way that we don't remember and no longer makes sense to us or place it in the wrong directory, as I often do, then we can spend a lot of time looking for it.

Encoding and the Camps

It is worth thinking for a moment about how those processes of encoding, storage, and retrieval may have been affected by the special conditions that existed in the lives of both survivors and liberators. One of the ways computers are different from people is that computers encode everything they "experience". Whatever I type into this keyboard, whether or not it is interesting, useful, stimulating, or true, gets encoded. Computers pay complete, constant attention to whatever is coming in through available input channels (keyboard or touchscreen or voice controller) and encode it all. Humans, on the other hand, selectively attend to a subset of the stimuli to which we are exposed. This strategy of selective attention makes good sense. We have far more elaborate sensing capabilities than do most computers and are constantly exposed to a staggering amount of information. As I stand here typing, my senses are filled with information: touch sensations as my clothes rustle against my skin, sunshine after a few days of rain, my dog slumbering cutely in one of her favorite places a few feet away, neighbors walking down the street, cars passing by. I am not attending to most of this (except, I did a little to write the last sentence). Now, my attention might be drawn to one of my neighbors walking down the street if I heard him/her through the open window talking about the shabby state of my lawn as he/she passes by. I might mention this to my wife later in the day and snarkily comment on the sad state of the offending neighbors' fence.

If you ask me at some point in the future about what happened on this particular morning (don't wait too long – see the next section) I'm not likely to remember very much other than perhaps the incident involving the overcritical neighbors. Why? Because we quickly forget things that we don't rehearse or elaborate. In a way, our evolutionary default is to remember by exception. We mostly don't bother to waste any more time or energy storing representations of things that don't break through the normal hum-drum routine of our sensory experience. If our attention is strongly focused on something then we may overlook even provocative or unusual things that happen. I may be so intent on my writing, for example, that I completely ignore my dog's loud and vigorous attempts to alert me to the dangers posed by the venerable but (to her) intolerable tradition of residential mail delivery in the United States, obliviously typing as she snarls, barks, and hurls herself against the door in a vain attempt to consume our extremely competent, reliable, and tolerant mail carrier.

With these thoughts in mind, let's reconsider the situations confronting camp survivors or liberators. By most accounts, survivors and liberators (or any soldiers in combat) have in common that they are intently focused on one thing: survival. When I read Primo Levi or other survivor accounts of life in the camps, I am struck by the amount of effort it took to survive. Survival was a constant and deliberate struggle. This intense and constant struggle took place against a backdrop of numbing routine: roll-calls and work-details and waiting in line for food. This routine was punctuated by extraordinary events completely outside the range of normal experience: public floggings or executions, arbitrary acts of extreme violence. This routine was experienced without watches or calendars or reliable access to news or information to demarcate or set apart any particular event. There was little or no access to paper, pencil, or any way to create a permanent record of anything.

What aspects of experience were most likely to be encoded and remembered, or quickly forgotten, in the concentration-camp world? Based on what we know about memory in other circumstances, I would guess that survivors would be most likely to encode and remember those aspects of their daily experience most directly related to their daily survival. In this connection, Primo Levi relates a story about standing in the soup-line at Auschwitz, a situation in which preparedness was extremely important. Prisoner-numbers were called out in

Polish, and he became acutely sensitive to the sound of the number of the prisoner ahead of him in line spoken in the Polish language, one which he did not speak. He remembered this otherwise trivial detail years later, because it was directly connected to his daily struggle for survival, and was repeated many times.

I would also surmise that survivors' memories would favor things that were rehearsed and elaborated: things that were common and frequent topics of conversation among inmates. We get inklings of what some these topics were by reading survivor accounts. No doubt survival itself was a primary topic, but inmates must also have shared stories about their varying experiences in the camps: what the different work-details were like, which guards were particularly vicious or unusually humane, where and how the necessities of life could be "organized". And rumors, stories, gossip, and speculation heard and passed on through the network of inmates who often had experience of many different camps as they wound their way through the lager archipelago, to paraphrase Solzhenitsyn's evocative term.

If we are wondering what the soldiers who were fighting in the headlong pursuit of the Nazi armies across Germany in April of 1945 might have encoded and remembered, we should begin with those things that occupied their attention most compellingly, and those things that they talked about most. American units were typically covering a lot of ground quickly in the last several weeks of the war. They encountered town after unfamiliar-sounding town, or bridge, or camp, or obstacle, attending most carefully to those that posed a potential threat, moving on when they could do so safely to begin the cycle anew at the next step in the march across Germany. The Nazis had many thousands of people in custody across Germany in a great many camps, prisons, and other facilities large and small. Political prisoners from Germany and across Europe, slave-laborers from Europe and the occupied territories, and prisoners of war were encountered constantly. Many of the details unrelated to the daily imperative of conducting military operations against a retreating but still very dangerous enemy were most likely quickly forgotten.

Anyone who has ever been associated with the military knows that soldiers spend a lot of time talking: griping, complaining, and rumor-mongering are especially popular verbal pastimes. Soldiers in WWII did not have access to the sources of news and information routinely available in modern conflict, and so there was a very active rumor-mill[239]. Stories passed from soldier to soldier and unit to unit, often undergoing significant transformations as they made their way

---

[239] Which is not to say that rumors are entirely a thing of the past.

from place to place. What would soldiers have encoded and remembered? Most likely things that were interesting or odd enough to rise above the daily tedium of repeated actions and emerge from the constant stream of new information to which they were exposed to provoke significant discussion and elaboration. Stories about lampshades made from human skin, for example, especially if such stories involved an SS temptress known as the "Bitch of Buchenwald" might well have risen to this level. Many soldiers visited Buchenwald while it was still in American hands, and the widespread publicity brought to the camp by the visits of Congressional and other high-level delegations ensured that Buchenwald was widely discussed: even soldiers who did not visit the camp might have been exposed to news stories, or first-, second-, or third-hand accounts from other soldiers. Forty years in the future, sorting out what they experienced directly from what they heard or read might not be so easy.

Storage

Information stored in computers seems to remain intact for a very long time. In fact, my computers seem to become obsolete and end up being replaced long before any information they store has degraded significantly. This is an area where human memory is very unlike computer memory: human memories mostly disappear quickly unless positive steps are taken to ensure their retention. One of the most reliable findings in psychological science is the general shape of the "forgetting curve". When people are exposed to information, and then tested at intervals to see how much of that information they have retained, the function that relates amount remembered to time since exposure has the general shape of the one below:

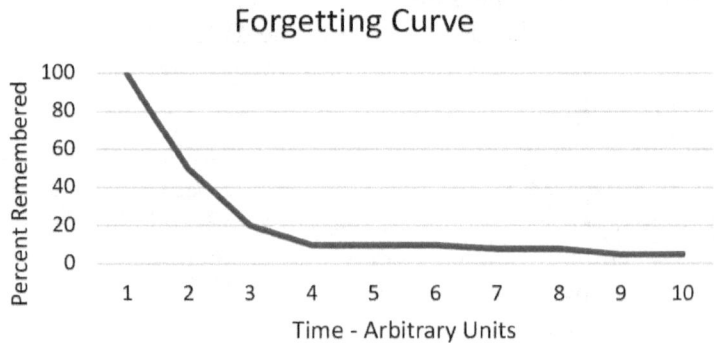

The steepness of the curve can vary depending on many factors, but in general, most forgetting occurs quickly: new information is lost within minutes, hours, days. The pace of forgetting slows significantly over time, however: those memories that do survive may last for years, decades, a lifetime.

Several factors are known to affect remembering: we have already mentioned rehearsal and elaboration. Thinking and talking about a remembered event after the event has occurred, especially soon after it has occurred, can help strengthen our recollection of the event and remember it longer. So-called "elaborative rehearsal" is known to be helpful in ensuring that memories are transferred into long-term memory. A special challenge for Holocaust survivors and liberators is that the events of those years were often avoided and not discussed (rehearsed or elaborated) for decades. Theresa Ast, whose book *Confronting the Holocaust: American Soldiers Enter Concentration Camps* is based on many liberator testimonies, notes that after the war, many people simply wanted to forget about it and move on: liberators' reports about the camps were met with disbelief, and much testimony was only made when the liberators were in their fifties, sixties, or seventies[240]. Leonard Lubin, a liberator of the Wels II camp, said that "from 1945 to 2006 he never discussed his personal contact with the Holocaust with anyone"[241]. John C. McManus, in *Hell Before Their Very Eyes: American Soldiers Liberate Concentration Camps in Germany, April 1945*, likewise mentions the reluctance of soldiers to discuss their camp experiences, as often they were doubted or disbelieved. According to McManus, "…the natural inclination of most men was to clam up[242]." Robert H. Abzug, in *Inside the Vicious Heart: Americans and the Liberation of Nazi Concentration Camps*, avers that:

"When the liberators came home they did try to tell people about the camps, but, most ended up responding to the disbelief, disgust, or silence of others with a silence of their own….Only as they got older and looked back upon the important events of their lives did the encounter with the concentration camps begin to loom large. For their own children and for the world in general, many of the liberators thought it important finally to set down their experiences[243]."

The fact that soldiers and survivors did not talk much about their memories

---

[240] Ast, Theresa. *Confronting the Holocaust: American Soldiers Enter Concentration Camps*. (Georgia, Nomenklature Publications, 2013). This book does not have page numbers, but the material is near footnotes 665-710.

[241] Hirsh, Michael. *The Liberators: America's Witnesses to the Holocaust.* (New York, Bantam Books, 2010) p. 299.

[242] McManus, John C. *Hell Before Their very Eyes: American Soldiers Liberate Concentration Camps in Germany, April 1945,* (Baltimore, Johns Hopkins University press, 2015) p 149.

[243] Abzug, Robert H. *Inside the Vicious Heart: Americans and the Liberation of Nazi Concentration Camps*. (New York, Oxford University Press, pp. 169-170.

in the interval between the war and the growing interest in the Holocaust in the 1980's and 1990's could also be seen as potentially beneficial in aiding accurate recall later: sometimes when we retrieve and discuss memories repeatedly, they change. Most of us can think have of stories that have gotten better with repeated re-telling. Holocaust memories are also distinctive: they occurred at a specific time, and generally speaking, nothing like them was experienced before or after. Insofar as these memories exist at all, then, later retrieval will be less affected by interference from competing, similar memories. These potential benefits may be outweighed, however, by the weak encoding and the lack of rehearsal also characteristic of these memories.

Age is also a well-known factor affecting memory. When we are very young, we do not form memories as effectively as when we are more mature; when we are very old, we do not recall memories as well. During the last few decades, survivors or liberators who began to think about and recall their experiences only much later in life were disadvantaged in that aging makes accurate recall of all memories more difficult. This, again, is unlike the case of computers: my relatively old computer, as long as it works at all, will store and retrieve information just as effectively as a brand-new one. If we think about survivors writing about the Holocaust for the first time now or in the recent past, we can appreciate that they are squeezed by age-related memory factors from both directions: they were quite young when they were in the camps, and are quite old when trying to recall their experiences.

Another factor affecting survivors selectively is the physical state they were in during their time in the camps. Most were starving, chronically exhausted, frightened, and confused; many were sick. Memories are physical changes that take place in our brains, and as such, require energy for their formation, consolidation, and maintenance. The dire straits in which many survivors found themselves, especially at war's end when the camps were liberated, likely also compromised their ability to store, consolidate, and retain accurate memories.

Retrieval

There are thus quite a few factors working against accurate encoding and storage of camp experiences. Liberators may not have encoded relevant aspects of their experience because those experiences were embedded in a fast-paced, action-packed drama, the significance of which might only have been made clear much later, and then did not talk or think much about these experiences for many, many years. Survivors may not have encoded and stored memories of significant experiences for similar reasons, and were further challenged by the poor physical, mental, and emotional state in which many found themselves at the time of liberation.

While the focus in this book is on failures of memory, it must be said that many liberators and survivors did successfully form, retain, and recall very accurate memories of their camp experiences despite these challenges. When interest in these historical events was rekindled (at least in the United States) a half-century after they had taken place, some liberators and survivors were able to look back and provide compelling and accurate testimony as to what had happened. Their stories are not the focus of this book, but of course there were and are many. Others, though, had only vague and uncertain hints in their recollection of their experiences. For these survivors and liberators, their memories of their camp experiences were a mostly blank slate. As we shall see, the immense interest and public discussion of the Holocaust that grew in the United States in the 1980's and 1990's would provide ample material to fill those blank slates.

Retrieval and Reconstruction

Another important difference between human memory and computer memory is the nature of the retrieval process. My computer retrieves exactly what was stored, so long as I can remember what I named the file, what directory it was in, and so on. We may talk about human memory as if it functioned in much the same way, but psychologists these days more often use the word *reconstruct* in referring to human memory.

One reason we think this way about memory is something called the misinformation effect. This happens when our memories are altered by the way we attempt to retrieve them. We saw earlier that when an interviewer asked Henry Herder about the gas chambers at Buchenwald, Herder at first didn't remember any (there never was one at Buchenwald) but immediately began to alter his memory to suit the interviewer's apparent certainty that there were gas chambers at Buchenwald. Had the interviewer instead asked, "Was Buchenwald one of the camps that had gas chambers?" Herder might have been less inclined to begin reconstructing his memory of Buchenwald to include gas chambers. He might simply have said, "No, I don't think so." Note the difference between human and computer memory here: if I make a mistake and type something incorrect into my computer's search bar, the computer does not begin to modify whatever it is I am looking for to match the query. But that is exactly what happens in human memory, because we are not simply reading back a verbatim copy of what was encoded and stored: we are rebuilding the memory using whatever information is currently available to us, and part of the information available to us is the way we interrogate our memory. There are many other examples of this sort of interference and distortion in our memories: suggestive or leading questioning, source confusion or misattribution, bias, imagination inflation, false memory creation, and intrusion are examples.

Elizabeth Loftus' path-breaking research on eyewitness testimony[244] has shown how sensitive our memories can be to this kind of post-event distortion. She had research participants view a film of a multi-car collision. She later asked them how fast the cars had been traveling when the accident occurred. But she asked the question five different ways: "How fast were the cars going when they (smashed, collided, bumped, hit, contacted) each other?" All the participants had seen the same film, but those who were asked how fast the cars were traveling when they *smashed* each other estimated the vehicles' speed as being about ten miles per hour faster, on average, than did those who were asked how fast they had been traveling when they *contacted* each other.

Some survivor and liberator memories may be especially vulnerable to confusion and distortion because of the combination of weak encoding at the time of exposure to the event, minimal rehearsal and elaboration for decades after exposure, and then the relatively sudden and widespread availability of post-event information. Older people reconstructing memories that were not that strong to begin with after many, many years will use whatever information they can to reconstruct the memory.

Before the internet, the potential aids available to us in reconstructing such memories were more limited than those available to us today. We could consult contemporaries (fellow survivors or Army buddies) though their memories are subject to the same potential problems as ours. We could search books, films, periodicals, or old letters and photographs to help us piece together our experiences. Often, these resources are very helpful. Reconstructing our own past can sometimes look like the same kind of detective work in which we might engage to investigate someone else's past. In a way, that is what we are doing: these are autobiographical memories, but after so much time and so much life they can seem distant and alien to us.

---

[244] Loftus, E. F., & Palmer, J. C. (1974). Reconstruction of automobile destruction: An example of the interaction between language and memory. *Journal of verbal learning and verbal behavior, 13*(5), 585-589.

False Memories May Have Both Individual and Social Origins

I distinguished earlier between social or collective memory, and individual memory. The *Selbstbefreiung* myth and the *Liberators* controversy are social phenomena in the sense that they were largely driven by societal- or cultural-level imperatives. These seem different to me than the errors of people like Leo Hymas, Henry Herder, or Rick Carrier. These individuals have dramatically misremembered their experience with the Holocaust, but the nature of their misremembering mostly serves no larger social cause or political purpose. This does not mean, however, that there is not a social dimension to their misremembering.

One cannot help but wonder, for example, where Leo Hymas got the idea that he had liberated Buchenwald. It seems that his outreach activities began in earnest in the 1990's, and grew in the last decades of his life – Leo Hymas died in 2016. Hymas' USC Shoah Foundation interview contains a segment near the end in which he displays and explains (sometimes incorrectly) several artifacts associated with his wartime service. The only items directly associated with Buchenwald are some photographs, but these photographs, Hymas points out, were taken or obtained by someone else: his friend, Ella Matson Lindsay. Ella Matson Lindsay was a nurse, a First Lieutenant in the 58th Field Hospital, who visited Buchenwald a few days after the liberation. Her group was transported from the nearby town of Gotha to Buchenwald on April 18 expressly to view the camp.

There is a memoir of Ella Matson Lindsay on the internet,[245] the opening words of which are:

"It has been 50 years since the liberation of Concentration Camps by Allied Forces which took place in Europe during World War Two. I kept a detailed journal of my activities as First Lieutenant Army Nurse, 58th Field Hospital, Third Army, during the war, though it was prohibited to do so.

After witnessing the horrors of Buchenwald Concentration Camp one week after it was liberated by my friend Leo Hymas of Issaquah, Washington, and his three buddies. I did a little writing in this journal, then stashed it away unread for the next 50 years. Recently I was asked to participate at the Silver Anniversary Annual Conference on the Holocaust and Churches held at Brigham Young University, Provo, Utah, March 5-8, 1995."

---

[245] Ella Matson Lindsay Recalls Holocaust, http://yanceyfamilygenealogy.org/holocaust.htm, retrieved 8 July 2019.

A bit later, Ms. Lindsay describes her reaction as she entered Buchenwald on April 18, 1945:

"None of this prepared us for what we later saw, April 17[246], 1945, when we were commanded by General Dwight D. Eisenhower and General George Patton to witness the unbelievable horror of the liberation of Buchenwald Concentration Camp. (My husband, Lt. Colonel M. Grant Lindsay, whom I met after the war, and I became close friends in 1983-84 with Leo Hymas of Issaquah, Washington).

Little did I know at that time that Leo and his three buddies, in April 1945 stumbled onto the barbed wire enclosure of Buchenwald, and Leo pushed a pipe-like bomb under the fence and blew it up. They were true liberators of this infamous killing camp. Leo and I including my cousin, Keith Davis of Springville, Utah, and several others gave our personal accounts of what we saw at the killing camps of Germany at the recent Holocaust Conference in Provo."

Ms. Lindsay's complete account offers a striking picture of what a visit to Buchenwald was like for a young Army nurse who had seen a lot, but nothing like Buchenwald. Her description is in general agreement with other contemporary accounts, and the emotional impact the camp had on Ms. Lindsay comes through clearly in her sometimes-emotional narrative. It is interesting that even in her short encounter of only a few hours in Buchenwald, she nevertheless heard and remembered stories about Ilsa (her misspelling) Koch and the human-skin lampshades, and passed on a story from a former prisoner asserting that the shrunken head displayed was of a Polish prisoner who had been decapitated as punishment after having been recaptured following an escape attempt. She passes on the extremely incorrect number of 5,000,000 prisoners having passed through Buchenwald, something she may heard from a prisoner, or misunderstood or misremembered.

It is impossible without first-hand knowledge of the timing and nature of Mr. Hymas' personal history of discussing his wartime experiences to do more than speculate, but there is certainly the possibility that meeting Ella Matson Lindsay in 1983 or 1984 may have led to discussions about her experiences at Buchenwald that contributed to the false memory he created about liberating Buchenwald himself. Perhaps Ms. Lindsay showed Mr. Hymas the photos of Buchenwald, and

---

[246] Ms. Matson reports elsewhere in her memoir that it was the 18th: "April 18, 1945: Yesterday Jean Krawcheski* and many of the others in our hospital went to Buchenwald. Today it was my turn, along with nurses, Eisen, Beebe, Coop, Alta, and about 16 of our enlisted men. We wrapped up in blankets in the back of a 6x6 truck. Weather extremely cold, drizzly rainfall. Roads very bumpy. It seemed we had been riding for ages when we reached Weimar, but actually Gotha, where our hospital is set up at a Hitler Youth Camp, only 12 miles away."

he later confused the pictures with images and events from his own experience: it appears that Hymas was in the vicinity of Siegburg prison on April 11, for example, and his Division participated in the liberation of Flossenburg on April 23, 1945. In both places there were conditions and people very much like the ones that obtained at Buchenwald. Tracing the natural history of memories like this can provide clues as to their origin. If Mr. Hymas did not discuss or write about Buchenwald until after meeting the Lindsays, then perhaps (and only perhaps) this is where the "memories" originated.

Without the internet, it would be much, much more difficult to sort through the various recollections of the liberation of Buchenwald and assess their veracity. But for the past few decades, the basic facts about the liberation of Buchenwald have been available to anyone with a computer, an internet connection, an open mind and a few minutes' time. This makes all the more mystifying the fact that people with elaborate false memories like Leo Hymas sometimes persist in their conviction that these memories are real even when information invalidating them is readily available. For example, Ella Matson Lindsay's 1995 memoir correctly identifies the date of liberation of Buchenwald as April 11, 1945, though Hymas persisted in reporting the date as April 5 or April 9. How is this possible?

Social factors probably play a very powerful role in the development and maintenance of false memories of this kind. Ella Matson Lindsay clearly believed Hymas' account: her memoir was written on the occasion of a Brigham Young University-sponsored conference on the Holocaust which she, Hymas, and others attended. The fact that Mr. Hymas (and the others) participated in such a prestigious conference at a prestigious university and apparently was not questioned or challenged on any of the details of his testimony can only have supported and perhaps increased Hymas' certainty of the truth of his memories. Such memories, false or not, are not likely to fade once they begin to be repeated at public events, are subjected to extensive elaboration and rehearsal in discussions with others, occasion heartfelt and sincere praise from thousands of people, are spread widely on the internet, and are validated by their presentation and celebration by reputable Holocaust-related institutions. In the last two decades of his life, Hymas spoke at innumerable Holocaust-related events, and was especially active with the Holocaust Center for Humanity in Seattle, Washington. Hymas was promoted by the organization and energetically and extensively shared his tale of the liberation of Buchenwald. Before references to Hymas were removed from the organization's website in the late summer of 2019, the Holocaust Center for Humanity's website contained a biography of Leo Hymas that related his story of the liberation, repeating errors in basic facts, including the incorrect date of liberation. [247]

Testimony like this can be visceral and riveting: it comes from a visibly sensitive and emotional man, a pillar of his community and church, often wearing his WWII uniform or displaying his medals and insignia, discussing heroic and horrific events he witnessed personally. Leo Hymas is visibly emotional, often moved to tears, during his interview recorded by the USC Shoah Foundation. Could there be a more credible-sounding and -appearing source? How can Mr. Hymas possibly have been so certain about these events if they didn't happen? And if they really didn't happen, was he deliberately lying? Could he really simply have been mistaken?

Knowing what I know about the psychology of memory, I think he was completely sincere in his beliefs. I think that his memories of the liberation of Buchenwald were as real to him as is my memory of what I had for breakfast this morning. I think the same is true of people like Harry Herder, Rick Carrier, and J. Ray Clark: these are not people fabricating stories to get attention, they are people who have, for reasons we hopefully can now better understand, constructed false memories of an event which are of tremendous interest to other people. To be fair, many of us develop such memories but also do our own detective work to weed them out: Leo Hymas could have read and studied what is known about the liberation of Buchenwald, appreciated the discrepancies between his recollections and those of so many others, and tried to resolve those conflicts, but apparently, he did not. He might have taken the time to learn a bit more about "Jimmy" DeMarco and puzzled over the apparent conflict in timing between the facts of DeMarco's death and his own memories. But apparently, he did not.

To be fair again, perhaps he felt no need to engage in this kind of self-reflection or analysis because his account was implicitly and indeed quite explicitly validated by prestigious Holocaust-related institutions. On at least two occasions he was formally interviewed about his experiences, and those interviews were recorded: his nearly three-hour USC Shoah Foundation interview is easily found in its entirety on the internet. Would they have devoted that much effort to obtaining his testimony if its veracity were in doubt, he might have thought? The Holocaust Center for Humanity presented his story for decades, and went so far as to revise the date of the Buchenwald liberation (which can be verified as April 11, 1945 in seconds) two days into the past to accommodate Hymas' story. I think it would actually be asking rather a lot of Leo Hymas, who was not a professional historian, or an academic, to apply the kind of rigorous, skeptical scrutiny to his story that the professionals involved apparently never thought necessary.

---

[247] Leo H., Holocaust Center for Humanity, https://www.holocaustcenterseattle.org/survivor-stories/leo-h, retrieved 8 July 2019.

Again, the boundaries between the individual and social dimensions of memory become blurred. Leo Hymas developed the memories he did because of his unique personal history and experience. The term "social privilege" is sometimes applied to situations like this: we are taught to respect our elders, we appropriately revere those who served honorably in defense of their country, as did Leo Hymas, we are overwhelmed by the magnitude and significance of the Holocaust, so we don't question or challenge the accounts of survivors or liberators, because to do so would be unseemly and inappropriate. And for many institutions, such stories are appealing, as they showcase the involvement of local citizens in these momentous events and help the institution further its worthwhile and socially responsible goals.

Involuntary Impostor Syndrome

Rick Carrier, Harry Herder, Leo Hymas – these are people who, under other circumstances, we might call impostors. They have (I believe) assumed an identity which is not theirs. They have (I believe) adopted a history that does not belong to them. To varying degrees, they have (I believe) benefitted from their assumption of this unearned identity. "Real" impostors, like Frank Abagnale, Jr[248]., the con man whose impostor life was chronicled in the film "*Catch Me If You Can*" labor under no delusions that they are who they say they are. It takes a great deal of talent and deliberate effort to pull off the impersonations Abagnale and others like him have accomplished. But they, too, are aided by the web of assumptions, beliefs, and social conventions that operate to assure and reassure others (us) that things are as they seem as we go through our lives.

Involuntary impostors are, to an extent, victims of a conspiracy of circumstances of which they are not the sole authors. Carrier, Herder, Hymas could become involuntary impostors only because they fell into a certain demographic category: they were men of a certain age who had served in the US Army in the European Theater in WWII. They were men who (most likely) did have some experiences related to concentration camps. They were men who were exposed to an avalanche of images and information about the camps, decades after their own experiences, which natural mechanisms of human memory commingled with their dim and fading memories to produce a new set of recollections which seemed as vivid and real to them as any other memories. They were men whose new memories went unquestioned, who were honored and lauded for possessing

---

[248] Frank Abagnale, Jr., https://en.wikipedia.org/wiki/Frank_Abagnale, retrieved 17 September 2019.

the identity these new memories bestowed upon them, who came (to varying degrees) to revel in the attention and adulation that accompanied the status that came with these new memories.

On the other hand, a more completely accurate name for the syndrome I am describing might be "Semi-Involuntary Impostor Syndrome", because it is hard to completely dismiss the feeling that men like Carrier, Herder, and Hymas have failed just a little bit in holding themselves to proper account. Carrier's apparent flights of fancy Gumped him into a world of meetings with famous World War II generals, exotic and beautiful spies, breakfasts with NYC mayors, praise from rabbis on the solemn and sacred grounds of Auschwitz, awards from France, tearful presentations in the Krakow Opera House. Was he perhaps seduced just a little bit by all the attention? He was an intelligent, literate, and creative man, the author of four books. Could he not have fact-checked himself, even a little?

Hymas was a Patriarch of his church, a man who was expected to provide moral guideposts for others, whose telling of his wartime experiences provided just such lessons. For many of the soldiers and survivors whose stories we have found to deviate from what we think is the historical record, there are hints of self-interest in the errors made. Sometimes their memories portray them in a heroic light, as did Leo Hymas', or work to justify their world-views, as do Jack Werber's. Conspiracies depend on conspirators, and most of the involuntary impostors we have discussed may remain unindicted co-conspirators only because of the social privilege they enjoy.

While involuntary impostors may benefit in various ways from their undeserved status, how and how much do those who encourage and promote them benefit? Holocaust-related organizations that sponsor and promote public outreach through mechanisms such as Speaker's Bureaus do a great public service by bringing these stories to public attention. That public attention helps to accomplish the goals of such organizations, preserving and perpetuating memories of the Holocaust and improving the public's understanding of what happened. Contributions and donations probably result from these outreach activities, which help these organizations continue their good works. Perhaps organizations who have access to speakers whose stories are very popular find it easy to persuade themselves that there is no real reason to engage in any fact-checking. But the explicit and seemingly unconditional endorsement of these organizations contributes to the involuntariness of the impostor role some of these speakers adopt. Perhaps everyone (save those with a scrupulous devotion to the truth) benefits when there is seemingly no need to ask searching questions about the validity of survivor or liberator testimony.

The Public Fate of False Memories of the Holocaust

It is instructive in this regard, though, to consider the case of Deli Strummer. Deli Strummer was a Holocaust survivor (no connection to Buchenwald) who, like Rick Carrier and Leo Hymas, was very active in reaching out to the public with her Holocaust memories. Coincidentally, she, too began sharing her memories of the Holocaust late in life and died in 2016. Strummer was part of the Speaker's Bureau of the Baltimore Jewish Council, and was in great demand for her eloquent and emotional presentations about her Holocaust experiences. At some point in the late 1990's, though, questions began to arise about the veracity of her memories. People knowledgeable about the Holocaust found elements of her story hard to square with the historical facts as they understood them. John Holzworth, a high school teacher whose class had been visited by Strummer decided that he would discontinue such visits, as he was skeptical of her story[249]. When Strummer wanted to produce a film about her story for use in schools, the Baltimore Jewish Council decided to commission an investigation of Deli Strummer's story by Lawrence Langer and Raul Hilberg, two distinguished Holocaust scholars.

Langer and Hilberg concluded that significant elements of Strummer's story were false. Strummer's Holocaust narrative began in 1941, for example, the year she claimed to have been deported to Theresienstadt. It turned out that she had not been deported until 1943, and that her Holocaust journey included fewer camps and less time in the camps than she reported. The nine months in Auschwitz she described, for example, was eight days, if she was there at all. She claimed to have escaped death in gas chambers on multiple occasions when SS guards turned on water rather than gas, though gas chambers were not plumbed for water and there are no known instances of individuals surviving entry into a Nazi gas chamber[250], though at least one other Holocaust survivor, Gena Turgel, also claimed to have survived a gas chamber at Auschwitz when water was released instead of gas. Turgel was later at Bergen-Belsen, where she also reported having comforted Anne Frank as she perished from typhus.[251]

---

[249] Holocaust Educator has Credibility Problem, https://www.jta.org/2000/07/27/lifestyle/holocaust-educator-has-credibility-problem, retrieved September 16, 2019.

[250] Myklos Nyiszli reported an incident in which a young girl did survive gassing at Auschwitz, but she was dispatched with a bullet soon after. Nyiszli, Miklos (2011). *Auschwitz: A Doctor's Eyewitness Account*. New York: Arcade Publishing.

[251] NBC News, https://www.nbcnews.com/news/world/auschwitz-survivor-gena-turgel-walked-out-gas-chamber-alive-n293496, retrieved August 20, 2019.

The Baltimore Jewish Council removed Deli Strummer from its Speakers Bureau and asked her to stop sharing her Holocaust story at schools, though she persisted in doing so. News articles published at the time (2000) wrestled with the mixed feelings her case provoked among survivors and historians, who struggled to balance compassion for Deli Strummer with commitment to the truth, and to preserving the integrity of Holocaust studies and institutions. Openly confronting problematic survivor testimony as did the Baltimore Jewish Council seems to many (myself included) to be the best way to assure the public of the integrity of the institutions they support and of defusing attempts by deniers to use such incidents to further their destructive narratives[252]. The cases of Deli Strummer and Leo Hymas illustrate two different kinds of institutional responses to the discovery of inaccuracies in personal testimony.

It is worth mentioning again that the liberation of Buchenwald was a conspiracy of circumstance that seems, in retrospect, tailor-made to create false memories of the sort I've described above. That so many divergent yet false versions of the liberation of Buchenwald have found their way into public discussion in the years since 1945 should not, therefore, be especially surprising. But why are so many of them still circulating unchallenged and unquestioned?

The Record Corrected: Selbstbefreiung and Liberators: Fighting on Two Fronts in WWII

To understand why so many false versions of the Buchenwald liberation remain current, it is helpful to consider those versions of the liberation that now lie outside the boundaries of the generally accepted consensus. The *Selbstbefreiung* myth and the *Liberators* story are examples of versions of the liberation that are now widely recognized as false. Why have these two versions been rejected by the court of public opinion, when so many other equally problematic stories seemingly go unquestioned?

In the case of the *Selbstbefreiung* myth, it was the political re-orientation that occurred with the collapse of the Soviet Union and the re-unification of Germany that occasioned the re-examination of the Buchenwald liberation story in Germany. Because the liberation story had been appropriated and adopted as a founding myth only in the DDR, and because the *Selbstbefreiung* conflicted

---

[252] Marego Athans and Jay Apperson, THE BALTIMORE SUN, June 22, 2000, https://www.baltimoresun.com/news/bs-xpm-2000-06-22-0006220189-story.html, retrieved August 20, 2019; Libby Copeland, THE WASHINGTON POST, September 24, 2000, https://isurvived.org/4Debates/SollyGanor/DeliStrummer-discredited.html, retrieved August 20, 2019.

with the version of the liberation accepted in West Germany, some kind of reconciliation between the competing versions of the story became necessary. In re-unified Germany, commitment to historical accuracy prevailed over devotion to ideological purity and the *Selbstbefreiung* myth is now widely (though not universally) seen as what it was: a distorted version of the liberation story created and sustained to serve political and social ends.

The *Liberators* story was apparently a victim of its own success. The film received a great deal of attention because of the uplifting message it conveyed, and it was nominated for an Academy Award. Because the film was squarely and prominently in the public eye, it invited attention to itself: people began digging more deeply into the story, and soon the loose arrangement of facts and vague memories unraveled. The film was revealed as tendentious and inaccurate, and it was decided to discontinue airing the film. The Oscar went to some other film. The producers of *Liberators* rejected the consensus among historians and critics and persisted in supporting the uplifting but false version of history promoted by the film, and to this day (late 2019) it is easy to find internet sites that remain committed to *Liberators* and seem to regard its critics as motivated primarily by revisionist racism. But the *Liberators* version of the liberation of Buchenwald lies far outside the historical mainstream.

Under the Radar, Into the Crosshairs

In America, it would seem that many stories "fly under the radar" as it were, and are publicized, quoted, and passed from source to source without any real scrutiny or fact-checking, until and unless they somehow become embroiled in high-profile controversies. The stories of Harry Herder, Leo Hymas, Rick Carrier, J. Ray Clark, Jack Werber, and Rabbi Lau, as examples, have not been seriously challenged in the way the *Liberators* was challenged. Some have received significant local attention, some even national and international attention, but none have been implicated in any significant controversies, as far as I am aware. The very different fate of Edward Daily, a soldier who seems to have developed a false memory of his role in the Korean War, is instructive in this regard. Daily flew under the radar, relating his story of participating in a massacre of Korean civilians during the Korean War without challenge, until the story gained a great deal of notoriety. As the story attracted media attention, and was nominated for (and eventually awarded) a Pulitzer Prize, Daily found himself in the crosshairs.

No Gun Ri

Edward Daily came into the public spotlight because of his personal testimony about events at No Gun Ri, a small village in central South Korea. A Korean novel written in the 1990's described a horrific massacre of Korean civilians that was alleged to have happened in the early days of the Korean War. This novel came to the attention of the Associated Press, which conducted an investigation of the events and published a story about No Gun Ri that was eventually nominated for and awarded a Pulitzer Prize. Daily was interviewed as part of this investigation and told an elaborate and detailed story about his participation in the massacre. He claimed to have played a central role in the killings, operating one of two machine guns that were trained on Korean civilians. Daily was very active in the 7th US Cavalry veterans' organization, and it was this unit that had been implicated in the murders at No Gun Ri.

The case itself remains controversial. In late July 1950, under-trained and over-matched American troops were being driven south across the Korean peninsula by advancing forces from the north. Between July 26 and 29, a number of Korean civilians were killed by American soldiers under a railroad bridge near the village of No Gun Ri. Estimates of the number killed vary, and the circumstances under which the civilians were killed and whether it was a deliberate act ordered from above, or an incident more attributable to the inexperience and poor training of the soldiers, remain unclear. The Associated Press concluded that several hundred civilians were killed as a result of direct orders from higher headquarters. Robert Bateman, a serving Army officer at the time, wrote a book that directly challenged these conclusions. Bateman argued that the number of civilians killed was probably fewer than one hundred, that there were no specific orders from above to kill these civilians, and that the firing had been triggered by rifle fire from enemy soldiers hiding among the group of civilians. There is a large literature on No Gun Ri, and the interested reader will find in this incident another fascinating historical story inextricably entangled with issues of human memory. The Army conducted an extensive and thorough investigation of the matter, which concluded that something terrible happened at No Gun Ri: some number of Korean civilians was killed by American soldiers, but the report failed to resolve the details clearly enough to settle the essential points of the controversy once and for all[253].

---

[253] History News Network, " Did the Associated Press Misrepresent the Events that Happened at No Gun Ri?", http://hnn.us/articles/3626.html, retrieved July 27, 2019. This article presents an exchange between Robert Bateman, who challenged the AP's story, and Charles Hanley, one of the authors of the story.

For our purposes, though, what actually happened at No Gun Ri during those tragic days is not the main point of interest: we can honor and respect those who died without attempting to adjudicate a case that is far more complicated than the liberation of Buchenwald. It is the role of Edward Daily in the story that may help us understand more clearly both the way veterans can come to believe false narratives about their wartime experiences, and the circumstances under which such stories may, or may not, be subjected to greater scrutiny.

Robert Bateman, initially an admirer of Edward Daily, became skeptical of the version of the massacre story told by the Associated Press, and specifically of the account of the massacre provided by Edward Daily. As he began to inquire more closely into Daily's Army record, Bateman found that Daily's service record did not square with the claims he had made. Bateman discovered that Daily was not even assigned to the unit that was implicated in the shootings, the 7th US Cavalry Regiment, at the time they occurred. Edward Daily was serving not on the front lines as a machine gunner with the 7th Cavalry in July 1950, but as a jeep mechanic with the 27th Ordnance Maintenance Company. He was not assigned to the 7th Cavalry until nearly a year later. As the story developed, it was also discovered that Daily had claimed that he had been awarded certain medals for heroism, including the Distinguished Service Cross, that he had never received, had been wounded and received three Purple Hearts when he had not, and that he had been a POW when he had in fact never been captured.

Edward Daily's vivid memory of firing a machine gun into a large crowd of Korean civilians from a distance of fifty yards after having been ordered to do so, of hearing the screams and cries of the victims as they died, was false: it didn't happen. He was not even in the area when the events at No Gun Ri transpired in July, 1950. How then, could Daily make such bold and vivid claims? Was he a liar, or did he genuinely believe the story?

Michael Moss' May 31, 2000, *New York Times* article entitled "The Story Behind a Soldier's Story"[254] offers some interesting insights about the evolution of Daily's false account of his involvement in the events at No Gun Ri. As we hear Daily's story, we can consider the possibility that similar processes may have been at work in the case of some of the Buchenwald survivors and liberators who developed false memories. Moss reports that Daily didn't speak about his experiences in Korea for many years, just as, as we have seen, many Holocaust survivors and liberators did not discuss their experiences after WWII:

---

[254] Moss, Michael. The Story Behind a Soldier's Story. *New York Times*, May 31, 2000. https://archive.nytimes.com/www.nytimes.com/library/national/053100korea-massacre-ap.html, retrieved 8 July, 2000.

"Married with a son, Mr. Daily seemed to have erased Korea from his mind," his former wife, Hilda Daily, said. "It was a shock to me," she said of the Associated Press report. "He never talked about the war."[255]

But in the mid 1980's, Daily began to experience significant life problems: a divorce, work difficulties, and treatment for mental health issues. At about the same time, he quickly became very active in a 7th Cavalry veteran's organization, and served as its President for a time in the early 1990's. Daily published three books on the history of the 7th Cavalry, and actively sought stories from other veterans. When the Associated Press became interested in the No Gun Ri story, Edward Daily played a pivotal role in helping the organization identify sources by providing the AP with lists of veterans and their telephone numbers.

Some veterans contacted Daily as the AP began calling them, and Daily may have called some himself before the AP contacted them. In any case, there was apparently a great deal of communication among the veterans as the AP began constructing its narrative, and Daily was in the middle of much of that communication. In retrospect, some veterans wondered whether their memories of the events at No Gun Ri may have been implanted by Daily:

"As Associated Press reporters tried to track down the story of what happened at No Gun Ri, Mr. Daily made his own calls to fellow veterans, several of them said. "He tried to inform me how things happened," said Norman Tinkler, who is 69, a Seventh Cavalry veteran who told the news service he had emptied a machine-gun clip on defenseless people."[256]

This was a situation tailor-made for memory suggestion and misattribution. Daily was an apparently credible source, a soldier who had allegedly been wounded, captured, and decorated in combat with the 7th Cavalry who played a central role in the 7th Cavalry veterans' organization. He contacted veterans and made leading and suggestive statements about what had happened at No Gun Ri. The prestige associated with the Associated Press investigation added another dimension to the apparent credibility of the story itself. Veterans on the receiving end of these advances might very well have begun to believe Daily's version of events and construct memories consistent with that version:

"So embedded is Mr. Daily in the memories of some veterans that they still find it difficult to believe he was not with them at No Gun Ri: 'I know that Daily was there,' insisted Eugene Hesselman, another key witness in the original Associated Press account. 'I know that. I know that.'"[257]

---

[255] Ibid
[256] Ibid
[257] Ibid

But he wasn't there: there is incontrovertible documentary evidence that Edward Daily was not at No Gun Ri in July 1950. Daily's aggressive networking with 7th Cavalry veterans nevertheless created a strong impression among them that he must have been at No Gun Ri:

"Robert Gray, 74, a former second lieutenant who spent five years with the Seventh Cavalry, recalled a reunion at Fort Meade, Md., in 1996. "Daily asked me, 'Who is that?' I said, 'That's Johnny De Borde, my mortar observer.' "

A few minutes later, Mr. Gray said, Mr. Daily walked up to Mr. De Borde and said: "How in the hell are you? It's been a long, long time, buddy."

Mr. De Borde recalled today, 'And he hugged me.

I had not seen Daily before in my life.'

Speaking of Mr. Daily's account of No Gun Ri, Mr. Gray said: 'Everyone assumed he was there.

No one questioned it. He wove such a damn web.'"[258]

It seems incredible that people can come to believe, and to induce others to believe, seemingly outlandish stories about public historical events. There were clearly doubters among the 7th Cavalry fraternity all along, some of whom were quoted in Moss' *New York Times* article. But Daily himself does not appear to have been a doubter, and later seemed as mystified as everyone else as to just how all this might have happened:

"For his part, Mr. Daily said he did not dispute Army documents that show he was not at No Gun Ri, but rather spent most of the war as a mechanic and clerk behind the front lines.

'I still remember it vividly,' Mr. Daily said in an interview at his home here today — Memorial Day, which he spent in seclusion. 'But they are saying I was with a different company. I've seen their documents. How do you deny that?'

'I feel,' he said, 'like I'm in a dream world.'

Mr. Daily denied fabricating or altering any records. 'No, no, no,' he said. Asked to explain how he came to show friends citations for some of the Army's highest medals, including the Distinguished Service Cross, he said, 'I can't explain it.'"[259]

---

[258] Ibid

[259] Ibid

The same memory pitfalls that are seemingly responsible for the false memories of the veterans and survivors we have examined above with respect to Buchenwald are likely to have contributed to the development of Daily's false memories, as well. Unlike the others, though, this false narrative played a dominant role in Daily's life, organizing his self-image and defining his social position. Because this narrative was so important to him, he apparently went to great lengths to support and sustain it. Daily eventually paid a high price for his involvement in this story: when it was determined that he had not been at No Gun Ri, the Army began to investigate compensation and medical treatment he had received on the basis of apparently false claims about his service. He was eventually convicted and sentenced to twenty-one months in prison as a result. While it may strain credulity under such circumstances to continue to think that he was not deliberately lying, I remain convinced that it is possible that he fully believed in the reality of his memories.

Individuals such as the ones we have discussed have powerful emotional and, to an extent, rational incentives to believe their memories. Placing oneself at the center of momentous historical events can be rewarding: one is immediately accorded honor, respect and approbation, and sympathy. And, one immediately becomes interesting to other people: people want to hear what one says. Attention is reinforcing: "Ed [Daily] likes the limelight, he always did," said his friend Mr. Down.[260]

Moreover, one can lay claim to some moral high ground. Edward Daily met with survivors of No Gun Ri and apologized for what happened to them and their families, and as President of the 7th Cavalry organization travelled to South Dakota "to help make amends for the 1890 massacre at Wounded Knee by the Seventh Cavalry. 'Daily has this thing about apologizing,' says David Hughes, 72, of Colorado Springs, a former Seventh Cavalry officer who believes The Associated Press exaggerated what might have occurred at No Gun Ri."[261] Rabbi Lau, on the occasion of President Obama's visit to Yad Vashem, related a story about Leo Hymas tearfully apologizing to him for not getting to Buchenwald sooner. Assuming the role of apologist for wrongs committed long ago is a way to cloak oneself in moral virtue, without confessing any real personal guilt.

The personal emotional rewards may be difficult to resist, but one might think that cold, hard reason could overcome the siren song of appealing but false memories by subjecting them to at least some analysis. The stories told by

---

[260] Ibid

[261] Ibid

Harry Herder, Rick Carrier, J. Ray Clark and Leo Hymas don't square with the facts, and it takes only a few minutes of cursory investigation to uncover the difficulties with these stories, much less effort than was required to discover that Edward Daily's story was false. The individuals themselves apparently don't do this detective work because they are not skeptical of their memories: in their eyes, there are no doubts about their recollections, so why go to the trouble to vet them?

Once these stories are spread by reputable media sources and Holocaust institutions, though, the individuals involved acquire an even better reason to believe themselves: if there is any question about the stories, why do reporters or historians publicize them without question or challenge? The fact that Harry Herder's story has been incorporated into children's books and scholarly works, or that Leo Hymas' story was so prominent on the Holocaust Center for Humanity's website for so long, or that Rick Carrier was the face of the United States Holocaust Memorial Museum's "Liberators" exhibit for years (and remains so as of this writing) must eliminate or at least diminish any need such individuals might feel to fact-check themselves. Today, twenty years after Deli Strummer's story was discredited, you can find on the United States Holocaust Memorial Museum website five examples of her testimony, including a speech made to the National Security Agency in 1997, in which she presents her mistaken memories. These materials contain no annotation or warning to the listener that her story was investigated and found to be false. Many people must think that reputable organizations such as these naturally verify and validate what they print and publicize, but that is just not so.

There have been lonely voices attempting to correct these false stories as they appear. Eric Schulte wrote about Buchenwald myths many years ago[262], and Flint Whitlock responded to a blog post in 2012, on the occasion of Rick Carrier's participation in the March of the Living at Auschwitz, to point out that Carrier did not liberate Buchenwald as he had claimed, citing some of the same inconsistencies in his story that I noted above[263]. But as we have seen, fact-checking such stories by journalists or institutions mainly seems to take place on an exceptional basis: sometimes when questions are raised in the context of a prestigious award, such as an Oscar or a Pulitzer Prize, but sometimes simply

---

[262] Buchenwald Liberation Myths: 1945-2013, https://blogs.timesofisrael.com/buchenwald-liberation-myths-1945-2013/, retrieved September 14, 2019.

[263] The American liberator who literally blew the lock off the Buchenwald gate, https://furtherglory.wordpress.com/2012/02/10/the-american-liberator-who-literally-blew-the-lock-off-the-buchenwald-gate/, retrieved September 14, 2019.

because alert consumers of information question or challenge them, as in the case of Deli Strummer. When the potential lack of credibility of a particular story threatens the credibility of institutions, a belated process of hard-nosed investigating may be begun. Otherwise, the public is left pretty much on its own to figure these things out. Time after time, we have seen false stories naively accepted by powerful media institutions unravel after they have been presented to the public as true. There have been several such instances in recent years related to the Holocaust, and there is no reason to think that there won't be more in the future.

We live in an era in which it is increasingly easy to produce and consume information. Most of this information is unfiltered. There were once barriers that made it difficult for an individual to publish books or produce television content, but now there is self-publishing, the internet, YouTube. The book you are reading is self-published: whatever scrutiny it was subjected to before publishing was organized by me, and you can and should judge for yourself how effectively that was done. If you have read this far, though, you perhaps realize that the scrutiny applied by traditional journalism and publishing may not be all that it has been cracked up to be by journalists and publishers.

The Buchenwald liberation story is, as I have mentioned, one that is especially susceptible to misremembering, for reasons that I have already outlined. This should not lead us to lower our guard when it comes to testimony about other events, however. The Buchenwald liberation was a kind of "perfect storm", or at least a pretty good storm, from the memory viewpoint, but there were many other events that were similarly vulnerable to misremembering. The reality is that some of the personal testimony we hear about the Holocaust, from survivors or from soldiers and "liberators", is mistaken. When we pick up a survivor or liberator memoir, we simply have no way of knowing how much of what it contains is accurate, unless we undertake to do our own due diligence to verify the contents. One take-away from this book ought to be that the survivor or veteran stories featured in your newspaper, or on your television, or on the internet, or even at a Holocaust museum or institution, may be true, or may not. The plain truth is that they have most likely been accepted at face-value by the outlet presenting them: the aging survivor or veteran has probably not been asked to provide any documentation or proof that his or her story is true.

A look at this one day in Holocaust history, April 11, 1945, the day of the liberation of Buchenwald, has revealed many, many mistakes, errors, and inaccuracies in the way that day has been presented to the public. Some of these mistakes have resulted from reporters or journalists innocently accepting the statements of survivors or liberators at face value; some have resulted from

Holocaust institutions failing to check even the most basic facts in the testimonies they present; we have found mis-labeled photographs, children's books that repeat false memories and inadvertently cite a Holocaust denier, even a web-page banner at the nation's most prestigious Holocaust-related institution, the United States Holocaust Memorial Museum, showcasing as the face of liberators a veteran whose memory of liberating Buchenwald is almost certainly false. These are but a few examples.

That mistakes of memory occur in circumstances like the ones in which survivors and liberators found themselves is not at all surprising: human memory can be expected to produce such errors. That these errors have been presented and perpetuated for as long as they have by reputable Holocaust institutions doing important work is a bit more surprising, but far from shocking. Preservation has been the first priority as survivors and veterans have grown older: testimony is a perishable resource, and as the number of living survivors and liberators diminishes each day, it is vital that we capture their recollections for posterity.

Insofar as posterity may be interested in knowing which of the testimonies (or which parts of testimonies) we bequeath to them are true and which are not, it seems especially important to me that we be open and honest when we find errors in the material we have preserved and presented. It is important for two reasons: First, publicly acknowledging those instances in which testimony can be shown to be mistaken should alert users of such material that they have a duty to fact-check such material as best they can. Second, openly acknowledging mistakes is vital to preserving the integrity of the very institutions on which we rely to transmit the lessons of the Holocaust to the future. A great many politicians and public figures have discovered that one's response to a mistake or misstep can be far more consequential than the mistake or misstep itself. One point of this book is that there is no need for defensiveness: mistakes, especially those involving memory, are frequent and natural occurrences. I will not be surprised (or pleased) to learn at some point that there are mistakes in this book: I hope when that happens that I will acknowledge them and apologize. Our duty is to push our egos to the back and keep our commitment to truth front and center. Better to embrace and explain our mistakes than to try to paper over them, sweep them under the rug, or quietly move on without acknowledging them.

Historians make considerable use of personal testimony, and some may bristle at the clearly (and deliberately) unbalanced picture of personal testimony this book presents. This book is about misremembering, so naturally the focus is on personal testimony that has been, to a greater or lesser degree, shown to be unreliable. I will repeat now that there is a considerable amount of personal testimony about Buchenwald, the liberation, and of course other topics that is accurate and reliable: perhaps most of it is. The trouble is that accurate and inaccurate accounts are not distinguished as such in search engine results, or in library catalogs, in your local newspaper, or even at Holocaust-related museums and institutions. It is up to you to evaluate and assess the information you consume, uncomfortable and awkward as that may sometimes feel: you can't depend on anyone else to do it for you. Not even me.

APPENDIX

Leon Adler

http://projects.leadr.msu.edu/usandtheholocaust/exhibits/show/american-jewish-liberators-mat/leon-adler

There is a brief video in the USC Shoah archive of Leon Adler recounting a moving story that does not involve Buchenwald. The above URL contains the following: "Leon Adler describing how he felt after liberating the Buchenwald concentration camp less than an hour after the Germans fled… I was enraged, especially when I saw what they did to those people in that burning shack setting it on fire. The cruelty. First I was shocked, then I remember walking around. I was kicking things. I was frustrated I couldn't do anything about it." This description may refer to the massacre at Gardelegen .

Andy Anderson

https://karakavensky.com/wwii-combat-medic-andy-anderson/

Andy Anderson reports that he was a medic who was part of 3rd Army and arrived at Buchenwald April 11, where he remained to care for the inmates for some time.

Kenneth Berthold

https://www.heritagefl.com/story/2014/03/07/features/incredible-reunion-buchenwald-survivor-and-his-us-army-liberator/2325.html

The above website contains the following: "By 3 p.m., on April 11, American soldiers walked into Roth's barracks. 'The messiah had arrived,' Roth proclaimed. 'These two young battle-hardened soldiers looked at this group of kids weighing 75-80 pounds who were nothing but mere skeletons. These two soldiers who had seen horrible death on the battlefield broke down, they could not comprehend the horror they saw at Buchenwald.' Unbeknownst to Roth or the audience, CUFI event planner Gabriel Aviles had received a call from an Orlando man who saw a community event listing in the Orlando Sentinel for Roth's talk. This Orlando man said he was part of the American unit that liberated Buchenwald on April 11, 1945.Corporal Kenneth Berthold, just three or four years older than Roth, was with the 6th Armored Division of the U.S. Third Army. He brought a photo album to the lecture with pictures he had taken inside the Buchenwald death camp."

Don Cote

USC Shoah Foundation Interview, reviewed onsite at the United States Holocaust Memorial Museum. Cote was not a liberator of Buchenwald, but passes on two incorrect stories he says he heard from prisoners: that the mayor of Buchenwald and his wife committed suicide after visiting the camp (this probably refers to the mayor of Ohrdruf) and that the camp commander was a woman named "Irma" who made lampshades of tattooed skin.

Martin Damgaard

http://www.fpp.co.uk/Auschwitz/Buchenwald/images_Damgaard/index.html

The above website contains the following: "ILLUSTRATED here are two examples of the collection which includes about 30 pictures. — the first is my father outside of the camp, on liberation day itself. My father was **Captain Martin J. Damgaard**, 602nd Combat Engineer Battalion (Camouflage)." The photo shows a number of soldiers, and appears to have been taken after liberation.

Leslie Leonard Fleisher

https://www.holocaustcenter.org/visit/library-archive/oral-history-department/oral-histories-f-j/fleisher-leslie-leonard/

This website lists Leslie Leonard Fleisher as a liberator of Buchenwald, but provides little detail, save the following: "They found that they were one and a half miles north of Buchenwald Concentration Camp. No one knew a thing about the camp. Mr. Fleisher said that the stench was so horrid that it "gets in your throat and tastebuds." He was in one of the first groups to enter Buchenwald. Mr. Fleisher saw piles of skeletons and bones, canvas cloths thrown over, millions of flies and a thick odor. They went into the hospital, wanting to remove the patients out of that "hell hole" to Weimar where medical staff could help as they were coming through. The hospital was like a dry-goods store. It was a wooden building filled with people wearing black and white striped pajamas, stacked up, feet against the walls and filthy conditions. 'Inhumanity of man to man.'".

Arthur Goldberg

https://www.holocaustcenter.org/visit/library-archive/oral-history-department/oral-histories-f-j/goldberg-arthur/

The above website contains the following: "Goldberg entered Europe at Le Havre about a month after D-Day and was involved in the European campaign through France and Germany as part of HQ Company, 1270th Combat Engineer Battalion, Third Army. While near the city of Weimar, his outfit came across a walled-in enclosure opposite a small, neat German village. The company was ordered to enter the enclosure. Until that point, Goldberg did not know that he was entering Buchenwald concentration camp, nor did he have knowledge of the existence of any concentration or labor camps. Goldberg believes his company was the second U.S. military unit after the initial liberators to enter the camp, probably a few hours after liberation."

Sol Goldstein

http://libraryguides.goucher.edu/c.php?g=321002&p=2354932

The above website contains a taped interview with Sol Goldstein and transcripts of the interviews. This is taken from the second transcript. CM/EG are the interviewers, SG is Sol Goldstein:

"And we made a left turn on this road, in this wooded area, and lo and behold, there was this big, high chimney, a red brick chimney, and white smoke billowing out of it, and as we got closer, the smell became more intense. We turned the corner, made a right turn, and there in front of us, it was maybe a quarter of a mile, half a mile away, was this fence, huge fence. And I took my glasses and I could see that there was like barbed wire on top and it looked like there were 3 fences, 1, 2. I could count only 3 fences, 1, 2, 3, and I—I couldn't imagine what it was, and I turned to one of my fellows, a corporal, and I said, "You know what? I think we're about to liberate a prisoner of war camp," because up to that point, no one had ever told us there was such a thing as a concentration camp...So, you have to understand something. This place where we were was Buchenwald concentration camp...Now, we were at one of the satellite camps, and when we saw these fencing and one of my guys said, "I think it looks like an entrance up there to the right," and I said, "No, we're not going to go up there. We're going through the fence. So I moved the cars around, put the half track in front, and we plowed right through the fences."

Herbert Gorfinkle

https://vitabrevis.americanancestors.org/2015/04/crossing-paths-two-stories-of-buchenwald/

The above website contains the following:

"In the fall of 1944 Herbert shipped out to London, then to France and Holland, where he was entrenched as an army photographer and Tech 5 combat engineer in an intelligence unit until the winter of 1945. On April 11 of that year, he arrived at Buchenwald with the 9th Armored Infantry Battalion. Herbert, who typically wrote open, guileless letters home, did not mention Buchenwald at all. It was not until two months later, in June, that he began to talk about what he saw: 'The people were slaves, in some factories I've seen the chains they used to tie the people to their machines.'"

Barry Lewis

https://hamodia.com/2013/05/26/holocaust-survivor-liberator-meet-for-first-time/

The above website contains the following:

"When Lewis first saw Buchenwald, he was a young man but an experienced soldier. He was born in Dover, England, left home and began his military service with the British merchant marines as a teen. He later landed in America and joined the army. As a staff sergeant, Lewis landed on the beaches of Normandy on D-Day and had been fighting for nearly a year. He was among the first wave of soldiers who liberated Buchenwald."

John Macinko

https://www.dailycamera.com/2012/06/01/john-macinko/

The above website contains the following:

"The highlight of his service was arriving at Buchenwald Concentration Camp the same day as the 5th Ranger Battalion liberated the camp. He gave a number of talks and slide show presentations on Nazi atrocities."

George "Butch" Newsom

http://chabadinfo.com/news/son-of-buchenwald-liberator-speaks-at-yeshiva/

The above website contains the following:

"A Few weeks ago, **Mr. George "Butch" Newsom**, Cincinnati Ohio, passed away at the ripe old age of 94 years old. Mr. Newsom was the first American soldier to enter Buchenwald during its' liberation. He was the one that took pictures of the carnage that he saw, so that the world should know and never deny the truth of what happened.

While liberating Buchenwald, Mr. Newsom met a young teenager of about 14 and became close with him. This young teenager later wrote a book about his experiences in the camps during the holocaust. He called Mr. Newsom to help fill in the blanks, as he suffered from malnutrition and could not remember certain details. Mr. Newsom helped him with his book. The name of the book is Night and this young teenager is Eli Weisel.[sic] They communicated over the years and would meet whenever Mr. Weisel came to Cincinnati."

Lucien Rego

http://archivesblog.lib.umassd.edu/2015/04/22/70th-anniversary-of-the-liberation-of-the-concentration-camps/

The above website contains the following:

"Lucien Rego was born in Fall River on April 15, 1925. Mr. Rego was drafted into the army on August 6, 1943. He spent most of the war overseas as a Private, PFC, seeing combat with the 5th armored division as a Demolition Man. From January to June 1944 he was responsible for packing parachutes on the planes with ammunition in front for the underground in England. He was with a tank force and also fought in the Battle of the Bulge from the 16th of December until January. As he approached Buchenwald in late March 1945, he remarked about the odor all around. His group was there long enough to take pictures. This was a camp of all men."

Tony Rossetti

https://www.azcentral.com/story/news/local/scottsdale/2014/11/02/arizona-republic-article-brings-together-holocaust-survivor-liberator/18393321/

This website contains the following: "Rossetti, now 89, was among the men interviewed for the article. He was assigned as a driver for one of Patton's colonels and was among the soldiers who liberated Buchenwald."

https://www.deseretnews.com/article/765618633/Arizona-mans-search-reunites-WWII-soldiers.html

This website places Tony Rossetti at Buchenwald the day after liberation: "They were there the morning after American soldiers liberated Germany's Buchenwald concentration camp in April 1945."

Don Schoo

https://www.youtube.com/watch?v=nKKwNCqt3bYGives

This video interview describes Don Schoo's experience at Buchenwald, which sounds as though it occurred several days after the liberation.

Milton Silva

http://archivesblog.lib.umassd.edu/2015/04/22/70th-anniversary-of-the-liberation-of-the-concentration-camps/

Milton Silva is listed as a liberator on this website:

"Some of the local liberators of Buchenwald from our area were Judge Milton Silva, Lucien Rego, and Martin Damgaard."

But it is clear from other sources, such as this one:

https://scholarcommons.usf.edu/cgi/viewcontent.cgi?referer=https://www.google.com/&httpsredir=1&article=1134&context=hgstud_oh

that Milton Silva arrived at Buchenwald a few days after liberation[265].

---

[265] The Liberators: America's Witnesses to the Holocaust (New York: Bantam Books, 2010) and Concentration Camp Liberators Oral History Project, University of South Florida Libraries, ©2010 Michael Hirsh. Milton R. Silva oral history interview by Michael Hirsh, July 18, 2008, https://scholarcommons.usf.edu/cgi/viewcontent.cgi?referer=https://www.google.com/&httpsredir=1&article=1134&context=hgstud_oh, retrieved 8 July 2019.

Works Cited

Abdul-Jabbar, Kareem. *Brothers in Arms: The Epic Story of the 761st Tank Battalion, WWII's Forgotten Heroes.* (New York, Harlem Moon, 2005).

Abzug, Robert H. I*nside the Vicious Heart: Americans and the Liberation of Nazi Concentration Camps.* (New York, Oxford University Press).

Ast, Theresa. *Confronting the Holocaust: American Soldiers Enter Concentration Camps.* (Georgia, Nomenklature Publications, 2013).

Baumslag, Naomi. *Murderous Medicine: Nazi Doctors, Human Experimentation, and Typhus.* (Washington DC, Baumslag, 2005).

Bender, Benjamin. *Glimpses: Through Holocaust and Liberation.* (Berkeley, North Atlantic Books, 1995).

Black, Robert W. *Rangers in WWII.* (New York, Ballantine Books, 1992).

Browning, Christopher.*Collected Memories: Holocaust History and Post-War Testimony.* (Madison, WI; University of Wisconsin Press, 2003).

Buchenwald: Mahnung und Verpflichtung (Dokumente und Berichte). Berlin, VEB Deustscher Verlag der Wissenschaften, 1983).

Burney, Christopher. *The Dungeon Democracy.* (New York, Duell, Sloan and Pearce, 1946).

Carlebach, Emil, Gurenewald, Paul, Roeder, Hellmuth, Schmidt, Willy, and Vielhauer, Walter. *Buchenwald: Ein Konzentrationslager.* (Berlin, Dietz Verlag, 1988).

Carrier, Frederick Goss. *A Teenager's Experience In the First Wave Assault Onto Utah Beach*, April 25, 1994. US Army Center for Military History Archive, Historical Resources Collection, Part II, 314.81.

Chamberlin, Brewster S., and Marcia Feldman, editors. *The Liberation of the Nazi Concentration Camps 1945: Eyewitness Accounts of the Liberators.* (Washington, DC: United States Holocaust Memorial Council, 1987).

Clark, J. Ray. *Journey to Hell: The Fiery Furnaces of Buchenwald.* (USA, Pentland Press, 1996).

Dawidowicz, Lucy S. *A Holocaust Reader.* (Springfield, NJ, Behrman House, 1976).

Elsner, P. (2017). 75 years after Erich Wagner's doctoral dissertation: "A Contribution to the Issue of Tattooing" - scientific misconduct in Nazi Germany.

Journal der Deutschen Dermatologischen Gesellschaft - Journal of the German Society of Dermatology : JDDG, (15)11, 1152-1154 .

Fleck, Egon and Edward Tenenbaum, *Buchenwald: A Preliminary Report.* Headquarters 12th Army Group Publicity and Psychological Warfare, 24 April 1945.

Gedenkstätte Buchenwald (Eds.) *Buchenwald Concentration Camp 1937-1945: A Guide to the Permanent Historical Exhibition.* (Gottingen: Wallstein Verlag, 2004).

Gerry, Maryanne, and Hayne, Harlene. *Do Justice and Let the Sky Fall: Elizabeth F. Loftus and Her Contributions to Science, Law, and Academic Freedom (Psychology Press Festschrift Series)*, (London, Psychology Press, 2006).

Greenberg, Cheryl Lynn. *Troubling the Waters.* (Princeton, Princeton University Press, 2006).

Gros, Louis. *Survivor of Buchenwald: My Personal Odyssey Through Hell.* (Brule, Wisconsin; Cable Publishing, 2012).

Gross, Jan, with Irena Grudzinska Gross, *Golden Harvest*, (Oxford and New York: Oxford University Press, 2012).

Hackett, David A. *The Buchenwald Report.* (Boulder: Westview Press, 1995).

Hirsh, Michael. "The Liberators: Americas Witnesses to the Holocaust". (New York, Penguin, 2010).

Hofmann, George F. *The Super Sixth: History of the 6th Armored Division in World War II and its post-war Association.* (Louisville, Kentucky: Sixth Armored Division Association, 1975).

Jacobsen, Mark. *The Lampshade: A Holocaust detective Story from Buchenwald to New Orleans.* (New York, Simon and Schuster, 2010).

Kathleen Shelby Boyett, "*Cannon Fodder on Utah Beach*", (Charlotte, NC, Searching Mink Publications, 2018).

Kenneth H. Garn, "*Storming Ashore: One Soldier's Adventures in the First Engineer Special Brigade 1942-1945 Including D-Day*", (Huntington, WV, University Editions, 1998).

Klotman, Phyllis R., and Cutler, Janet K. *Struggles for Representation: African American Film and Video.* (Bloomington, Indiana University Press, 1999).

Kogon, Eugen. *The Theory and Practice of Hell: The German Concentration Camps and the System Behind Them.* (New York: Farrar, Staruss and Giroux, 1950).

Langbein, Hermann. *Against all Hope: Resistance in the Nazi Concentration Camps.* (St. Paul, MN: Paragon House, 2009).

Lau, Israel Meir. *Out of the Depths: The Story of a Child of Buchenwald Who Returned Home at Last.* (New York: Sterling, 2005).

Levi, Primo. *If This is a Man.* (London, Abacus, 2013).

Levi, Primo. *The Drowned and the Saved.* (New York, Simon and Schuster, 1988).

Loftus, E. F., & Palmer, J. C. (1974). Reconstruction of automobile destruction: An example of the interaction between language and memory. *Journal of Verbal Learning and Verbal Behavior,* 13(5), 585-589.

Mastroianni, George. *Of Mind and Murder: Toward a More Comprehensive Psychology of the Holocaust.* (New York, Oxford University Press, 2018).

McManus, John C. *Hell Before Their Very Eyes: American Soldiers Liberate Concentration Camps in Germany, April 1945,* (Baltimore, Johns Hopkins University Press, 2015).

Moeller, Juergen. *Konzentrationslager Buchenwald Weimar im April 1945: Die amerikanische Besetzung von Weimar Wer befreite Buchenwald?,* (Bad Langensalza, Verlag Rockstuhl, 2017).

Moser, Joseph F., and Baron, Gerald R. *A Fighter Pilot in Buchenwald: The Joe Moser Story.* (All Clear Publications, 2009).

Neurath, Paul Martin. (Christian Fleck and Nico Stehr, Eds.) *The Society of Terror: Inside the Dachau and Buchenwald Concentration Camps.* (Boulder: Paradigm Publishers, 2005).

Niven, Bill. *The Buchenwald Child: Truth, Fiction and Propaganda.* (Rochester, Camden House, 2007).

Nyiszli, Miklos. *Auschwitz: A Doctor's Eyewitness Account.* (New York: Arcade Publishing, 2011).

O'Donnell, Patrick. *Beyond Valor.* (New York, Touchstone, 2001).

Oster, Henry, and Ford, Dexter. *The Kindness of the Hangman: Even in Hell, There is Hope.* (Manhattan Beach, CA, Higgins Bay Press, 2014).

Overesch, Manfred. *Buchenwald und die DDR: oder Die Suche nach Selbstlegitimation.* (Goettingen, Vandenhoeck and Ruprecht,1995).

Porat, Dan. *The Boy; A Holocaust Story.* (New York, Hill and Wang, 2010).

Potter, Lou. *Liberators: Fighting on Two Fronts in World War II.* (New York, Harcourt-Brace Jovanovich, 1992).

Robinson, Donald B. Communist Atrocities at Buchenwald. *The American Mercury,* October, 1946.

Roseman, Mark. (1999). "Surviving testimony: Truth and Inaccuracy in Holocaust Testimony". *The Journal of Holocaust Education,* **8(1)**, 1-20.

Schacter, Daniel L. *The Seven Sins of Memory.* (Boston, Houghton Mifflin, 2001).

Seipp, Adam R. "Buchenwald Stories: Testimony, Military History, and the American Encounter with the Holocaust". *Journal of Military History,* **79,** 721-744.

Sherman, Jill. *Eyewitness to the Liberation of Buchenwald.* (Mankato, MN; The Child's World, 2016).

Solasko, F. (Ed.) *War Behind Barbed Wire.* (Moscow, Foreign Languages Publishing House, 1959).

Stein, Sabine and Harry. *Buchenwald: A Tour of the Memorial Site.* Weimar/Buchenwald, 1993. Brochure in the author's possession.

Stern, Kenneth S. *Liberators: A Background Report.* The American Jewish Committee, Institute of Human Relations, 165 E. 56th Street, NY 10022. Feb. 10, 1993.

Suderland, Maja. *Inside Concentration Camps: Social Life at the Extremes.* (Cambridge, Polity Press, 2013).

Weindling, Paul. Victims and Survivors of Nazi Human Experiments: *Science and Suffering in the Holocaust.* (London, Bloomsbury, 2015).

Weinstock, Eugene. Beyond the Last Path.: *A Buchenwald Survivor's Story.* (New York, Boni and Gaer, 1946).

Werber, Jack. *Saving Children: Diary of a Buchenwald Survivor and Rescuer.* (New Brunswick, NJ; Transaction Publishers, 2014).

Whitlock, Flint.Buchenwald: *Hell on a Hilltop,* (Brule, WI, Cable Publishing, 2014).

Wilson, J. P., Hugenberg, K., & Rule, N. O. (2017). Racial bias in judgments of physical size and formidability: From size to threat. *Journal of Personality and Social Psychology,* 113(1), 59-80.

Index

Military Units

4th Armored Division 11, 15, 16, 17, 18, 19, 20, 21, 22, 23, 25, 29, 30, 31, 49, 50, 80, 101, 115, 122
5th Ranger Battalion 82, 156
6th Armored Divisions 11, 15, 16, 19, 115
7th US Cavalry 144, 145
9th Armored Infantry Battalion 13, 15, 30, 156
12th Army Group 11, 25, 29, 42, 43, 160
12th Army Group Headquarters 25, 29
21st Army Group 11
37th Tank Battalion 17, 18, 19, 20, 30
58th Field Hospital 135
80th Infantry Division iii, 12, 15, 16, 29, 80, 86, 100, 105, 110, 112
97th Infantry Division iv, 89, 90, 92
120th Evacuation Hospital iii, 31, 51, 53, 86
183rd Combat Engineer Battalion 56, 65, 72, 122
761st Tank Battalion 61, 64, 65, 70, 71, 80, 122, 159
1981 Liberator's Conference 37

A

Aachen 104
ABC miniseries Holocaust xiv, 36, 56
Academy Award 61, 143
Adam Seipp iv, 55, 112, 113
African-Americans 65, 71, 81
Alexandra Przyrembel 34
Alex Gross vii, 69, 72, 73, 74, 108
Alfred Toombs 43
American Jewish Committee 62, 63, 162
Andernach 102, 103
Anne Frank 141
anti-Semitism 78
Apollo Theater 61
Appelplatz 74
Arbeit Macht Frei 33, 36, 57, 83
Army nurse 136
Asa R. Gordon 64
Associated Press 144, 145, 146, 148
Association Francaise Buchenwald Dora et Kommandos 21
Atlanta Daily World 72
Augsburg 35
Auschwitz 3, 4, 6, 7, 40, 74, 75, 77, 83, 97, 111, 128, 140, 141, 149, 154, 161

B

badges 6
Bad Sulza 25
Baltimore Jewish Council xvi, 141, 142
Benjamin Bender vii, 59, 63, 69, 71, 115
Bergen-Belsen 2, 33, 77, 78, 141
Bill DeBlasio 97
Bill Justis 82
Bill Niven 40
Binjamin Wilkomirski 124
binoculars 5, 26, 27, 28
Bitch of Buchenwald 34, 74, 106, 130
Bonn 92
Bristol Productions 91
Bruno Apitz 40, 58
Buchenwald iii, iv, vii, viii, xii, xiii, xiv, xv, xvi, 1, 2, 3, 4, 5, 6, 7, 8, 9, 10, 11, 12, 13, 14, 15, 16, 18, 19, 20, 21, 22, 23, 24, 25, 26, 27, 28, 29, 30, 31, 32, 33, 34, 35, 36, 37, 38, 39, 40, 41, 42, 43, 44, 45, 46, 47, 48, 49, 50, 51, 52, 53, 54, 55, 56, 57, 58, 59, 60, 61, 62, 63, 64, 65, 67, 68, 69, 70, 71, 72, 73, 74, 75, 76, 77, 78, 80, 81, 82, 83, 84, 85,

86, 87, 88, 89, 90, 91, 92, 93, 94, 95, 96, 97, 98, 99, 100, 101, 102, 103, 104, 105, 106, 107, 108, 109, 110, 111, 112, 113, 114, 115, 116, 122, 123, 125, 126, 130, 133, 135, 136, 137, 138, 141, 142, 143, 145, 148, 149, 150, 151, 153, 154, 155, 156, 157, 158, 159, 160, 161, 162
bulldozers 33, 77, 78
Buna rubber 4
Bundesrepublik Deutschland BRD 38
Buttstadt 25

C

Camp Elder Hans Eiden 12
Captain Davidson 23, 25
Carl Vaernet 5
Charles Davidson 24
Charles Rangel 61
Chevalier of the Legion of Honour 97
Christopher Browning 125
Christopher Burney 40, 43
clandestine home-made radio 114
Claude Lanzmann 56
clinicians 124
clock over the main gate 12, 109
Cold War 36, 38, 41, 45
Collective Memory 38
Cologne 77, 93, 94, 102
Combat Engineer Battalions 104
Commandant 5, 27, 33, 48, 113
Communism 40, 42, 43
computer memory 127, 130, 133
computers 127, 130, 132
Creighton Abrams 18
crematory 33, 111
Criminals 1

D

Daasdorf 18
Dachau xiv, 3, 10, 33, 34, 56, 61, 62, 65, 84, 161

Daniel Schacter 79
Dan Rather 97
Dan Stone 87
David Dinkins 61
David Hackett 10, 25, 30
DAW 3, 5, 99
D-Day 101, 102, 103, 104, 155, 156, 160
death marches 2, 60, 93
Deli Strummer xvi, 141, 142, 149, 150
Dennis Wile 58
Denstedt 19
Denzel Washington 61
DEST 3, 5
Deutsche Demokratische Republik DDR 38
Displaced Persons 79
Documentary evidence 122
Donald R. Robinson 43
Donald Trump 77
Douglas Kelling 56
Douglass Institute of Government 64
Driesch 117, 120
Dr. Rutherford 78
dysentery 9

E

East Germany iii, vii, xiv, xv, 8, 35, 36, 38, 39, 41, 42, 45, 46, 47, 50, 51, 52, 54, 55, 59, 63
Edmund Coates 24
Edward A. Tenenbaum 25, 26
Edward Daily 143, 145, 146, 147, 148, 149
Edward R. Murrow 32
Effektenkammer 15
Egon W. Fleck 25, 26
Eisenach 67, 72
elaboration 130, 131, 134, 137
elaborative rehearsal 131
Elie Wiesel 69
Elizabeth Loftus 134
Ella Matson Lindsay 135, 136, 137
Emmanuel Desard 18, 21, 22, 31
Emory University 57, 72

encoding 126, 127, 132, 134
epidemiology 79
Erfurt 16, 50
Erich Wagner 34, 159
Ernst Haberland 51
Ernst Thälmann 52
Erpeler Ley 102
Ettersberg iii, 1, 14, 15, 19, 46, 68, 78
Eugene Weinstock 110, 115
eugenics 78
Eugen Kogon 10, 38, 42
experimental psychology 125
extermination camps 3, 4
Eyewitness testimony xi

F

False Memories vii, viii, 33, 135, 141
Fascism 40
Federal Republic of Germany
 FRG 8, 38
Field Marshal Bernard Montgomery 11
Field Marshal Walter Model 11
Final Solution 5
First Army 11
First Engineer Special Brigade 103, 104, 160
F.L. Alcindor 64, 70
Flint Whitlock iv, xii, 10, 115, 149
Flossenburg xiv, 90, 137
forgetting curve 130
Fort Eben Emael 103, 104
Frankfurt 115
Franz Eichhorn 16
Fred Crawford 57, 58, 72
Frederic Keffer 13, 14, 18, 30, 75, 123
Frederick Goss Carrier 96, 101
Free French 21, 31, 48, 50
Freezing and re-warming experiments 84

G

gas chamber 85, 141
Gauleiter 98, 100

Gedenkstätte Buchenwald 1, 10, 46, 160
Gena Turgel 141
General Dwight D. Eisenhower xii, 4, 38, 113, 114, 136
General George Patton 11, 77, 105, 136
General Omar Bradley 11
General Theodore Roosevelt 101
George Blackburn 37
George Hofmann 14
Georgia Commission on the Holocaust 67
Georg Konrad Morgen 109
Gerald Myers 110
German Army Group B 11
German Democratic Republic 8, 9, 38
 GDR 8, 9, 38
Germany iii, vii, xiv, xv, 1, 8, 11, 13, 15, 32, 33, 34, 35, 36, 37, 38, 39, 41, 42, 43, 44, 45, 46, 47, 48, 50, 51, 52, 54, 55, 59, 63, 72, 77, 81, 82, 88, 90, 91, 104, 105, 110, 116, 117, 120, 129, 131, 136, 142, 143, 155, 158, 159, 161
Gestapo 43, 46
Goethe 26, 70
Gottschalk 15, 18, 30, 75
greens 6, 8
Grosskromsdorf 19
Gunskirchen Lager 64
Gustloff-Werke 3
Gypsies 6, 8

H

Haberndorf 18
Hans 12, 16, 17, 21, 23, 31, 47, 50, 108, 109
Hans Eiden 12, 16, 17, 21, 23, 31, 47, 50
Harry Stein 10
Haus Buchenwald 109
Heinrich Nett 109
Henry Kamm 71, 72
Henry Oster vii, 69, 75, 77
Hermann Langbein 114
Hermann Pister 5, 12, 48

Herschel Schacter 36
history iii, xii, xv, xvi, 2, 9, 10, 38, 39, 40, 41, 54, 58, 63, 64, 66, 72, 79, 81, 84, 87, 101, 105, 136, 137, 139, 143, 146, 150, 154, 155, 158
Hitler xiv, 5, 77, 94, 102, 105, 136
Hitler Youth 94, 136
Hollis C. Alpert 13
Holocaust Center for Humanity 95, 137, 138, 149
Holocaust denial xii, xvi, 87
Holocaust doubters and deniers xii
Holocaust Encyclopedia 6, 96
Holy Cross Cemetery
  Malden 120
homosexuals 1, 6
Hottelstedt iii, 12, 15, 17
Hoyt 15, 18, 30
human memory 54, 78, 79, 124, 127, 130, 133, 139, 144, 151

I

Ilse Koch 33, 34, 35, 58, 74, 77, 84, 104, 106, 108, 109, 110, 115
Individual Deceased Personnel File 116
individual memories xiv, 35, 81
Institute for Historical Review 87
international camp committee 17
Internationale Lagerkomitee
  ILK 39
internet 56, 57, 75, 82, 86, 88, 95, 97, 105, 107, 134, 135, 137, 138, 143, 150
Involuntary Impostor Syndrome viii, 139, 140
Irving Roth 97
Israel 64, 65, 69, 70, 71, 95, 161
Ittenbach 117

J

Jack Werber viii, 107, 115, 140, 143
James V. DeMarco iv, 91, 116, 120, 125
Jan Gross xv

Jedem das Seine 36, 74, 83, 98, 111, 112
Jeffrey Goldberg 63
Jehovah's witnesses 1
Jehovah's Witnesses 61, 108
Jena 5
Jesse Jackson 61, 62
Jewish Community Relations Council 63
Jews 1, 4, 6, 8, 26, 27, 60, 63, 72, 74, 77
Jim Crow 67
John C. McManus 34, 131
John Glustrom 58
John Holzworth 141
John Tagliabue 59
Jorge Semprun 26
Journal of Historical Review 87
J. Ray Clark viii, 105, 138, 143, 149
Jürgen Möller 15, 19, 21

K

kapos 39
Kareem Abdul-Jabbar 64, 65, 70
Karl Koch 5, 109
Kenneth Stern 62
Klaus Trostorff 46
Kommunistische Partei Deutschlands
  KDP
    German Communist Party 40
Krakow Opera House 97, 140
Kristallnacht 1
Kubelwagen 101, 102, 105

L

labor camps 3, 4, 155
lager archipelago 129
lampshades 4, 34, 58, 75, 84, 106, 130, 136, 154
Lawrence Langer xvi, 141
Le Havre 104, 155
Lehesten 82
Leonard Lubin 37, 131
Leonard Smith 64, 67, 71
Leon Bass 56, 57, 63, 67, 68

Leo Pine 57, 58
Leopold Hansen, 50
Liberators: Fighting on Two Fronts in WWII viii, xiv, 61, 142
lie detectors 123
Little Camp 3, 9, 41, 60, 93, 97, 99, 100
Lucius Clay 34
Lucy Dawidowicz 78
Ludendorff Bridge 92, 101, 102
Ludwigsburg 109
Lynn Ramsey 100

M

M-1 Abrams Main Battle Tank 18
Maja Suderland 8, 10
Maj Reed 29
Manfred Overesch 46
March of the Living 97, 149
Margaret Bourke-White 33, 100
Margraten 117, 118, 119
Marianne Ellenbogen 124
Mark Roseman 124
Mark Schulte 61, 62
Mary DeMarco 118, 119
Maurice Halbwachs 41, 50
Mauthausen xiv, 37, 64
medical experimentation 5
memory wars 124
Michael Dukakis 62
Michael Hirsh 111, 158
Michael Moss 145
misinformation effect 133
Mittelbau-Dora 4
Mittweida 13
Monowitz 4
Morton Silverstein 62
Moscow 52, 53, 162
myth xv, 39, 40, 41, 45, 48, 50, 52, 54, 55, 63, 73, 77, 79, 114, 135, 142, 143
myth-building 41
Myth-making 41

N

Naked Among Wolves 58
Naphtali 69
National Archives and Records Administration 14, 20, 22, 23, 25, 29, 30, 90, 116
New York Times 59, 61, 62, 71, 72, 145, 147
Nina Rosenblum 61, 62
Ninth Army 11
NKVD 9
No Gun Ri viii, 143, 144, 145, 146, 147, 148
Nordhausen 105
Nuremberg Tribunals 92

O

Ohrdruf xii, 4, 26, 33, 36, 38, 50, 67, 68, 92, 113, 114, 122, 154
Old Overholt 101, 105
Oprah 124
Orson Welles 55
OSS 26, 102
Otto Roth 17
Ottstedt 18, 19

P

Pacific theater 104
partisans 73
pass 21, 23, 24, 31, 50, 58, 74, 103
Paul Bodot 18, 21, 22, 31, 48, 49
Paul Martin Neurath 10
Paul Schneider 40, 52
Peggy Tishman 63
perfect storm 150
PFC Dee Eberhart 34
Phyllis Klotman 65
Pierre C.T. Verhaye 115
Poland 1, 101
political prisoners, 1, 6, 9
President Harry Truman 118
President Obama 148

Primo Levi 4, 10, 128
prison 47, 75, 88, 90, 137, 148
Psychological Warfare Division 20, 38
psychology xv, 124, 125, 138
public television 61, 62
Pulitzer Prize 143, 144, 149
PWD team 20, 29, 30

Q

QUERFURT 25

R

Rabbi Hershel Schacter 109
Rabbi Israel Meir Lau 69
RASTENBURG 25
Raul Hilberg xvi, 141
Recht oder unrecht – mein Vaterland 83
Reconstruction viii, 133, 134, 161
recovered memories of trauma 124
reds 6, 8
Red Triangle 115
rehearsal 131, 132, 134, 137
Reichstag Fire Decree 1
Remagen 92, 101, 102, 103
retrieval ii, 126, 127, 132, 133
re-unification of Germany 142
Revere, Massachusetts 120
Rhine 11, 33, 90, 92, 101, 102, 103, 105
Rick Carrier viii, 96, 97, 98, 100, 101, 102, 104, 105, 125, 135, 138, 139, 141, 143, 149
Robert Bateman 144, 145
Robert Bennett 13
Robert H. Abzug 131
Robert W. Black 82
Roma 1, 6, 40
Roma and Sinti 1, 6
Ruhr Pocket 11, 90, 105, 116

S

Saul "Pete" Pryor 103, 104
Schindler's List 36, 56
Schutzhaft 1
Schwabsdorf 19
Scott Stiffler 100
Selbstbefreiung viii, xiv, xv, 39, 40, 41, 48, 49, 50, 52, 54, 55, 59, 63, 73, 79, 98, 114, 135, 142, 143
Sergeant Blowers 84
SHAEF 98
Shoah 56, 60, 73, 74, 77, 87, 89, 91, 92, 93, 94, 108, 109, 110, 135, 138, 153, 154
shrunken heads 4, 33, 34, 35
Siegburg 90, 91, 116, 125, 137
Sieg river 90
soap 77, 109
Sobibor 4
Socialist Unity Party 45
socially privileged 78, 96
social privilege 139, 140
Solzhenitsyn 4, 129
Sophie's Choice 36, 56
South Dakota 148
Southern Poverty Law Center 87
South Korea 144
South Station Boston 119
Soviet Special Camp No. 2 1, 9, 51
Soviet Union xiv, 1, 9, 36, 38, 41, 54, 81, 142
Sozialistiche Einheitspartei Deutschlands 45
SS vii, 3, 4, 5, 6, 9, 12, 14, 16, 17, 18, 19, 22, 25, 28, 31, 33, 34, 35, 40, 43, 46, 47, 53, 55, 59, 71, 73, 74, 75, 77, 78, 89, 92, 94, 98, 99, 100, 107, 108, 109, 110, 115, 125, 126, 130, 141
SS WIKING 25
Stalingrad 1
Stanley Milgram 55
Stefan Jerzy Zweig 40, 58
storage 46, 126, 127, 132

T

tattoos 33, 34, 35, 58, 84, 108, 109
The American Experience 61
The American Mercury 43, 162
The Buchenwald Report 10
The Fight for Fifteen. See Fight for $15
The New Republic 63
Theresa Ast 131
Theresienstadt 45, 141
The Villager 100, 101
Third Army 11, 12, 39, 60, 81, 115, 135, 154, 155
Third Reich 4, 9
transit camp 3, 4
transit camps 4
transmitter 114, 115
Treblinka xv, 4
typhus 5, 27, 69, 90, 141
Typhus 5, 9, 27, 84, 159

U

Underground 108
United States Holocaust Memorial Museum iv, xiii, xiv, 1, 3, 6, 12, 13, 15, 26, 28, 32, 35, 58, 60, 67, 68, 72, 73, 74, 75, 76, 77, 84, 87, 89, 96, 97, 99, 107, 108, 114, 149, 151, 154
University of Southern California School of Dentistry 78
US Army Air Corps 108
US Army Center for Military History 12, 15, 57, 67, 80, 101, 159
USC Shoah Foundation 56, 60, 73, 74, 77, 87, 89, 92, 108, 109, 135, 138, 154
USS Barnett 101

V

V-2 rocket 5
Venn diagram 123
VFW 105
VJ Day 117

W

Walter Bartel 45, 46, 47
Ward 15, 18, 30
Weimar iii, iv, 1, 9, 15, 16, 19, 20, 25, 26, 33, 35, 46, 48, 70, 71, 84, 88, 89, 92, 98, 99, 100, 104, 105, 109, 112, 114, 125, 136, 154, 155, 161, 162
Wels 37, 131
Westerbork 37
West Germany 35, 36, 38, 45, 143
William C. Hoge 29
William Daniel Grey 100
William Miles 61
William Scott 57, 67, 73
Willy Blum 40
WNET 61
work-shy 1
Wounded Knee 148

X

XX Corps 14, 19, 20, 23, 25, 31

Y

Yad Vashem 87, 95, 148
Yale University Press 87

Z

Zeiss 5

www.ingramcontent.com/pod-product-compliance
Lightning Source LLC
Chambersburg PA
CBHW021950290426
44108CB00012B/1014